8.00/ 5.60

POLITICS IN AN URBAN AFRICAN COMMUNITY

D0729407

PLATE I

African Miners coming off shift

POLITICS IN AN
URBAN AFRICAN COMMUNITY

by

A. L. EPSTEIN

*Professor of Anthropology in the Australian National
University, Canberra*

Fitz Memorial Library
Endicott College
Beverly, Massachusetts 01915

PUBLISHED FOR
THE INSTITUTE FOR AFRICAN STUDIES
UNIVERSITY OF ZAMBIA
BY
MANCHESTER UNIVERSITY PRESS

© 1958 INSTITUTE FOR AFRICAN STUDIES, UNIVERSITY OF ZAMBIA
Published by the University of Manchester at
THE UNIVERSITY PRESS
316–324 Oxford Road, Manchester M13 9NR

ISBN 0 7190 1041 1

Distributed in the U.S.A by
HUMANITIES PRESS INC.
450 Park Avenue South, New York, N.Y. 10010

First published 1958
Reprinted 1960, 1973

HN
800
.R6
E6

Printed in Great Britain by Butler & Tanner Ltd., Frome and London

To
the memory of
CHARLES AND PAULA EPSTEIN

Calo cesu cileya pantanshi
Na 'fwe bantu tuleya pantanshi.

Our country is going forward,
And we the people, too.

CONTENTS

LIST OF TABLES

LIST OF PLATES

INTRODUCTION

I

THE developments that have been taking place in Africa in recent years rank among the most striking events of our age. African peoples over an entire continent have become involved in a process of social upheaval and radical social change. One aspect of this great transformation has been the increasing incorporation of peoples, traditionally rural in their economy and way of life, into the wage-earning economy of the towns.

In Northern Rhodesia the process is particularly well marked. Little more than a generation ago, Northern Rhodesia was a country still largely unknown to the outside world. True, the British South Africa Company had established its administration there just about the turn of the century, and many Africans had already left their tribal homes to seek work in the Belgian Congo, in Southern Rhodesia, and even in the mines of the Witwatersrand in what is now the Union of South Africa. But· in the main, tribal life continued to run in its accustomed paths. African men and women still lived out their lives with their kinsmen in small villages dotted about the countryside; they gave allegiance to their tribal chiefs and headmen, and ordered their existence in accordance with time-hallowed customs.

Today this general picture is altered considerably. In the late twenties vast mineral resources were discovered in the area now known as the Copperbelt (see Map 1) across the border from the Katanga Province in the Belgian Congo.[1] Since then Northern Rhodesia has become one of the richest copper-mining areas in the world. Where once there was only bush with scattered African villages linked by a network of winding paths, there are now large towns of multi-racial composition, linked with one another, and with the outside world, by road and rail, telephone and wireless. In his rural village the African was a subsistence cultivator, a hunter and, in some tribes, a herdsman. Now, in the towns, he

---

[1] For a general account of these discoveries see E. A. G. Robinson, 'The Economic Problem' in J. Merle Davis, *Modern Industry and the African*, Macmillan, London (1933). Cf. K. G. Bradley, *Copper Venture*, published privately for the Rhodesian Selection Trust (1953).

earns his livelihood as a labourer in a copper mine, as a brick-layer or carpenter, a tradesman or owner of a transport service. In his social relations he is no longer largely confined to members of his own tribe; he works for, and enters into social intercourse with, his fellow Africans of other tribes, and also Europeans and Indians.

II

Clearly, the process of urbanization is an exceedingly complex one; it raises problems which, if they are to be handled effectively, require the co-operation of workers in many disciplines. Given this fact, and the limiting circumstances in which my own field-work was undertaken, I have considered it more profitable at the present stage to select a limited problem for analysis rather than to attempt a more thoroughgoing examination of the question in all its varied aspects. The present book, therefore, represents an attempt to apply anthropological methods to the study of the administrative and political system involving Africans in an urban community on the Northern Rhodesia Copperbelt.

Northern Rhodesia today is a society divided by many cleavages, of which the dominant cleavage is that between Europeans and Africans. This dominant cleavage affects very closely every aspect of the social system. Nevertheless, these cleavages do not follow simply the lines of colour. As we shall see, there are many divisions within the African community, while the White community is also divided within itself by various sectional and class interests.[1] But underlying these cleavages, there is interdependence between all sections of the population, whose interaction make up the social system and keep it working. Various devices in the form of economic barriers and social convention may serve to emphasize the separateness of the different racial groups, but there are also bonds of co-operation which link Africans and Europeans together within a single field of social relations.[2] It is

---

[1] For an excellent illustration of these divisions see, for example, the debate on a motion to appoint a Commission of Inquiry following the strike of European artisans on the Copperbelt in 1946, *Northern Rhodesia Legislative Council Debates*, no. 55 (1946), pp. 104–42.

[2] Cf. M. Gluckman, 'Malinowski's "Functional" Analysis of Social Change', *Africa*, March, 1947, republished in *Malinowski's Sociological Theories*, Rhodes-Livingstone Paper No. 16 (1948).

in this sense that I speak of a Copperbelt town as an urban community. The material presented in this study relates almost exclusively to the African section of such a community. It must be emphasized at the outset, therefore, that this range of data pertains only to a narrow sector of the field. The movements I describe in succeeding chapters have always to be viewed and understood within the wider system of social relations which embraces both Africans and Europeans, and the social divisions which exist within both racial groups.

In thus setting the limits of my study within a single local community—and, indeed, within a section of that community—I am aware that I may be exposing myself to a criticism that has been brought against the 'community study method' developed and followed by a number of American anthropologists.[1] That method operates on the assumption that the local community is a 'microcosm of culture' or a 'world-in-little' which can be approached in the same way that the anthropologist approaches the tribe. In fact, as Goldschmidt points out, one cannot view the community as a microcosm because the community is only a part of a wider system with a 'generalized organization'. Events within the local community are being continuously and increasingly influenced by forces which operate from without.[2] Therefore although I have taken the community as my unit of study, I must make it clear that I do not imply that the various developments which are described below can be explained solely in relationship to the social structure of the town itself. The towns of the Copperbelt—indeed the whole of Northern Rhodesia—are today part of a world-wide economy. Therefore, many events, such as the recent incorporation of Northern Rhodesia within the Federation of Rhodesia and Nyasaland, or the establishment of African trade unions, can only be satisfactorily explained within a much wider and more-embracing politico-economic system. In this study such events have been taken as given; the problem I have set myself is to show how, for example, given the existence of trade unions, their present organization fits in with the other processes of growth I outline, and to describe their relationships with other bodies within the local administrative and political

[1] See, for example, W. Goldschmidt, 'Social Class in America—a Critical Review', *American Anthropologist*, vol. 52, no. 4 (1950), pp. 483-97.
[2] Ibid., p. 486.

structure. Thus the community, as conceived here, is not a microcosm, but a field of social relations the limits of which have been arbitrarily set for convenience of study.

III

In presenting their analyses of tribal social systems, some anthropologists have proceeded by 'sealing off' the social system in time as well as in space. Working in relatively stable and homogeneous communities, where time itself appears as a 'cyclical rhythm of eternal repetition', they have been able to employ the synchronic method to analyse the interrelations of the elements within the system during the period of time their observations were recorded.[1] I believe that this mode of approach is inadequate for describing the administrative and political institutions in the developing social system of the Copperbelt. For example, when I was engaged in a study of African Urban Courts in Northern Rhodesia in 1951, Tribal Representatives were a flourishing institution in all the mine compounds. When I returned to Northern Rhodesia on a second tour some eighteen months later, the Tribal Representatives had been abolished at the instance of the newly-established African Mine Workers' Trade Union. Similarly, when I commenced work on the present study at Luanshya in August, 1953, there was no branch of the African National Congress then in existence in the town: a few months after a branch had been formed which later organized a boycott of the European-owned butcheries in the town. Given this degree of institutional instability, I was led to thrust my inquiries into the past, and to analyse the administrative system as a system in the process of growth.

In a Copperbelt town, the mine itself, the local Municipal Council, and the Office of the District Commissioner provide between them the fixed points in the social framework. For the rest, the social system presents an appearance of continuous flux in which new groups and associations are constantly springing up. Often they are ephemeral, and die away as quickly as they came into being. The social system thus appears, to borrow a phrase of the late Justice Cardozo, as a kind of 'endless becoming'.

---

[1] See M. Fortes, *The Dynamics of Clanship among the Tallensi*, Oxford University Press, London (1945), p. xi.

Yet despite the fluid and ephemeral quality of many African social institutions on the Copperbelt, they do not emerge and die without leaving some trace upon the social fabric. Each leaves behind some deposit upon which the social system is gradually built. Thus when we survey the scene as a whole over the past twenty-five years, a pattern does begin to emerge. Order emerges out of the chaos of particular events, and social regularity is seen to exist in the movement of the system through time. I have attempted here to examine the urban administrative system from this point of view.

In order to study the process of growth, I have followed the method outlined by Gluckman,[1] and have examined the working of the administrative system at three successive periods of Copperbelt history. The division of the total period into decades is to some extent arbitrary, but I believe that this division does coincide with the major nodal points of Copperbelt development—the commencement of mining operations and the first production of copper, the disturbances of 1940, and the more recent emergence of the African Mine Workers' Trade Union. Thus the study falls into three main parts. I begin by outlining the social structure of Luanshya where I carried out my field-work; here I indicate some of the major social characteristics of the town, and conclude by passing in review the local administrative system. I then pass on to a discussion of the emergence of the African urban community in the period 1930–40. The period was marked by a good deal of groping in the dark and experimentation, but by the end of the decade the foundations of the present system of urban administration had been laid. At the same time, forces were already at work making for social and economic differentiation amongst African urban dwellers. Africans in the towns were now beginning to group themselves, and thus to distinguish themselves from their fellows, in terms of their relative skills, their degree of education, and their general social values. Gradually, new associations came into being to express these different interests, and clashed with existing bodies in a struggle for power within the existing administrative order.

The course of this struggle during the period 1940–50 is

---

[1] M. Gluckman, 'Analysis of a Social Situation in Modern Zululand', *Bantu Studies* (March, 1940), pp. 1–30 and (June, 1940), pp. 147–60.

traced out in Chapter III. Here I have examined the way a small group of urban leaders, composed largely of younger and better educated men, organized their protest against what they conceived to be an 'intrusion of tribal government' into the urban areas. I show first how, through the Welfare Societies, they challenged the Tribal Elders who hitherto had dominated the 'official' African representative bodies in the towns; and later, when the new leaders had secured a foothold in these bodies, how they attacked the existing organization of the African Urban Courts, the members of which were nominated by Native Authorities in the tribal areas.

The final part deals with the period 1950–4. Although much of my material here relates to such organizations as African trade unions and the African National Congress, I would emphasize that this is not a study of trade unionism or African nationalism as such. Consequently, I have supplied only so much of the general historical and economic background as I considered relevant for the understanding of their rôle within the local community. The development and internal organization of the African trade unions is described first. I then discuss the continuation of the processes described in the earlier periods, and show how the system of tribal representation was abolished on the mines at the instance of the new urban leaders, who had become the principal office-bearers in the African Mine Workers' Trade Union. I have argued that at this time the leadership of these men was accepted by urban Africans because, by virtue of their education, their proficiency in English, and their more obvious approximation to European standards in dress and habit, they not only were the natural intermediaries between the mass of the African people and the European authorities, but also because they pointed the way forward to a new order of society. The further account then describes how cleavages have developed within the African Mine Workers' Trade Union, and how the very factors which brought the Union leaders into their position of power have now come to be regarded by many Africans as an index of the distance which separates these leaders from the people.

Chapter V attempts to bring out the relations between the Unions, the African National Congress, and 'official' representative bodies by describing the 'social situation' created by the boycott of the European butcheries, which was organized by the National Congress while I was in Luanshya. Here I have tried to relate certain organizational differences, and differences of policy, between Congress and the African Mine Workers' Union to the different principles of social organization operating in the Mine Township and the Municipal Township, which together make up the social structure of a Copperbelt town. As a territorial organization, the National Congress is anchored to no one local community, and is tied to no one set of economic or social interests. I have suggested that one of the functions of a body such as Congress is, by a kind of paradox, to make itself available in a formative period as an instrument for promoting sectional interests, or the interests of dissident factions within existing organizations.

There follows finally a discussion of the normative system of the urban community in so far as it is revealed in the work of the African Urban Court. Here, too, we find evidence of social change. But in the main, the evidence from the Urban Court suggests that urban Africans continue to order their behaviour over a wide area of their social life in accordance with tribal norms and values. This conclusion would appear to contradict the general picture presented in the earlier chapters, where the emphasis was on the movement away from 'tribalism'. I have suggested that the contradiction is to be explained partly in the ambiguity in the concept of 'tribalism' itself, and partly in the fact that ambiguity and inconsistency are themselves important factors in the urban social process. My present data suggest that the urban social system is made up of many different sets of social relations or spheres of social interaction. The factors making for social change and development operate over the whole of this field, and are present in every sphere; but they do not impinge upon these spheres with the same weight, or at the same time. Thus the developing urban social system appears to be marked by internal inconsistency. In the discussion of 'tribalism' in the towns I have tried to show how such inconsistency may be resolved through the operation of the principle of situational selection.

IV

The material presented here is based upon field-work which I carried out at Luanshya between August, 1953, and June, 1954, as a Research Officer of the Rhodes-Livingstone Institute. Initially I

B

was able to secure the full co-operation of the Mine Management at the Roan Antelope for the study. Shortly afterwards, as a result of a series of unfortunate misunderstandings, this support was withdrawn, and for the greater part of my stay in the town I was denied personal access to the mine compound. Inevitably this has meant that at many points my data are not as full as I would have wished. However, while aware of the book's many inadequacies, I am persuaded that the present paucity of material on African urbanization provides some justification for its publication. I hope, too, that it may be found to have some value as a record of some aspects of the social development of the Copperbelt at a particular point in its history.

At the time the study was undertaken, the issue of Central African Federation was still an item of major concern to many people throughout Northern Rhodesia. Through their leaders in the African Representative Council, in the African Mine Workers' Trade Union, and in the African National Congress, the African people had expressed their bitter opposition to the incorporation of Northern Rhodesia in the proposed Federation. I am all the more conscious, therefore, of the heavy debt I owe to those many Africans on the Copperbelt who gave me their co-operation and support at a time when suspicion and distrust of European motives were widespread amongst all sections of the African population. To all of them, and to Mr. L. Katilungu and the members of the Supreme Council of the African Mine Workers' Trade Union in particular, I can only say that I hope they will find in this analysis of the difficult problems which face them, some measure of re-payment for the confidence they reposed in me.

I wish to thank Mr. G. Fane-Smith, Senior Provincial Commissioner, who kindly allowed me access to the relevant documentary material in the office of the District Commissioner, Luanshya. I owe a special debt of gratitude to Mr. F. M. N. Heath, District Commissioner at Luanshya. His advice and personal encouragement were often of inestimable value to me. No one could have been more helpful and co-operative. I would also like to thank Mr. H. F. Hilson, Town Clerk at Luanshya, Mr. Jack Finnigan, the Location Superintendent in the Mikomfwa Housing Area, and Mr. F. Spearpoint, African Personnel Manager on the Roan Antelope Copper Mine, all of whom gave me invaluable assistance.

I should like to pay tribute here to the work of my two African Research Assistants, Mr. Ackson Nyirenda and Mr. Simeo Mubanga. The material I have been able to present in this study owes much to their keenness and quick perception of what was significant for the problems in which I was interested.

I am heavily indebted, both intellectually and personally, to Dr. (now Professor) J. C. Mitchell, then Director of the Rhodes-Livingstone Institute. The whole direction of my thought on African urbanization has been to a considerable extent guided, and certainly sharpened, by his own earlier work on the Copperbelt, and by continuous discussion with him at every stage of the research. On the personal side, at a time when the prospects of continuing my research at Luanshya appeared dim, it was a constant source of reassurance to me to know that I could always count on the full weight of his support.

In the writing up of my material I owe much to Professor Max Gluckman of the University of Manchester. Through close personal association as pupil and friend, through his own writings and the constant stimulus provided by his seminars, I have gained more than I am able to say. Professor Ely Devons of the University of Manchester and Professor I. Schapera have read an earlier draft of the manuscript, and made many invaluable and pertinent criticisms, which I hope I have been able to meet. To both of them I am extremely grateful. I would like to thank, too, Dr. Ellen Hellmann of the South African Institute of Race Relations, and Professor J. A. Barnes of the University of Sydney, for their careful reading of my manuscript and their comments on it. My acknowledgments would not be complete without a special word of thanks to my colleagues in the Department of Social Anthropology in the University of Manchester and in the Rhodes-Livingstone Institute, in particular Dr. V. W. Turner, who have all helped to clarify my thinking at a number of points. For myself, working with them has always been an exciting and rewarding experience. Finally, I should like to thank Mrs. V. W. Turner for her assistance in the drawing of the maps and diagrams.

RHODES-LIVINGSTONE INSTITUTE,   A. L. E.
LUSAKA.
    MAY 10, 1956.

CHAPTER I

THE SOCIAL LANDSCAPE OF A COPPERBELT TOWN

I

THE town of Luanshya, on which this study concentrates, lies about twenty miles from the main railhead at Ndola. Luanshya, the neighbouring communities of Kitwe (Nkana mine) and Mufulira, and the more distant Chingola (Nchanga mine), together make up the area now known as the Copperbelt, for which Ndola serves as an administrative and commercial centre. In this chapter I set out, as background to the later analysis, a brief account of the growth of Luanshya, its major topographical features, and social characteristics. I conclude by considering briefly the system of government within the town.

Like the other towns of the Copperbelt, Luanshya owes its recent growth and expansion entirely to the copper-mining industry. An outcrop was discovered in the area as early as 1902; but it was not until 1926 that major drilling operations revealed the presence of great sulphide deposits, and led to the establishment of the Roan Antelope Copper Mine.[1]

Elsewhere on the Copperbelt similar developments were also taking place, and for a time the whole of this area was in the midst of a construction boom. There was a sudden rapid influx of European immigrants, the greater proportion of whom came from the Union of South Africa. The flow of African labour to the new townships was even greater, and by the end of 1930 some 30,000 of them were in employment on the mines alone. Commerce followed to supply the wants of the new urban agglomerations, and trade flourished.[2]

These developments were halted almost as suddenly by the world depression, the worst effects of which were felt on the Copperbelt in 1931. Soon the mines at Bwana M'kubwa, near

---

[1] For the financial and technical reasons underlying the delay in developing the industry see K. G. Bradley, op. cit.

[2] Merle Davis, op. cit., p. 143.

Ndola, and at Mufulira had closed down, while development at Nchanga mine was curtailed. Nkana mine and the Roan Antelope mine alone remained active. For a time there was widespread unemployment. The numbers of Africans employed on the mines had fallen by mid-1932 to 7,500.[1] Europeans were also affected and many who were engaged in commerce were forced to close their businesses and leave the country.[2]

By 1936 there was a general improvement in the situation and trade began to revive. This movement has continued. Throughout the period of the war the mines were producing at full capacity, and the total production was bought up by the British Government.[3] More recently, there has been a return to conditions of boom, and the rapid expansion of Luanshya and the other Copperbelt towns within the past few years reflects the prosperity that the mining industry has enjoyed in the post-war period.

II

The accompanying sketch map of Luanshya throws into relief the major topographical features of the town. An important feature, to which we will recur constantly, is the dichotomy between the Mine Township and the Government Township. The Roan Antelope Township is the private property of the Company and is governed under the terms of the Mine Townships Ordinance.[4] The Government Township, which was first declared and

---

[1] Merle Davies, op. cit., p. 151. It is difficult at this stage to estimate the extent of unemployment and, in particular, to learn what happened to those who were dismissed their employment. Coulter (in the *Merle Davis Report*, p. 79) speaks of the 'jobless tenth' who borrowed rent money under the freemasonry of tribal obligation and lived on the surplus mealie porridge of those who were more fortunate than themselves. On the other hand, Robinson (at p. 176) points out that although there were cases of real hardship, the great majority of the unemployed had returned to their villages. In their evidence before the Commission of Inquiry into the Copperbelt disturbances of 1935 (see below, p. 21), Africans frequently referred to the incidence of unemployment. See, for example, *Evidence*, vol. ii, pp. 749, 892.

[2] R. R. Kuczynski, *Demographic Survey of the British Colonial Empire* (1949), ii, p. 419.

[3] Indeed, copper did not come on to the free market in London until 1953. At this point the price of copper was about £250 per long ton. This compares with the figure of £90–100 in 1939, and £20–30 at the depths of the slump.

[4] Cap. 121 of the Laws of Northern Rhodesia (1952 edition).

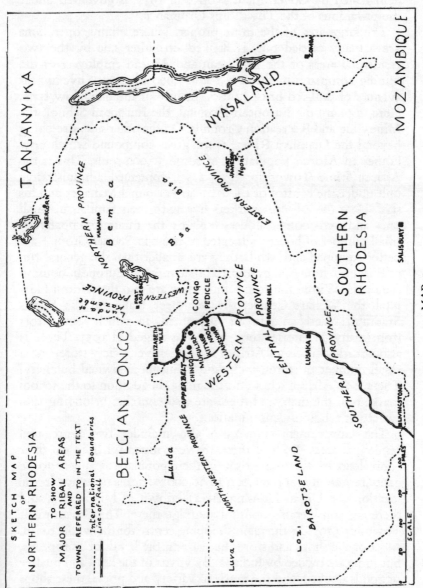

SKETCH MAP
OF
NORTHERN RHODESIA

TO SHOW
MAJOR TRIBAL AREAS
AND
TOWNS REFERRED TO IN THE TEXT

International Boundaries --------
Line-of-Rail

SCALE

MAP I

demarcated by Government Notice in 1930, is governed under the provisions of the Townships Ordinance.[1]

The large area of the mine proper, where mining operations are actually carried out, is flanked on either side by the two residential areas of the European and African employees of the mining company. In the one, some 3,000 Europeans live in neat avenues of dull-red brick houses, mainly of the bungalow type. Here, too, are the European Hospital, the European School, the Mine Club and Recreation Grounds. On the other side, stretching beyond the Luanshya River, is the great compound which now houses an African population of some 30,000 souls. This is the African Mine Township. It is a self-contained administrative unit under the control of the African Personnel Manager and his staff. Here the African workers live with their families in small one- and two-roomed houses built by the mining company. A small number of houses, allocated to those in Special Group,[2] are better equipped and, while they are smaller than the general run of European houses, they approximate more to European housing standards. Within the compound there are also the African Hospital, the Welfare Centre, the Sub-Beer Hall, and the Sports Stadium, where an African Olympiad, in which competitors from many Territories took part, was staged in 1953. There is also a market-place, an African Co-operative Society store, and a small number of stores, including a European-owned butchery. There is an African school on the mine, in addition to the school marked on the map, and there are also churches belonging to a variety of religious denominations.

The Government Township also includes two segregated residential areas. Both of these are very much smaller than their equivalents on the mine, though their populations appear to be growing rapidly. Some 8,000 to 10,000 Africans now live in the location (or Urban Housing Area) known as Mikomfwa, and there is a considerable housing shortage there. The Government Township provides the main shopping centre for the whole town. Most of the shops and stores here are in the hands of Europeans, but some are owned by Indians. By virtue of the kind and quality of goods stocked, and the range in variety and prices, these shops

---

[1] Cap. 120 of the Laws of Northern Rhodesia (1952 edition).
[2] See below, p. 16.

cater very largely for a European trade; some of them refuse Africans permission to enter, while others insist that Africans make their purchases through a hatch at the side of the shop. As we shall see, the treatment of Africans in these stores has been a source of much irritation and has raised complaint. The Post Office, the Office of the Municipal Board, the Office of the District Commissioner with which is associated the African Urban Court, the main Police Station, the Magistrates Court, and the various business premises and offices, are also situated in the Government Township.

Between the Mine and Government Townships there is the Second Class Trading Area, which caters almost exclusively for an African trade. A few of the shops and tea-rooms are owned by Jews, but most are in the hands of Indian business men, and the area forms a kind of Indian quarter.

III

Thus the population of the whole town—Europeans, Africans, and Indians—is almost entirely an 'immigrant' one. The Africans, both on the mine and in the location, are drawn from most of the seventy tribes of the Territory, and also from neighbouring Territories. Since I refer to these tribal divisions from time to time in the course of this study, I discuss here briefly certain characteristics of some numerically significant tribal categories.

The Bemba-speaking peoples, who include a large number of the tribes of the Northern and Western Provinces, make up by far the most numerous category in the town. The Bemba proper are the largest and one of the most strongly organized tribes in the whole Territory. When Livingstone visited their Paramount Chief Chitimukulu Chitapankwa in 1867, the Bemba were at the zenith of their military power. After successfully repelling the advance of the Ngoni, they exercised a suzerainty over large areas of the plateau. The Bemba are a proud people, conscious of their military past, and are known to Europeans and their fellow Africans alike for their 'arrogance'. Convinced of their own superiority over other tribes, the Bemba tend at times to claim an inherent right to leadership in the towns.[1]

---

[1] See, for example, the remarks of the Bemba member of the General Workers' Trade Union quoted below, p. 152.

Another important group is drawn from the Eastern Province. Here, the Ngoni, another warrior people who migrated from the present region of Natal in the earlier part of the nineteenth century, are regarded as the dominant tribe. Their own language has now almost completely disappeared in Northern Rhodesia, and Ngoni culture has been deeply influenced by the matrilineal peoples whom they conquered, and with whom they inter-married. Nevertheless, it is still common in the towns for Tumbuka or Kunda people to speak of themselves as Ngoni. Richards quotes the remarks of some African women, with whom she once talked in Broken Hill, that the Bemba and Ngoni were the only two tribes in which the women still desired to have many children and to build up families. It was because of their aristocracy, they said.[1]

The Nyasaland group is made up for the most part of people from a number of small tribes, none of which had developed a centralized political organization. On the mines these Nyasalanders have always occupied an important position out of all proportion to their numbers. This may be related to Nyasaland's earlier experience of European administration and missionary activity. The much earlier establishment of missions in Nyasaland gave the Africans there a long lead in education over their fellows in Northern Rhodesia. For a long time most of the African clerical posts on the mines and in the Government service were filled by men from Nyasaland. Moreover, the mines of Southern Rhodesia were more readily accessible to the migrant labourers from Nyasaland than they were to the men of the Northern and far Western Provinces of Northern Rhodesia. By the time that the mines

---

[1] A. I. Richards, *Bemba Marriage and Present Economic Conditions*, Rhodes-Livingstone Paper No. 4 (1940), p. 16. A similar notion is expressed in a song sung by members of the Bemba Dance Society, *Mbeni*, one verse of which runs:

Filuti aleipusha muno Luanshya munange mushobo
Munange mushobo
Number one BaBemba
Number two BaNgoni, aba bantu basaini ofu.

The Compound Manager asks: show me the tribe here in Luanshya,
In Luanshya show me the tribe.
Number one—Bemba:
Number two—Ngoni, these people are 'sign off' (i.e. are absolutely without fear).

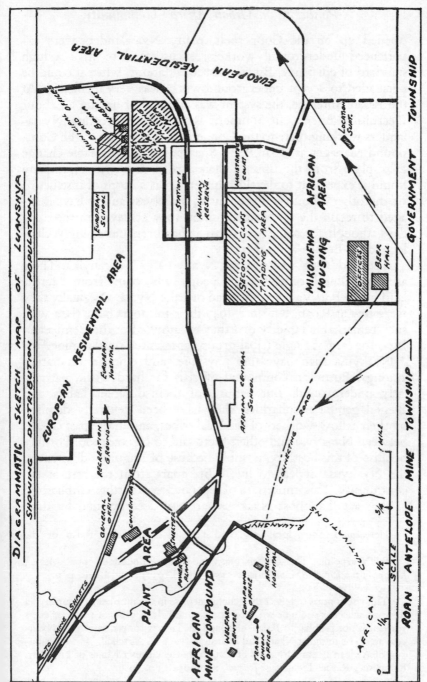

MAP 2

DIAGRAMMATIC SKETCH MAP OF LUANSHYA
SHOWING DISTRIBUTION OF POPULATION.

EUROPEAN RESIDENTIAL AREA

GOVERNMENT TOWNSHIP

AFRICAN AREA

Location Supt.

Mikomfwa Housing

Offices   Beer Hall

Second Class Trading Area

Magistrate's Court

Railway Reserve

Station

Municipal Offices

Blmard

Bomat

B...t
Flats
C...

European School

EUROPEAN RESIDENTIAL AREA

European Hospital

Recreation Ground

African Central School

General Office

Connecting Road

PLANT AREA

Conveyor
Smelter

Power Plant

African Mine Compound

Welfare Centre

Compound Office

African Hospital

Trade Union Office

To Mine Shafts

R. LUANSHYA

AFRICAN CULTIVATIONS

SCALE

0   1/4   1/2   3/4   1 MILE

ROAN ANTELOPE MINE TOWNSHIP

opened up on the Copperbelt, many Nyasalanders were experienced underground workers, accustomed to give a high
standard of efficiency. By contrast local labour, when it could be
persuaded to accept underground work, was very inefficient. At
the Roan Antelope, the system was adopted of having a Labour
Recruiting Agency in Southern Rhodesia re-directing Nyasalanders working there to the Copperbelt. According to the Compound Manager at Roan,[1] Mr. Spearpoint,[2] a noticeable change
took place from the time of their arrival. Later, the Company
found it expedient to develop this group as a corps of instructors
of the other labourers. In the main, the Nyasalanders have managed to retain the dominant position they achieved in the early
days, though for some years past it has been increasingly challenged by Bemba and others.[3]

A second 'alien' group is the Nyakyusa of Tanganyika. These
are a patrilineal, cattle-keeping people who come from a fertile
land in the Rift Valley at the head of Lake Nyasa. Originally they
were few at Roan, but since 1947 their numbers have risen with
such remarkable rapidity that they are now, after the Bemba and
Bisa, the largest single tribal group represented on the mine.[4]

Nyakyusa men have fine physique, and enjoy a reputation
amongst European compound officials for hard work, particularly underground. But because of their different habits and
alleged genital peculiarities, they have been generally despised
by their fellow-workers of the local tribes, and in the past clashes
between Nyakyusa and others were said to be common. Possibly
because of this hostility, possibly because of linguistic differences,
the Nyakyusa appear to live a life apart from the rest of the
community. This impression of separateness is further emphasized
in the fact that most Nyakyusa are not accompanied by their

---

[1] Hereafter I follow local usage and speak of the mine as 'Roan' or 'the
Roan'.

[2] F. Spearpoint, 'The African Native and the Rhodesia Copper Mines',
Journal of the Royal African Society, xxxvi (July, 1937) supplement, p. 9.

[3] See below, p. 235.

[4] This rise appears to reflect the general increase in the number of Tanganyika
Africans who have sought work on the Copperbelt in the past seven or eight
years: it is not peculiar to Roan, although the largest concentrations of Nyakyusa are to be found at Nkana and Luanshya. See J. C. Mitchell, 'The Distribution of African Labour by Area of Origin on the Copper Mines of Northern
Rhodesia', *Rhodes-Livingstone Journal*, xiv (1954), pp. 30–6.

wives, and thus tend to live contiguously in the men's single quarters.[1]

But the ties which link Africans in the towns together as members of a tribe, and thus divide them from other tribes, operate only in certain situations. In order to support himself and his family, indeed to get a house in the location or on the mine, the African in the town must have a job. Fundamental to the urban situation is the fact that Africans of many tribes now participate in the common wage economy of the towns. They are linked and divided within new sets of relations which involve them as wage-earners and urban dwellers rather than as tribesmen.

This fact is emphasized particularly in the work situation itself. So far as I am aware, no attempt has ever been made on the mines to fit members of a given tribe to particular kinds of work. The gang, which forms the unit of labour on the mines, is usually made up of members of many tribes. There are cases where certain tribes do predominate in particular kinds of work. For example, the work of night-soil removal is usually undertaken by members of the Luvale-speaking group of peoples from the far west of the Territory. But this reflects the unwillingness of other tribes to be employed in this kind of work, rather than any deliberate act of Management policy.

A similar position also exists outside the work situation. For while a man may choose his friends, he cannot always choose his neighbours. There are no tribal sections either in the mine compound or in the Government location. Everywhere people of many tribes are intermingled, and new bonds of co-operation based on propinquity and neighbourliness are constantly being formed.

I will touch on the question of work and wages later in discussing the internal organization of the mine. It is in the leisure-time activities of the people that one gains perhaps the clearest impression of the emerging urban communities of the Copperbelt, based on these new sets of relations, and coming to possess their own distinctive culture. The Beer Halls, of which there is one in each section of the town, form an important focus of

---

[1] As further evidence for this view, Dr. Mitchell has sent me reports, which appeared in the local Press in 1955, that the Nyakyusa at Nkana were seeking to form their own Trade Union. See below, p. 235.

African community life. One's first impressions of a visit to the Beer Hall are apt to be confused amid the constant clamour and jostling going on all around. But, with repeated visits, a pattern begins to emerge. Young men, dressed in gaily-coloured open-necked shirts, and wearing cowboy hats, squat on the ground or move around strumming a guitar and singing the latest Copper-belt 'hit-numbers'[1] or otherwise seek to gain the attention of the *bakapenta*,[2] the 'young ladies of the town'. Elsewhere a group of Tribal Elders are sitting together, and complain of a member of their tribe who has just bought a present of beer for an Urban Court Member of another tribe. In another group, some of the town's leading personalities, all smartly dressed in lounge suits, are engaged in quiet conversation in English with a well-known African visitor from Kitwe or Lusaka. They gossip about person-alities and discuss the political news from other towns, and they make arrangements for later meetings in their private homes.

Sport forms another important leisure-time activity. Football is the most popular game, and thousands of Africans will turn up to shout their support for their local heroes. Once I saw a young African petrol-pump attendant holding the attention of his fellows by miming in the most vivid way the wizardry of the Newcastle United team which had visited the Copperbelt a few years previously! The holding of the Central African Olym-pics aroused much interest in athletics, and it soon became com-mon to see children in the compound seeking to emulate the efforts of one very fine high-jumper from Uganda.

Yet, while Copperbelt life has its own distinctive flavour, in the main people pass their time after working hours in much the same way as people do in urban areas all the world over. They visit their friends and relatives: they listen to the wireless relayed from the Welfare Centre, or on their own 'Saucepan' radios which were produced specially for the African market; they go to the cinema (bioscope); they visit the reading-rooms at the Welfare Centre; or they simply 'loaf' around the house.

---

[1] Many of these songs derive from the 'hill-billy' type of cowboy song, but are re-interpreted in terms of African musical idiom. Gramophone records of these songs have a very wide sale.

[2] From the English word 'to paint', i.e. to use cosmetics. The term is often used as synonymous with 'prostitute', though here the term *lihuli* (from the Afrikaans word 'hoer', a whore) is more common.

PLATE II

The African Beer Hall at Roan

IV

I have spoken of Luanshya, and the other towns of the Copper-belt, as emerging communities. For they are young communities, little more than a generation old, and as yet they have developed few stable institutions. They are young in another sense, too. For one of the things which must strike the observer as he moves

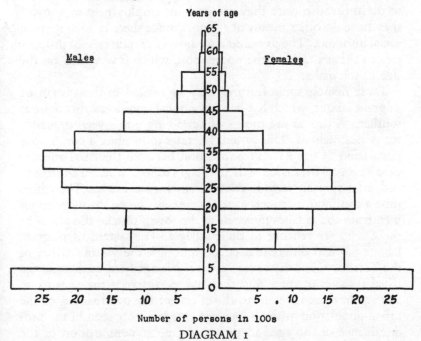

DIAGRAM I

AGE AND SEX DISTRIBUTION: ROAN ANTELOPE COPPER MINE AND OTHER LUANSHYA AREAS

(*Source:* Rhodes–Livingstone Institute Survey, 1951)

around a town is the relatively small number of older people to be seen. To illustrate this point I have produced a population pyramid of Luanshya, which is based upon material collected by Mitchell in the course of the Rhodes–Livingstone Institute Social Survey of the Copperbelt.[1]

We can see clearly from the pyramid the heavy loading of the

---

[1] J. C. Mitchell, *African Urbanization in Ndola and Luanshya*, Rhodes–Living-stone Institute Communication No. 6 (1954).

working-age population in both sexes. Apart from the very young children, the vast majority of the people fall within the age category 20-40. After the age of 45 in the case of men, and somewhat earlier in the case of women, their numbers begin to fall off rapidly. Many Africans feel that, at this age, they have 'worked' enough, and they decide to return to their villages. Others, who would be content to stay in the towns, are unable to do so because, once they are without employment in a town, they have no other means of support, since there is no system of social insurance. The pyramid also shows a certain lack of proportion in the sex ratio of the population, which is weighted on the side of the males.

These demographic features may be related to the system of migrant labour, which has become almost traditional throughout southern Africa as the means of supplying employers' demands for African labour. This system operates to produce a continuous circulation of the African population between the rural and the urban areas. Africans leave their villages to seek work in the towns and, after varying periods, return to their rural homes. The whole time a continuous process of replacement is going on, as younger men from the villages move in to the towns to take the places of those who are retiring to their villages. The system of migrant labour has had differential effects amongst the various tribes of the Territory, but over wide areas it has operated to denude the tribal reserves of men, and their wives, between the ages of 20 and 40. In these rural areas, the effects of the overloading of the urban population in the lower age categories are seen in the predominance of the aged in the demographic composition of the villages.[1]

Circulation of the population between town and country forms only part of the picture. For there is also continuous movement within any particular town, and between different towns. The rate of labour turnover is high, particularly amongst manual labourers, who move from job to job, sometimes after working for only very short periods. Once I was present while a Com-

---

[1] It may also be noted that the rapid and continuous increase of the African urban population must be at the expense of the rural areas. As Moore has remarked, the labour flows, like a syphon going on and on, regardless of whether the reservoir is getting empty or not. See R. J. B. Moore, *These African Copper Miners* (1948), p. 25.

pound Official interviewed a group of men seeking employment on the mine. After examining their identity cards, and questioning them briefly, he commented to me that most of them would stay on the job for only six months.

Some indication of the length of service of Africans at the Roan is given in Table 1.[1]

TABLE 1

LENGTH OF SERVICE OF AFRICANS IN EMPLOYMENT ON THE ROAN ANTELOPE COPPER MINE, JUNE, 1954

Cumulative length of service to date, in ticket-years	Underground workers	Surface workers	Total
0–1½	2,481 (43·4%)	1,283 (31·1%)	3,764 (38·2%)
1½–5	2,017 (35·3%)	1,603 (38·9%)	3,620 (36·8%)
5–10	969 (16·9%)	847 (20·6%)	1,816 (18·5%)
10 plus	254 (4·4%)	387 (9·4%)	641 (6·5%)
Total	5,721 (100%)	4,120 (100%)	9,841 (100%)

N.B. Length of service on the mines is counted in 'tickets'. A 'ticket' consists of 30 working days, and it usually takes about 34 days to complete a 'ticket'. Length of service in calendar years will be somewhat longer than is indicated in the table, where I assume that 12 'tickets' = 1 ticket-year.

Movement and instability are major characteristics of the urban scene, and are reflected in the high degree of residential and occupational mobility. Yet the urban situation is not wholly fluid and ephemeral: it also contains elements of persistence and continuity. Within Luanshya there is a small but hard core of citizens who have lived in the town for twenty years and more; their children have been begotten there, and have grown up and married in the towns. In his pioneer study of Broken Hill, Godfrey Wilson [2] drew attention to the tendency towards the increasing stabilization of the urban population there. More recently,

[1] Based on figures kindly supplied to me by Mr. F. M. N. Heath, Assistant Labour Commissioner, Kitwe. The figures are as at June, 1954.

[2] Godfrey Wilson, *The Economics of Detribalization in Northern Rhodesia*, Rhodes-Livingstone Papers Nos. 5 and 6 (1941 and 1942).

C

Mitchell [1] has attempted to document this process in his studies of African urbanization on the Copperbelt, and to work out in quantitative terms an index of urban stabilization. My own research stresses the need to see the administrative and political system of a Copperbelt town as a process of growth. In so far as this claim is justified, the present study may be regarded as providing a further index, in qualitative terms, of the increasing commitment of Africans to the urban way of life.

V

I conclude this introductory survey of the local community with a brief sketch of the system of administration in the town as it touches upon African affairs. The dichotomy of Mine and Government Township, to which I have already referred, sets the pattern of local government in Luanshya. As we have seen, the mine is a self-contained administrative unit, with its own elaborate internal organization. The Government Township has its separate administrative organization.

The mine is divided into seven main departments, each of which has its allotted sphere of responsibility, and its own form of internal organization. Here I confine myself to the African Personnel Department, which constitutes a kind of secretariat for African Affairs. The African Personnel Department is under the control of the African Personnel Manager and, as we shall see, all matters affecting Africans in the Mine Township are ultimately his concern and responsibility. The African Personnel Manager acts as adviser to the General Manager of the mine in all matters relating to African labour. He submits estimates on which expenditure appropriations are made for the African Township; he represents Management in negotiations with the Roan branch of the African Mine Workers' Union; and he is the representative of African interests on the Mine Township Council, which deals with matters, outside the mining process itself, affecting the general running of the Township. The position of the

---

[1] 'Urbanization, Detribalization, and Stabilization in Southern Africa: A Problem of Definition and Measurement', Working Paper prepared for the Abidjan Conference on the Social Impact of Industrialization and Urban Conditions in Africa, 1954. See also Mitchell's *African Urbanization in Ndola and Luanshya*.

Department within the organization of the mine is indicated briefly in the diagram below:

DIAGRAM 2

MINE ORGANIZATION SHOWING POSITION AND INTERNAL ORGANIZATION OF AFRICAN PERSONNEL DEPARTMENT

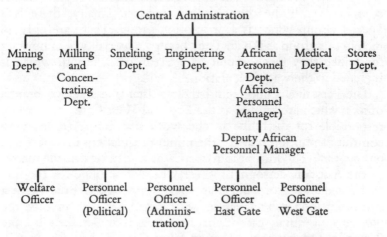

The African Personnel Department handles all matters which affect the African labour force, both inside and outside the work situation. The labour force itself is divided into nine groups, according to the degree of skill, and responsibility attaching to a job, and length of service. Groups 1 and 2 are composed entirely of unskilled labourers, and together they make up more than half of the total labour force. Men in these groups are employed on the surface as compound sweepers and night-soil collectors, and underground (where they begin in Group 2) as lashers, that is labourers who shovel out rock after blasting. Groups 3 and 4 are also labouring categories, and serve as promotion groups for those with long service. The rank and file of the African Mine Police, watchmen and caretakers, and others performing work which requires more knowledge for the job (e.g. boiler attendant or stoker in the power plant) are also included in Group 4. Groups 5 and 6 may be regarded as semi-skilled categories. They include such workers as carpenters, bricklayers, painters, plumbers and tin-smiths, but none has undergone any apprenticeship. Groups 7 and 8 are made up of boss boys or African foremen.

They are in charge of gangs, which form the basic labour units, of between 10 and 15 men, and they act as intermediaries between the members of their gang and the European supervisor in charge. Mine clerks are also found in these categories. They are employed as interpreters, storekeepers, record keepers, and so forth; but, as we shall see, the mine clerk enjoys a special social significance as compared with the other skilled workers. Finally, there is a Special Group which is a promotion group. There are only 28 men in this group at Roan. They occupy a special type of housing for which they pay a rental of £2 10s. 0d. a month which is included in the wage calculation.[1]

The Personnel Officers and their assistants at the two branch offices, which are known as the East and West Gates, are largely responsible for discipline in the work situation. Africans who commit flagrant breaches of the mining regulations may be 'fined on the spot'. The European Mine Captain then reports the matter to the Assistant Personnel Officer who will arrange for the fine to be deducted from the man's next pay-packet. But where a complaint lodged by the European Supervisor may involve the worker's dismissal, careful investigation is undertaken by the Personnel Officers at the East or West Gate. The final responsibility for dismissing an African worker rests with the African Personnel Manager, but in practice he delegates it to his Deputy and to the Personnel Officers at the East and West Gates.

Apart from its two branch offices, the African Personnel Department is also divided internally into a number of sub-departments. The Administration Department deals with the problem of housing and feeding. All African employees are housed by the mining

---

[1] Obviously there is a multiplicity of tasks to be performed on a mine, many of which have their own technical names. Here I have attempted only to indicate broadly the characteristics associated with each labour group. African wage differentials are set out in the Appendix. The average cash wage of the African surface worker has been estimated by C. G. Guillebaud at £74 a year, plus free housing and food. In the Special Group the average annual cash wage works out at £222 for the surface, and £243 for the underground, worker. The latter also receive a cost-of-living allowance, but no free housing or rations. The average annual cash wage of the European underground worker is estimated by the same authority at £1,400 a year. This figure does not include a fluctuating copper bonus which, at the beginning of 1954, augmented the cash wage of Europeans by about 70 per cent. Mr. Guillebaud was the Special Arbitrator in the wage dispute of January, 1953: see below, p. 97.

company, and those up to Group 4 are also entitled to regular rations, which they draw from the Feeding Store. Those in the higher labour groups receive an inclusive wage; but they are also allowed to buy at the Feeding Store, and there is a ready sale of meat, vegetables, and other items because the purchasers are able to buy on credit, the money being deducted from their wages on the next pay-day. The Administration Department is also responsible for African Control, which is concerned with the allocation of workers in the proper categories to the various mine departments; for the Induction School, where Africans are given a period of preliminary training before proceeding to their different jobs; and for carrying out tests designed to fit the workers to jobs for which they seem best fitted. There is also a Department of Welfare which deals with the running of the Welfare Centre and the library, and with the provision of sports, educational, and other facilities. Recently a 'Political Officer' was appointed whose principal function was said to be the planning of new schemes, for example in the field of compound local government. To some extent his position overlapped with that of other officers, particularly the Welfare Officer, and it was the subject of much discussion in the African Personnel Department during my stay in Luanshya.

One of the major functions of the African Personnel Department has always been the maintenance of discipline among the workers living in the compound. For long this function was exercised partly through the agency of African compound police. This was a purely mine body, with few legal powers. More recently, in line with general Government policy, a Police substation has been built within the compound, and a detachment of regular Northern Rhodesia Police based there.

The compound police are now reduced to the status of uniformed messengers, though they continue to serve the function of keeping the African Personnel Manager informed of changes in the current of local opinion. A further means of communication between the Africans and the mine management was provided by the system of Tribal Elders, which was introduced at Roan as early as 1931. The Elders were later replaced by Tribal Representatives [1] who were themselves abolished in 1953, at the instance

---

[1] See below, p. 62.

of the recently established African Mine Workers' Trade Union. Now, since the Union is confined, by virtue of its constitution and the terms of its agreement with the mining companies, to matters affecting labour conditions alone, there exists no representative body through which the Africans may express directly their views on the general running of the compound.

In the Government Township, authority is vested in the Luanshya Municipal (formerly Management) Board. Until 1952, when an electoral system was introduced, appointment to the Board was by nomination.[1] In the past it has included the District Commissioner, the Labour Officer, and representatives of the local branch of the Chamber of Commerce, of the mining company, of the ndian Association, and of the European women residents of the Township. Since Africans do not as yet own property in the trading and residential areas of the Township they do not rank as   payers, and therefore cannot qualify for inclusion on the local electoral roll. They have no direct representation on the Municipal Board.

Local authorities in Northern Rhodesia work on the principle that the African communities in the locations under their control should be self-supporting. Broadly speaking, this aim is achieved by the provision of municipal Beer Halls the profits from which are used to provide social services and welfare facilities.[2] At Luanshya the responsibility for expending these funds for years vested in a small sub-committee of the Management Board called the Native Welfare Committee. The Committee had little power, and acted in a purely advisory capacity. The Township location was administered, first by the Town Manager, and at a later date by a Location Superintendent, both appointed and employed by the Municipal Board; as on the mine, the Location Superintendent had the assistance of his own compound police and a body of Tribal Elders.

By 1947 these arrangements were being questioned. The Africans themselves began to ask why, if they were now thought capable of taking their seats in the Legislative Council, they should

---

[1] *Report of a Committee appointed to consider the Constitution of Management Boards*, Government Printer, Lusaka (1949).

[2] *Report of the Commission appointed to inquire into the Administration and Finances of Native Locations in Urban Areas*, Government Printer, Lusaka (1944), pp. 22–3. Hereafter referred to as the Report on Urban Locations.

be excluded from sharing the responsibilities of local government. In the same year, the Conference of Copperbelt District Commissioners discussed a proposal for establishing an Urban African Treasury. It was pointed out that throughout the Territory, Native Authorities had been given a measure of financial responsibility, but that the Copperbelt African had none, and that it was quite time he was taught how to spend public money. The Conference found itself unable to accept the proposal for an Urban Treasury, but suggested that official policy should be to encourage a more liberal outlook on the part of Management Boards in order to get them to agree to include one or more Africans in their membership.

This policy has still only been partially achieved. In 1951 building began in Mikomfwa, a new area set aside by the Luanshya Board under the terms of the Urban African Housing Ordinance,[1] and elections to the Urban Housing Board, for which the Ordinance provides, were held two years later. The Municipal Board's administration of African affairs was re-organized to bring it into line with the new conditions, and its Native Welfare Committee was replaced by an African Affairs Committee.

The present African Affairs Committee, a much larger body than the older one it replaced, includes two Africans, one a delegate from the African Urban Advisory Council, the other representing the Urban Housing Board. But only the latter is entitled to vote. Only three other members, all direct representatives of the Board, have a vote. Apart from the Town Clerk and the District Commissioner, who until now has acted as chairman, the other members (the Location Superintendent, the Beer Hall Manager, the Welfare Sister and the Labour Officer) are all co-opted and are without power to submit recommendations. The vote given to the one African member on the Committee represents a big concession by the Board, but on the Board itself the Africans are still represented by the District Commissioner.

The office of the District Commissioner constitutes a third centre of power within the community. In Luanshya this office dates from 1936 when, following the *Report on the Copperbelt Disturbances of 1935*, it was decided to excise the mining areas from the Ndola District, and each was declared to be a separate

---

[1] Cap. 234 of the Laws of Northern Rhodesia (1953 edition).

Administrative District. The District Commissioner is the local representative of Central Government, and he is ultimately responsible for the maintenance of law and order in the District. But he also has more specific duties. As a member of the Provincial Administration he is ultimately responsible to the Secretary of Native Affairs. Thus he is charged, in his office, with a special obligation to protect the interests of the Africans falling within his jurisdiction. More particularly, he may be called upon to act as a Court of Appeal against decisions of the African Urban

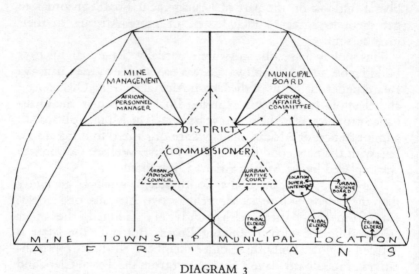

DIAGRAM 3

THE FORMAL STRUCTURE OF AUTHORITY INVOLVING AFRICANS IN LUANSHYA, 1953–4

Court, for the general supervision of which he is also responsible. The District Commissioner also sits as chairman of the African Urban Advisory Council, through which African opinion is transmitted to the appropriate authorities.

The formal structure of authority involving Africans in Luanshya may thus be presented as in Diagram 3.

An account of the various bodies plotted on the diagram, and an analysis of their interrelationships, form the subject matter of succeeding chapters. Here I confine myself to a discussion of the position of the District Commissioner in relationship to the other formal centres of power within the community—the Mine

Management on the one hand, and the Municipal Board on the other.

The District Commissioner has no voice in formulating policy on the mine about the running of the Mine Township. His position there was once summed up for me in the remarks of an informant who was himself an employee of the mining company: 'The District Commissioner is tolerated, but not welcomed. . . . We try to keep him out of the picture as much as possible.' These words were not intended to reflect upon any particular District Commissioner, for they were not describing any new phenomenon. Generally speaking, the structural position of Administrative Officers vis-à-vis the mine has remained constant since the earliest days of Luanshya, and their 'lack of contact' with mine affairs has been a constant theme of Government spokesmen. For example, when the Chief Secretary to the Government gave evidence before the Commission of Inquiry of 1935,[1] the whole of his argument centred on the lack of contact existing between the African mine-workers and the District Officer. Speaking on the general implications of the disturbances which occurred in that year on the Copperbelt, he said:

'Of course the whole lesson is that Government has not got the contact or the influence or the prestige by which alone we govern the native tribes. . . . No such thing would be possible I think in any tribal area as an outburst so sudden as that without any information reaching the Government or without attempt on the part of the natives to make representation, without any attempt to discuss matters with the local District Officer.'

Chairman: 'I understand from you that administrative officers have no duties in the mine compounds?'

Chief Secretary: 'They have duties. Unfortunately their duties are those which are most unwelcome to the mine employees, as they would be elsewhere. . . . Their duties consist in collecting taxes, in functioning as Magistrates. They have no paternal duties in the compound.'

The Copperbelt disturbances of 1935, which ended at Luanshya in the storming of the Mine Compound Office by a wild mob,

---

[1] *Evidence taken by the Commission appointed to inquire into the Disturbances on the Copperbelt, Northern Rhodesia*, Government Printer, Lusaka (1935), i, p. 55. Hereafter, the Commission is referred to as the Commission of 1935.

and the killing of six Africans and the wounding of many more, caused considerable perturbation to the Government. Innumerable conferences and discussions followed, and the present system of urban administration gradually took shape. Yet no measure could be devised to overcome what Administrative Officers saw as the central problem of maintaining a close contact with the African employees of the mine. In fact, as the years went by, the position of the District Commissioner grew worse in this respect, since Labour Officers were assuming more of his functions. Thus in 1947 the mining company refused the District Commissioner at Luanshya permission to attend ordinary meetings of the African Tribal Representatives on the mine, at which the Labour Officer was usually present. This attitude was determined, the General Manager at Roan explained,[1] by the desire to maintain an atmosphere of normality and proper balance of representation at the ordinary meetings of the Compound Manager and the representatives of African employees. At a meeting with the Chamber of Mines in the following year, the Deputy to the Provincial Commissioner again gave expression to administrative fears that contact between the Administration and the African mine-workers was inadequate. He said that District Commissioners were regarded by Africans as remote Olympian beings who resided in the Government Offices some distance away from the all-important mine compound. The Companies agreed at this meeting to make available suitable office accommodation near their Compound Office for the District Commissioner. It was further agreed that District Commissioners would not listen to complaints from Africans regarding their work or living conditions on the mine. As soon as the District Commissioner realized that the complaint was about these conditions, he would refer the matter to the Compound Manager. Clearly the effect of this concession by the Chamber of Mines could only be to demonstrate even more plainly the ineffectiveness of the District Commissioner in an industrial community.

The reasons underlying mines' policy in this matter are not difficult to determine. From the very outset the mine managements had exercised all functions of administration themselves,

---

[1] Letter of August 4, 1947, filed in the Office of the District Commissioner, Luanshya.

including many of those normally associated with Government. When the Government Administration became more firmly established, management showed some resentment at the Government's threatened expansion of influence.[1] For, where immediate interests tend to conflict, the presence of an influential District Commissioner would constitute a very real threat to the position and prestige of the Compound Manager. The Compound or African Personnel Manager controls nearly every sphere of the worker's life while he is on the mine. Furthermore, he is charged with the task of maintaining discipline amongst a large labour force which is concentrated within a single compound. The existence of an alternative authority, in the person of a District Commissioner, would render impossible the successful discharge of these functions.[2] So insistent, indeed, is Management on the need to avoid anything which might tend to undermine the authority of the Compound Manager that at Roan the General Manager himself is said very rarely to visit the compound.

The position of the District Commissioner vis-à-vis the Municipal Board has always been stronger than on the mine. Yet here too there appears to be an unmistakable tendency towards the weakening of this position. By virtue of his office the District Commissioner has always held a seat on the Municipal Board, and in the past at Nkana and Mufulira acted as chairman.[3] In the past he also provided the only link between the Board and the Central Government. Now, with the establishment of a Department of Local Government at Lusaka, the Board is able to by-pass the District Commissioner and communicate directly with the Central Government. Even within the sphere of African affairs, which are pre-eminently within the District Commissioner's province, more

---

[1] Major G. St. Orde-Browne, *Report on Labour Conditions in Northern Rhodesia*, Colonial No. 150 (1938), p. 5.

[2] This point was referred to both by administrative and mine compound officials in their evidence before the Commission of 1935. Mr. John Moffat, at that time District Officer, Mufulira, touched on the need for closer contact between administrative officers and the people, but pointed out that it was extraordinarily difficult to achieve: 'The last thing I think that one should aim at is trying to reduce the prestige or the importance of the Compound Manager in his own compound' (*Evidence*, i, p. 278). Mr. Scrivener, the Compound Manager at Nkana mine, spoke in similar terms (ibid., p. 464).

[3] *Report of a Committee to consider the Constitution of Management Boards*, op. cit., p. 12, esp. appendices G and I.

and more responsibility is coming to vest in the Municipal Board, which has now established its own Department of African Affairs. Hitherto, the District Commissioner has acted as chairman of the African Affairs Committee. But this arrangement lies within the discretion of the Board: during my stay in Luanshya some members of the Board had come to question it.

The office of the District Commissioner has its origins in the conditions of rural administration. In the past, and even today on many out-stations, the District Commissioner and his staff, and possibly a handful of missionaries, were often the only Europeans in the area. In this situation the functions of the District Commissioner affected nearly every aspect of African life. But in the urban areas, and particularly in an industrial community, he is rapidly divested of most of his traditional functions. His District Messengers no longer act as constables, for these duties have been taken over by the Northern Rhodesia Police who are directly responsible to their own Commissioner. His judicial functions are considerably reduced by the presence of a stipendiary magistrate and the establishment of an African Urban Court. Labour officers and trade union officials have taken his place in industrial councils, while his responsibility for civil affairs has been much modified by the development of local government in the Government Townships. In presenting the diagram of formal authority involving Africans within the town, I have placed the District Commissioner right at the centre. This might be taken to suggest that the District Commissioner is the hub around which the whole urban administrative system revolves. In this respect perhaps the diagram is misleading. For while he is in theory responsible for the whole District of which he is in charge, the District Commissioner in the town sits rather uneasily between the two local authorities of Mine Management and Municipal Board.

This has important consequences for the District Commissioner in his relations with the African community. His principal link with that community is through the Urban Advisory Council, which is composed of African representatives from both the mine and the location. In an article on the growth of African councils on the Copperbelt, Mr. Heath, a District Commissioner, has noted that 'in the eyes of Africans the primary function of Urban Advisory Councils in their present form is to act as a pressure group applied to local administrative units and members of the

Territorial Legislative Council'.[1] I cannot take this point further at the present stage, but it is relevant to note here that, since the Council's major link is with the District Commissioner, the pressure which it can exert is in large measure coincident with that which he himself can bring to bear. Since the position of the District Commissioner in the industrial areas itself appears precarious, it follows that in many situations the Urban Advisory Council is rendered completely ineffective, and its members are left with keen feelings of frustration. This lack of effective power, together with the fact that the Councils rest upon the principle of separate political representation for Africans, has now led to a demand, voiced at a meeting of the African Provincial Council at Ndola in 1954, that the system of Urban Advisory Councils should be abolished.

---

[1] F. M. N. Heath, 'The Growth of African Councils on the Copperbelt of Northern Rhodesia', *Journal of African Administration*, v (1953), pp. 131–2.

CHAPTER II

THE BEGINNINGS OF URBAN ADMINISTRATION
(1930–40)

ONCE when I was living in Bemba country in the Northern Province, I invited a class of schoolboys, who had never been to town, to write an essay for me on whether, when they left school, they would prefer to live in towns or remain in their villages. The majority of the boys expressed a preference for town life. Tales of town, with its sports and amusements, its economic advantages and educational facilities, and its wider opportunities for learning of new ways and people, excited in these lads expectations which could not be matched by the current monotony of village life. Yet they did not make their choice wholly unaware of the disadvantages of urban conditions. There was one point upon which the whole class was agreed—the violence and general lack of discipline which seemed to them to mark urban living. 'If you are not careful and you get drunk, you may be killed on the roadway. For on the Copperbelt the lion is a man, and not an animal as it is at home.'

The accounts I have received in the towns from informants who remember the Copperbelt in the days of its infancy describe similar conditions. They speak of hatred and fighting between the tribes; of the killing that went on in the paths leading from the Beer Hall; and of the gangs of young men who prowled around the compound at night, making it unsafe for people to appear outside their homes after dark. As we shall see shortly, the widespread disturbances which broke out on the Copperbelt in 1935 aroused considerable anxiety among Government officials; and the basis for the present system of urban administration emerged from the many formal and informal discussions that then took place. Nevertheless, violence is a feature of urban life which it is very easy to over-emphasize; in itself the prevention of violence forms only one aspect of the more general problem of achieving social control in a rapidly-growing, heterogeneous, and highly mobile population. The Africans who were now flocking to the

26

Copperbelt in search of work came from a multitude of tribes, spoke a wide variety of languages and dialects, and observed different customs. In the circumstances it was necessary to devise some form of channel of communication between the White authorities and the Black workers. In the absence of any lead from Government, the mining companies and the town Management Boards themselves were forced to take the initiative in providing the rudiments of a system of local administration.

Although there had always been small detachments of Northern Rhodesia Police stationed on the Copperbelt, the compound staff at most of the mines preferred to police their compounds themselves. For long, indeed, the police never entered the mine compounds unless they were asked, or unless some crime had been committed which required investigation.[1] The mine 'police boys' served not only as a disciplinary force, but also as intermediaries between the Compound Manager and the people. They received no adequate training in police duties, yet moved about armed with sticks, and were responsible to no other authority than that of the Compound Manager. As a body they were generally detested by the mass of the people, and there is little doubt that they abused the considerable power that their position on the mine gave them.[2]

These factors of themselves did not necessarily make compound police unsatisfactory as an agent of the mine administration. However, through the position they enjoyed, they also controlled the right of access to the Compound Manager. Every African who had a complaint to lodge, or who wished to raise some matter with the Compound Manager, had first to convince the compound police that he had good reason for 'troubling' the Compound Manager. This meant that the Compound Manager's opportunities for meeting people and hearing their grievances were themselves reduced. It was this consideration which led Mr. Spearpoint, at that time Compound Manager and now African Personnel Manager at the Roan Antelope, to introduce there in

---

[1] *Evidence*, i, p. 13.

[2] Spearpoint, op. cit., p. 19. Cf. the statement of the witness quoted in the *Report on Urban Locations*, p. 18, who described compound police as 'an absolute menace: they abuse authority, receive bribes and discriminate against tribespeople other than their own'.

1931 the system of Tribal Elders. The various tribes in the compound were approached with the suggestion that they might welcome the idea of having representation on a Council of Tribal Elders, and that the people selected to represent each tribe should be chosen at an election conducted entirely by members of the tribe working on the mine. The suggestion appears to have been well received, and ten Elders were elected. Elders of the larger tribes represented the interests of smaller, related, groups. Not long afterwards the lead given by Spearpoint was followed in the Township location.

The Council of Elders on the mine was designed primarily to provide a link between the Compound Manager and the African population of the compound. At meetings of the Council, Elders were able to state general grievances and raise complaints. The Compound Manager, for his part, was able to communicate to them the latest pronouncement of Management policy, and could feel 'certain of a true and comprehensive explanation being made to the tribes'.[1] The Elders also assumed judicial functions so that, through the hearing of innumerable petty cases, largely of a domestic character, they were able to supplement the compound police as an agency of social control. The position of the Elders in the Township location differed in certain important respects from that of their confrères on the mine, in ways whose significance will emerge at a later stage of the analysis. The Township location housed a very small population in comparison with the mine, and was under the control of the Town Superintendent. The Town Superintendent was responsible for the allocation of housing and housing sites, for the collection of rents, and for the general care of the location. He had some responsibility, too, for the maintenance of law and order, and here he was assisted by the Tribal Elders who would gather in the evenings to hear and attempt to settle the various minor cases that were constantly cropping up. Unlike the Compound Manager, the Town Superintendent had no wide responsibility in matters affecting the employment or working conditions of location residents, and the function and interests of the location Elders were correspondingly less extensive.

This then was the situation when the first major disturbances

[1] Spearpoint, p. 20.

broke out on the Copperbelt in 1935.[1] Unemployment was still widespread amongst the Africans in the towns but, since few opportunities for earning money existed in the tribal areas, many continued to come to the towns where they were supported in some fashion by their relatives.[2]

The disturbances themselves began at Mufulira as a strike of African miners. The immediate cause, according to the findings of the Commission of Inquiry, was the abrupt and incomplete announcement, throughout the compound, that African poll-tax had been increased all round, in the middle of the year. News of these events soon spread to Kitwe (Nkana mine), and there too there was a strike. The most serious incidents, however, took place at Luanshya where the disturbances culminated in the storming of the Mine Compound Office by an infuriated mob. There was general confusion, and some of the police appear to have lost their heads. Firing began in the course of which six Africans were killed and twenty-two injured.

It is unnecessary here to enter upon any detailed analysis of these events. It is sufficient for my present purpose merely to record their implication for the growth of the urban administrative system. There can be little doubt that the disturbances came as a profound shock to Government officials and Administrative Officers whose training and background had left them ill-equipped to handle the problems of an industrial community. The Senior Provincial Commissioner at Ndola (Mr. Goodall) was himself led to confess to the Commission of Inquiry that what had developed was something quite outside his experience. The Government's analysis of the situation was given by the Chief Secretary in his evidence before the Commission, parts of which I have already quoted. He argued that the disturbances were not primarily over tax, but that the causes were more fundamental.

'I say without any fear of contradiction at all, that if it transpires that if the tax was in any sense a direct cause of the disturbance it is proved to me as an Administrative Officer of very long experience, beyond all doubt, that a situation existed on the mines which was particularly

---

[1] Riots had occurred a few years earlier at Ndola. See *Evidence*, i, p. 13, and Merle Davis, p. 95. The Merle Davis Report refers to 'near-riots' in 1932 at Livingstone, Lusaka and Ndola.
[2] *Report of the Commission of 1935*, para. 90.

D

dangerous, undesirable, and quite unique in my experience. Because if natives riot on occasion of tax without any indication that they are dissatisfied, with no attempt to make representation of their grievances, without even making an attempt to evade payment, then I say that a spirit prevails among these natives which is altogether novel. . . . Somehow that spirit and that situation have to be accounted for and it cannot be accounted for by any situation created by Government unless we were at fault in having not sufficiently insisted that our administration of the natives on the mines must be conducted on lines similar to those prevailing elsewhere and customary under Crown Colony Government. Of course, the whole lesson is that the Government has not got the contact or the influence or the prestige by which alone we govern all native tribes. We govern vast areas in this country where to all intents and purposes we have not got a single armed man to enforce law, and we do it because of our close contact, influence and prestige, and more particularly with the leaders of the people. No such thing would be possible I think in any tribal area as an outburst so sudden as that . . . without attempt on the part of the natives to make representations, without any attempt to discuss matters with the local District Officer. . . .' [1]

A similar point of view was expressed by the Senior Provincial Commissioner. He pointed to the difficulties created for the Administration when the ordinary functions of the District Officer were inevitably replaced in an industrial centre by the Compound Manager: 'Whereas in their own homes for this, that, and the other matter they would go to the District Officer, here they find him engaged, or they are told that it is the function of the Compound Manager—as many of the matters are.' He suggested that what was necessary was a complete re-organization to bring Government into closer contact with the people.

Thus for many Administrative Officers the emergence of the urban communities on the Copperbelt did not appear to involve the posing of administrative problems very different in kind from those they were accustomed to handling in remote tribal areas. Rather, they tended to explain events on the Copperbelt in terms of their own failure to follow closely the principles and methods which already prevailed elsewhere. They saw their problem as the need for re-organization so as to reduce the 'distance' that had grown up in the towns between Administrative Officers and

---

[1] *Evidence*, i, p. 55.

the people. The basic assumptions underlying administrative policy were left unimpaired. The point of reference for administration remained the tribe, and not the town. Thus the Senior Provincial Commissioner himself raised the question whether it would not be a good thing to institute Native Authorities in the compounds, along similar lines to those already existing in the tribal reserves. Mr. Goodall did not develop these ideas at the time, but he appears to have envisaged a system whereby men of authority—'some sort of chiefs'—whom the people could respect, would be imported to the mine compounds from the tribal areas.

Mr. Goodall's suggestion, which was also considered by other witnesses in the course of the hearings of the Commission of Inquiry, involved the assumption that the dominant ties linking Africans together in the towns were still those of a tribal society, and that Chiefs or their nominees could still effectively exercise political control over their subjects as wage-labourers in the distant towns. Therefore, it is important to consider here the part played by the Tribal Elders on the Roan during the disturbances.

After the strike at Mufulira and Kitwe, and foreseeing that the trouble could quite easily spread to Luanshya, Mr. Spearpoint immediately consulted the Elders who assured him that no disturbances would take place at Roan. It may well be—and indeed it seems probable—that the violent form the disturbances took at Luanshya was unpremeditated; nevertheless, it is clear that in the strike situation the Elders lost completely whatever influence they had with the people. This emerges most distinctly in the evidence which Mr. Spearpoint himself gave before the Commission of Inquiry. He said that he summoned several of the Elders, and spoke to the Bemba Elder in particular. He told him to go among the Bemba people in the compound and try to ascertain whether there was any talk about possible disturbances on the following day. Later that evening an African clerk reported to him that the Bemba Elder had attended a gathering of his tribesmen and had been 'discredited'. The tribesmen accused the Elder of being in league with the Europeans and drove him away. Subsequently, when the riot started, and a mob stormed the Compound Office, the Elders fled, and, together with the compound police, sought safety within the Compound Office. Asked how the Elders behaved during the strike, Spearpoint replied: 'They appeared to be refugees as far as I can make out.'[1] Discussing the point in its Report, the Commission of Inquiry commented (para. 95):

... there appears to be an increasing amount of stabilization of the native mining population, involving their detribalization and indus-trialization. Such tribal control as still existed in the mines appeared to be entirely inadequate for the control of the position. At Luanshya there is a system of Elders both in the mine compound and the Govern-ment compound: these Elders are chosen by different tribes and have no legal authority over the natives. They do not appear to have been of much assistance, nor did they in any way succeed in controlling the disturbances when they had arisen.

Few Administrative Officers regarded these remarks as in-validating in any way the basic assumptions on which they worked. In terms of those assumptions, what the rejection of the Elders' authority in the strike situation showed was not the pos-sible ineffectiveness of 'tribal control' in an urban and industrial milieu, but the inevitable ineffectiveness of Tribal Elders who lacked the legal powers with which to enforce their authority. Hence came the proposal to institute some form of Native Authority in the towns. However, the proposal appears never to have gone beyond the stage of discussion. Opinion in the matter amongst Administrative Officers was divided, and there were those who saw the urban areas as 'White man's country, and no place for experiments in Indirect Rule'. The mining companies were also opposed to the development of such a system on the grounds that it would tend to undermine the authority of the Compound Manager.[2] The idea of establishing urban Native Authorities was dropped, and attention concentrated on the possibility of setting up properly constituted African Courts in the towns. In examining briefly the way in which these Urban Courts came eventually to be established, we will gain a clearer idea of how these assumptions affected the development of urban Native Administration.

In his evidence before the Commission of Inquiry, the District Commissioner, Ndola (Mr. Keith), had expressed the view that something more than mere Elders appointed by Chiefs was needed in the urban compounds. He pointed out that many of the Afri-cans in the town were 'advanced' and looked down on the illit-

---

[1] *Evidence*, ii, p. 594.   [2] See below, p. 39.

erate type of man, the old-fashioned type, who would be 'put in' by the Chief. He wanted to see these advanced Africans have a say in the selection of the Elders. After giving this evidence, Keith worked out some of the ideas he had put before the Commission. Following the disturbances of 1935, there had been set up a Native Industrial Labour Advisory Board to keep under constant review the general problems arising out of the increasing employment of Africans in industry. Early in 1936, a Sub-Committee of this Board examined a memorandum which Keith had prepared, setting out proposals to establish Urban Courts. Stressing that native administration tended to fall into the hands of the police to an unnecessary extent because there were no other means then available for dealing with disputes and assaults, the memorandum made certain concrete suggestions about the composition, organization, and jurisdiction of the Courts.[1] Two points were made which are important for the present discussion. First, it was emphasized that the Urban Courts thus envisaged had nothing to do with the system of Compound or Tribal Elders who formed part of the internal organization of the mine. What was wanted was a system which would cater for the needs of all urban Africans wherever they were employed. Second, the principle of the direct appointment of Court Members by Native Authorities was expressly disavowed. The composition of the Courts was to be decided by each urban District Commissioner himself after consultation with the local people.

Keith's argument rested upon the premiss that the urban agglomerations would develop into communities distinct from those from which the urban populations sprang. He opposed the selection of Court Members or representatives in local government by Chiefs in tribal areas because it would discourage the idea that the conduct and social life of urban Africans were their own responsibility. In any case, he argued, any attempt to foist the tribal system upon the urban communities was bound to fail, for sooner or later their desire to run their own affairs would be asserted.

Keith's views were attacked from a number of angles. Some

---

[1] For a more detailed account of the establishment of these courts see A. L. Epstein, *The Administration of Justice and the Urban African*, Colonial Research Studies (1953), chs. 1 and 2.

Officers urged that certain of his proposals, particularly those relating to the composition of the new Courts, were not practicable. Others had doubts about the applicability of Native law and custom in the urban areas. They questioned whether law administered in circumstances where many of the customs had become confused and all was in a state of flux could ever be said to be 'known' and 'capable of proof'. Application of the law could only be arbitrary, since it could not fulfil the basic condition of 'certainty' in the law. But underlying all these differences, there was a more fundamental division of opinion over Keith's major premiss. Senior Officers of the Provincial Administration had all gained their first experience of the Territory and its problems on outlying stations in the reserves, many of them long before the opening-up of the Copperbelt. They saw the African essentially as a subsistence cultivator, and a member of kinship-group and tribe. In the same way, they saw the towns as a place of temporary sojourn where a man would come to work for a short while and then return to his land, his family, and his chief. But more than this, 'town' and 'country' came to be charged with moral implications: they stood at opposite poles of a moral order in which country implied 'good' and town implied 'evil'. Like the schoolboys whose essays I have referred to, many officials tended to see the towns as a kind of 'jungle' wherein it was all too easy for a man to slough off the personal restraints imposed by tribal custom and controls. As Major Orde-Brown has pointed out,[1] the 'urbanized' African was frequently regarded with considerable suspicion and disfavour, and in some parts strenuous efforts were made to discourage his existence.

Discussion of these questions went on throughout 1936, and at the Conference of Provincial Commissioners held in that year it was agreed that the policy of introducing Native Courts in urban areas should be evolved only gradually. It was agreed further that the appointment of Africans to act as assessors might go some way towards meeting existing difficulties. The Conference considered that the presence of assessors at sittings of the Magistrates' courts might provide them with experience on the basis of which, in the future, it might be possible to develop fully constituted African Courts.

---

[1] Op. cit., pp. 29 ff.

The original idea appears to have been that the Urban Courts would be composed of honorary judges who would take their place on the Bench after the fashion of lay justices. But mine Compound Managers were reluctant to allow employees to have anything to do with such litigation, on the grounds that they would be taken away from their legitimate work. The Compound Managers also claimed that such duties might expose Court Members to temptations which would bring them before the criminal courts. Accordingly, it was now thought best that certain of the Chiefs in tribal areas be invited to send down to the various mine-centres, representatives who would be paid assessors attending daily on the District Officer.

In advocating the establishment of Urban Courts, Keith, the District Commissioner at Ndola, had considered the use of assessors in this way, and argued that it was a waste of time for the District Officer to sit with assessors who might just as well hear the cases themselves. And, in point of fact, it would seem that as soon as the assessors felt themselves to be firmly established, they began to function to some extent independently of the District Officer, operating as a Court *de facto* if not *de jure*. Thereafter the proper establishment of the Courts was only a matter of time, and in 1938 the Conference of District Commissioners of the Western Province agreed that immediate steps should be taken to constitute a Court at Mufulira. By the end of the following year similar Courts were operating at all the other mine centres and at Ndola, the commercial centre of the Copperbelt.

Although the mines had shown an unwillingness to co-operate in this matter, it is clear that the whole character of the Urban Courts was initially determined by the attitudes of Administrative Officers towards the question of stabilization of the urban population. The appointment of Court Members by the Native Authorities in the tribal areas operated to remove the responsibility for the maintenance of law and order in the towns from the hands of the urban residents themselves. At the same time, it gave tacit recognition to the view that a body of law, which had developed over the centuries and in conditions specific to tribal societies, was equally applicable in the new industrial communities emerging on the Copperbelt. Indeed, the aim in administering justice to the 'temporary' urban resident came to be formulated as:

'to maintain and strengthen him in his tribal background'.[1] In consonance with this policy, it was later decided that no Court Member should be appointed for more than six years, and that at the end of his first three years he should return for a period to his own tribal area in order to keep in touch with tribal law at its source.

The view that principles of social control deriving from the tribal system were equally operative in an industrial environment was also accepted at certain of the mines. Although the Elders at Luanshya had failed to exercise control in the strike situation, this did not mean that their authority was rejected by the people in all spheres of their work. As we shall see shortly, the system of Tribal Elders operated satisfactorily in the main, and was appreciated by the mass of the people. At Roan the system was persisted in, and even extended. By 1937 there were some forty accredited Elders on the mine.

There can be little doubt that the system of Tribal Elders proved of great value and assistance to the Compound staff. Meetings of the full Council of Elders were not held regularly because the Compound Manager wished the Elders to feel that they could approach him at any time. Individual Elders were also called upon from time to time to advise on points of native custom. Again, in order to claim married quarters and rations for his wife and children, the employee had to show that he was legally married. In Northern Rhodesia the only form of union legally recognized amongst Africans is marriage according to Native law and custom. Moreover, there is as yet no form of compulsory registration of African marriages for the whole Territory. With their knowledge of custom and their wide range of acquaintances amongst the people, the Elders were often of great assistance to the Compound Manager in establishing the validity or invalidity of a couple's claim to be married. In this way, through formal and informal contact with the Elders, the Compound Manager was able to build up a satisfactory medium of communication between his Department and the African employees. According to Spearpoint, the system was a great success and enjoyed the full support of Management. Thus a man who came before the Elders and was guilty of insulting behaviour was liable to be

---

[1] Quoted in Epstein, *Administration of Justice and the Urban African*, p. 11.

discharged from his job. The Elders had badges of office. They were also provided with larger houses, and were given larger rations in order to feed and shelter new arrivals on the mine, until they were able to trace their own kinsfolk.

There is also little reason to doubt that on the whole the system of Elders was popular with the people. Spearpoint describes the great use that was made of the Elders at this time as 'remarkable'.[1]

The office of Elder carried considerable prestige, and elections to the Council were often accompanied by much intrigue. Amongst themselves, they set up standards of decorum and propriety, and Mr. Spearpoint has told me of cases where individual Elders, whose behaviour had fallen short of those standards, were relieved of their office at the instance of the Council itself.

Many, perhaps most, of the Elders were related to tribal royal or chiefly families, and they were drawn from all departments of the mine. They included in their number ordinary labourers, as well as some senior boss boys and mine clerks. Their houses were scattered over the compound, and Management made no attempt to concentrate members of the same tribe in their own sections of the compound. Similarly, in the work situation, men of many tribes worked together in the same gang. There were instances where men of one tribe tended to predominate in a certain type of job, as in the case of the Luvale and the Nyakyusa considered in the previous chapter; but this was a matter of chance rather than deliberate policy on the part of the Management. Thus in selecting Elders of royal lineages the workers themselves reaffirmed their tribal ties.

The work of the Elders extended to almost every aspect of African life in the compound. Complaints, whether about social or working conditions, were dealt with through the Elders. When distinguished visitors came to Roan, it was the Elders with whom they would talk. When news was received of the death of a Chief, his tribesmen looked to their Elder to make arrangements for carrying out the traditional mourning ceremonies. But perhaps the most important aspect of their work lay in the settling of disputes between Africans. The Elders had no legal powers in

---

[1] Spearpoint, p. 19. I had the good fortune to be able to clarify many of the points made in his article in a number of interviews with Mr. Spearpoint himself.

this respect, and their jurisdiction rested mainly on the litigants' willingness to submit to their judgment. Every case was reported to the Compound Manager, who decided whether it was serious enough to warrant reference to an Administrative Officer. The few examples given by Spearpoint in his article suggest that the Elders were empowered to adjudicate only on very minor issues. Thus one case was brought by a native doctor who claimed payment for medicine to produce fertility in a barren wife. The women had refused payment, and in fact counterclaimed on the grounds that she had borne twins. This matter was reported for settlement to the District Officer. Later, cases involving claims for damages or compensation had to be referred to the Urban Court. But there were still many cases, often of a domestic character, where advice and moral instruction rather than any specifically legal remedy were sought, and here the Elders played an important part within the administrative system. I will attempt to examine this rôle in greater detail in a later chapter.

II

In an earlier chapter I spoke of the dichotomy which divides the whole town into two more or less distinct communities. From the discussion of the Elder system, we see further how this dichotomy is emphasized in a dual system of local administration. Mr. Keith had touched on this point in his memorandum on Urban Courts, when he remarked that what was needed was a body which would cater for the needs of all Africans in the town wherever they were employed. To some extent the newly-established Urban Court did provide a link between Africans on the Mine Township and their fellows in the Government location, for the Court Members were all representatives of the most important Chiefs in the Territory. It was customary at this time for the Court Members to take upon themselves the names of the Chiefs they represented, and they regarded themselves as being responsible for the general moral welfare of their tribesmen wherever they were living in the town. There was here a source of friction between Court Members and certain Tribal Elders, for each claimed to be the 'true' representative of his respective Chief. I was told that the Lozi Elder at the Roan was recalled to Barotseland in 1939 because of a dispute over precedence with the Lozi Member of the Urban Court.

Keith's memorandum envisaged a form of organization which would have had more complete governmental powers, and which would have been a more effective help to the Administration in its task of maintaining law and order among urban Africans. On Keith's argument, the Native Authority would have been made up of representatives from the mine, and from the Government Township. But whatever the composition of the proposed Authority, it would presumably have functioned as an instrument of local government, with certain executive, legislative, and possibly fiscal powers, as well as the judicial powers exercised by the Urban Court. It would have exercised jurisdiction in both mine and location, and represented African opinion in the town as a whole. In fact Native Authorities were never set up in the towns. As we have already noted, opinion amongst Administrative Officers was divided on the question, and the mines were also unwilling to co-operate. In a speech made in the Legislative Council in 1936, a Government spokesman referred to the difficulties of instituting a form of Native Government in compounds which were under discipline, with European officers in charge of them. 'We are proposing for those natives not in compounds to set up African townships which will be governed by Native Councils. I have been advised that the authorities, the mining authorities, are not in favour of their labourers being part and parcel of these Native Authorities. On the other hand, the residents of these African townships will undoubtedly be in touch with the residents of the mine townships and they will reflect the opinions of the natives in those mine townships.'[1] Instead therefore of Native Authorities, with powers broadly similar to those granted to the tribal authorities in the recent re-organization,[2] Government was led to introduce gradually the system of Urban Advisory Councils.

There appears to be some doubt about the date when these Councils were first introduced.[3] At all events, there was an Urban Advisory Committee in Luanshya in 1938, and at its very first

---

[1] Northern Rhodesia Legislative Council Debates, 1936, p. 91.
[2] Under the Native Authorities Ordinance, cap. 157 of 1936.
[3] See F. M. N. Heath, 'The Growth of African Councils on the Copperbelt of Northern Rhodesia', p. 123.

meeting the Provincial Commissioner explained what were to be its functions. He pointed out that Africans who came to the Copperbelt did so of their own free will. But once there they had to work for Europeans and submit to European regulations. It was impossible to preserve in the mine towns those native customs and that independence which prevailed in the villages, but at the same time Government wished Africans who were in the towns to have some means of expression. He said that it would be a great help to know the feelings of Africans on the Copperbelt on various matters. The Committee could also be of help in advising on the expenditure of the Beer Halls funds, and in the dispelling of false rumours which circulated so rapidly. In conclusion, the Provincial Commissioner explained that, unlike the Urban Court Members, the members of the Committee would not be paid as they would meet only at intervals, and this would not interfere with their ordinary work. It was an honour to be on the Committee, and that should be a sufficient reward. The Committee would not be concerned with working conditions. No grievances between employer and employee would be brought by the Committee, as there were other adequate channels.

The Advisory Committee was comprised of eight nominated members, and sat under the chairmanship of the District Commissioner. They were drawn almost entirely from the ranks of the Tribal Elders on the mine and in the location, though these included a few of the more highly educated Africans in Luanshya at the time. One of them was the son of a leading councillor in Barotseland in the time of the Paramount Chief Lewanika (d. 1916) and had matriculated at a college in the Union of South Africa, where he had been sent by the Chief. He was the first Lozi Elder on the mine, where he was employed as a clerk, and was able to produce before the Commission of Inquiry of 1935 a letter from the Paramount Chief showing the authority he had been given over all Barotse subjects living in Luanshya. Shortly after taking his seat on the Advisory Committee, he became involved in a dispute over precedence with the Lozi Urban Court Member, and he was recalled to Barotseland. Another clerk, employed by the Management Board to collect the rents of Africans living in the location, represented the Nyasaland section of the community. He too became involved in a case, was dismissed his employment, and was replaced on the Committee.

The minutes of the meetings of the Advisory Committee, which met at irregular intervals, show that the members concerned themselves almost entirely with matters of local or domestic interest. At one of its first meetings, the Committee drew attention to the situation and problems of African marriage in the urban areas. Members expressed their deep concern about the increasing laxity of the marital tie, and asked for a firmer control of marriage by a system of registration. They suggested that parties wishing to marry in the towns should first appear before the Tribal Elders, and then go to the 'Boma'[1] for the proper registration of their marriage. At this same meeting they discussed what measures could be taken for keeping prostitutes out of town, and the difficulties arising over the custody of children on divorce in the case of inter-tribal marriages, and they concluded with a demand that the compensation awarded to a husband in a case of adultery should be at a fixed rate. But in addition to the discussion of such broad topics, the Committee also dealt with more specific matters. These included requests for financial assistance for the local football teams, for the improvement of water supplies and washing facilities which operated on the 'communal tap' principle, and for the introduction of a stopping place for railway passengers at the smelter on the mine instead of at the station, as it was too far for women and children to walk from the station.

In this way the Committee served the District Commissioner as a ready channel of communication with the mass of the people. At the same time, he was able to pass on through the members new pronouncements on Government policy, and to inform the public of changes in the law. Indeed, even the most casual perusal of the minutes at this time suggests that a high proportion of the matters discussed in the Committee were initiated by the District Commissioner himself.

After a few years the Advisory Committee gave way to the Urban Advisory Council. The original members were replaced by others who were again drawn mainly from the ranks of the Tribal Elders. But now all the educated members had dropped out, and the Advisory Council took on more the appearance and character of the 'traditional' council of elders.

---

[1] The term commonly used to describe a Government station or District Office.

III

Thus by the end of the Copperbelt's first decade the foundations for a system of urban administration had been laid. The dichotomy of the town had become an administrative trichotomy. Mine, the Management Board, and the office of the District Commissioner, provided the fixed points of the administrative and political structure, and with each of these was associated its own form of local administration. The Elders on the mine and in the location formed quite distinct bodies and, though there may have been interaction between them in certain situations, for the most part they acted independently. But they had this in common, that while they owed their position as Elders to the prestige they enjoyed within a traditional tribal polity, their authority derived from sources within the urban community itself. By contrast, the Members of the Urban Court were associated with Government and, although they too enjoyed high prestige in terms of tribal political values, their authority stemmed from sources extraneous to the urban situation. As a senior Administrative Officer once commented, they were the 'representatives of the more important Chiefs in the urban areas, carrying out in those areas the work of the Native Courts in the rural areas'.

It should be clear, I think, that the developments I have been describing here were not the product of any clearly articulated programme. On the contrary, what is most striking is the lack of co-ordination in the building up of the urban administrative system. As I was able to show in greater detail in my report on the Urban Courts,[1] solutions to administrative problems were often of an *ad hoc* character, and had to be abandoned as their limitations in other situations became apparent. The circumstances were novel both for the Africans themselves, and the Europeans who were called upon to handle difficult administrative problems. The period might best be summed up as one of 'experimentation'.

Nevertheless, I believe that it is possible to discern a common theme running through these various developments, and appearing in the institution of Tribal Elders, Urban Courts, and Urban Advisory Councils. All sprang initially from the administrative

---

[1] *The Administration of Justice and the Urban African*, p. 9.

need to find some workable means of communicating with the inchoate mass of African workers who had flooded into the town from tribal areas in every part of the Territory, and even beyond. More than this, they all rested upon the common assumption that the social ties, the norms, and the values which had served to regulate behaviour in the tribal societies from which all the new urban dwellers had come, could continue to operate in the different conditions of an industrial community. Implicit in the employment of Tribal Elders, and the importing of Urban Court Members from the Native Authorities, was the view that the dominant ties between Africans in the towns were still the ties of the village and the tribe. This major proposition had as its corollary the assumption that the respect accorded to 'tribal' leaders and the authority they wielded in some situations, could also operate in other situations where African interests of a different order were involved.

In the conditions of the day, there was undoubtedly considerable justification for these views. Hostility between tribal groups was still marked by frequent brawls; and fights between individuals sometimes developed into serious affrays as tribesmen came to the support of their fellows. Tribal stereotypes developed around the unusual customs or alleged practices of particular groups, and many of these still persist. Labour was still almost entirely migrant, and the constant circulation of population between town and country militated against the development of ties which would have cut across those of tribalism. The institution on a tribal basis of a system of Elders and of Urban Courts itself served to emphasize and perpetuate these divisions.

In the disturbances which took place at Luanshya in 1935, the authority of the Elders was rejected by the people, and they were themselves forced to seek refuge in the Compound Office. In the circumstances, it is conceivable that those responsible for formulating policies might have been led to re-examine the major assumption, or at least its corollary, on which their policies were built. This did not happen. In the first place, it was possible to argue that the situation was of such an explosive character that any alternative form of authority would also have been rejected. But I believe that a more cogent reason why the assumption continued to be held by officials was that the failure of the Elders in the strike situation could itself be explained within the system of ideas of which the major assumption formed only a part. For Administrative Officers, the ineffectiveness of the Elders in controlling their people was satisfactorily explained in the lack of proper legal support for the Elders, and in their own lack of contact with the people. Thus it is significant that, immediately after the disturbances, Government brought the Bemba Senior Chief Mwamba, his 'son' Chief Munkonge, and a number of Bemba hereditary councillors, to the Copperbelt so that they might ascertain the nature of the people's grievances, and at the same time express their condemnation of a set of events which had brought the name of their tribe into disrepute.[1] Their later evidence before the Commission of Inquiry is most illuminating.[2] Chief Munkonge referred to the increasing stabilization of the urban population:

'The number of people who are staying here for longer periods is increasing,' he said. 'I think that we [Chiefs] lose power over these people because they are not under our direct jurisdiction: they are under Europeans here, and we cannot control them ourselves. . . . I cannot say anything about the Elders at Luanshya. I think if I took this matter to [Paramount] Chief Chitimukulu and told him about the Elders, all he would say is that the matter rests in the hands of the Europeans. It is entirely a European concern. I do not think the Elders can control the people because the people are not afraid of them. . . . They do not respect them because they have no power.'

A similar point was made by Councillor Munuka: 'If the Elders had no power the people would say, "You came here for work, we came here for work—why should we obey you?" '

Munkonge and Munuka had here struck on vital points. Administration in the towns was a European concern. Tribal Elders, the Urban Court, and the Urban Advisory Council all served various African interests, but they were also the creation of the European authorities. They were, in a sense, the 'official' instruments of administration. And it is here, I believe, that we

---

[1] Throughout the hearings of the Commission of Inquiry the term Bemba (or Wemba) was used very loosely and included, as indeed one witness pointed out, not only the Bemba proper but also all the cognate Bemba-speaking peoples of the Northern and Western Provinces from which the mine labour force was largely drawn.

[2] *Evidence*, i, pp. 127 and 131.

find part of the reason for the rejection of the Elders' authority in the strike situation. They appeared to be 'refugees', Spearpoint had said, and they were accused of being in league with the Europeans. The Elders indeed were caught up in a position which was fraught with conflict. To begin with, the Elders owed their prestige amongst the people to the fact that they were representatives, and often close kinsmen, of tribal chiefs, and to personal qualities which were traditionally admired; but they were at the same time employees of the mining company, and they owed to Management the various privileges which they enjoyed on the mine. As Tribal Elders they stood as representatives of the people, voicing their needs and complaints to the Compound Manager. But in other situations they acted as a kind of advisory body to the Compound Manager, on whose continued recognition their authority ultimately rested.

There was a further source of conflict. Africans in the towns were no longer simply linked together in a complex set of customary face-to-face personal relationships. Outside the work situation, it was possible for an African to restrict his social contacts to members of his own tribe, with whom he would intervisit, drink beer, and exchange gossip and news from home. But, as Munuka had pointed out, Africans had come to the towns for work, and in the work situation men of many different tribes were brought together in the common task. Through the new wage-economy of which Africans had now become part and parcel, they were linked with the Europeans and Indians who employed them and, through the structure of industry itself, were brought into social relationship with the world at large. In this kind of social system, where the dominant nexus was the relationship of master and servant, or employer and employee, the traditional gradations of prestige became essentially meaningless and irrelevant in certain situations. Working underground in a mine, the labourer had to obey the orders of his boss boy, even though he himself were the son of a Chief and the boss boy only of commoner stock. But there were other sectors of the social field where tribal values could continue to operate, and here Tribal Elders were esteemed for their ability to settle quarrels, to advise husband and wife on details of domestic ritual, and so forth. The different kinds of situation I have just outlined involved essentially different sets of social relations: the difficulties facing the

E

Elders in the strike situation stemmed from the fact that these different sets of relations were confused. The Council of Elders was a body founded on tribal lines, and its very existence was thus rooted in cleavage and division among African workers. By its very nature, therefore, it could not function effectively in a situation where people were involved in their rôle of workers, and not of tribesmen.

The nature of this confusion over the rôles of the Tribal Elders at the Roan is well brought out in the events following the disturbances. The Elders there were restored to public favour, and thereafter continued to receive the respect and regard of the mass of the people. The extension of the system of Elders at Roan took place after the disturbances and, according to Spearpoint, operated with great success. This is not so puzzling as at first sight it might appear. The nature and extent of urban 'tribalism' raises important problems which we shall have to consider in detail at a later stage, and we shall see that the term 'tribalism' covers a wide range of phenomena. Here we may note that, in one of its aspects, 'tribalism' refers to certain social categories through which Africans in the towns are able to organize their relationships with one another, and in terms of which they interact. But inter-tribal relations constitute only one sector of the total field of social relations in which the urban African is involved. As a wage labourer on the mine, or as petty trader and the like, he also becomes involved in new sets of relations which are independent of, and indeed cut across, tribal ties. Stated briefly, the urban African is involved in a number of different sets of social relations which stem from forms of social organization distinct from, and in many respects opposed to, one another. Nevertheless, because they operate for the most part in different spheres of his social life, the African in the towns is able to handle the various sets without obvious difficulty. It is only in situations of crisis, such as the disturbances of 1935, that the inherent conflicts emerge, and the radical opposition between these different principles of social organization is brought into the open.

The conflict between these opposed principles of social organization goes on through time. It is marked by the emergence of new associations, societies, and groups, which claim to be more truly representative of the urban community than the established bodies, with which they become joined in a prolonged struggle for power.

Already in this early period of Copperbelt history we find some indication of such a development through the growth in the towns
of Native Welfare Associations. Welfare Societies, indeed, appear
as a very early feature of African urban society,[1] and they were
the subject of some comment at a Conference of District Commissioners held in 1936. The District Commissioner, Broken
Hill, spoke of them as 'a representative body of educated native
opinion'. At Broken Hill, the Welfare Association appears to have
been treated as a kind of advisory board, and was consulted by
the District Commissioner before he made his recommendations
about the new tax-rates. When the new rate was announced he
again invoked the assistance of the Association to explain the
change to the general public. The District Commissioner, Broken
Hill, added that while the Association undoubtedly represented 'the
thinking and politically-minded Africans', he himself regarded it
as 'an excellent barometer of native opinion'. Other speakers took
a less favourable view of the Welfare Associations. One spoke of
them as 'debating societies which gave the educated native an
opportunity to get up before his fellows and air his English'. The
general opinion seemed to be that since the members of the
societies were drawn from the educated class, and were mostly
clerks and capitaos (foremen), they could not be considered
representative of the African population as a whole. The feeling
of the Conference was that the Associations should be allowed to
develop along the lines of debating societies, but that they should
not discuss political matters. In the following chapter I will show
how, as the Welfare Societies developed, they immediately began
to assume political functions which brought them into conflict
with the established bodies. Here my theme will be the prolonged
struggle that went on between them for power within the existing
administrative order.

---

[1] See, for example, Charles W. Coulter ('The Sociological Problem' in the
Merle Davis Report, p. 87), who refers to a Conference held with officials of the
Native Welfare Associations in Ndola, Livingstone, and Roan Antelope. This
was in 1932.

CHAPTER III

CONFLICT AND GROWTH IN THE URBAN COMMUNITY (1940–50)

I

IN his evidence before the Commission of Inquiry of 1935, Mr. Spearpoint [1] referred to the Elder system as filling a big blank. Indeed, until its abolition on the mines in 1953, the Elders, or Tribal Representatives as they had now come to be known, continued to be the primary agent of administration over Africans on the mine, outside of mining processes. Here, therefore, it is necessary to examine in closer detail the position the Elders occupied in the community during the period 1940–50. The direct evidence I was able to assemble on the question is not entirely adequate. At the time I began my field-work in Luanshya in August, 1953, the African Mine Workers' Union had recently succeeded in effecting the abolition of the Tribal Representatives, and I felt it might lead to misinterpretation of my motives if I pressed my inquiries too far in this direction. On the other hand, I had frequent discussions with Elders in the Municipal location; most of them were residents of Luanshya of long standing, and they continued to operate with the values and attitudes they had been bringing to their duties as Elders for more than a decade. I believe, therefore, that an analysis of the Elder system as I saw it operate in the Municipal location can shed considerable light on the position of their confrères on the mine in the earlier period.

There were twenty-three Elders in the Municipal location, representing some twenty tribes. With one or two exceptions, they all fell within the social category known in Bemba as *bakalamba*. They were the 'big ones', men of age and maturity who had seen their children grow up, marry, and in their turn produce a family. Some of them could claim a year or two at a Mission School, but in the main they were without formal education.[2] They were employed in a variety of occupations:

---

[1] *Evidence*, ii, p. 594.
[2] The expansion of educational facilities for Africans in Northern Rhodesia

as capitaos (foremen) in charge of gangs of labourers, as night-watchmen, and as piece-work tailors or shop assistants in the Indian stores in what is called the Second Class Trading Area. One or two had begun to engage in private trading and claimed to earn about £10 a month, but most of the Elders were usually to be found among the poorer section of the community. Moreover, the office of Elder in the location did not confer the privileges of a larger house and larger rations, as it did on the mine.

On what did their prestige depend? How did they come to be elected as Elders? All the Elders with whom I was able to discuss these questions were in complete agreement that tribal status in itself mattered little in their appointment. Any man, they used to say, who was wise and intelligent and well known among his people might be chosen as an Elder. Nevertheless, as the following table clearly indicates, most Elders did in fact claim close relationship with chiefly families, and indeed it was not unusual for them to describe themselves as Chiefs. Thus on one occasion an Elder was complaining to me that the Members of the Urban Court were given greater respect by the public than the Tribal Elders. He said that people knew that one day they might have to

TABLE 2

TRIBAL STATUS OF LOCATION ELDERS IN MIKOMFWA (1953) [1]

Brother of a Chief	4
Son or Maternal Nephew of a Chief	8
Grandson of a Chief	6
Brother-in-law of a Chief	1
Son of a Tribal Councillor	2
Ordinary Commoners	2
	23

has taken place only comparatively recently. Prior to 1925, with the exception of the Barotse National School, founded in 1907 and financed from the Barotse National Trust Fund, no schools received assistance from public funds. African education was undertaken by a wide variety of missionary societies who 'received no financial encouragement from Government to engage in education, and concerned themselves primarily with their evangelical work'. See *Annual Report on African Education* (1947), Government Printer, Lusaka.

[1] Of the 97 men interviewed in the course of a sample survey in Mikomfwa, 12 claimed to be the sons of Chiefs, 7 to be the grandsons of Chiefs, and 4 claimed to have classificatory ties with Chiefs. The remaining 74 were all ordinary commoners. The survey consisted of interviews conducted by my two Research Assistants on a 10 per cent random sample of houses in Mikomfwa.

go to court, and they were afraid that if they did not show proper
respect for the Court Members the case might go badly with them.
'Look at the [Court] President,' the Elder exclaimed. 'He is only
the son of *Cilolo*, a mere councillor; and even the Bemba man
is *Kasomposhi wa mfumu*, a remote relative of the Chief. So,
although they are greatly respected they are not as Chiefs at
home. But most of the Elders are Chiefs even at home.' That this
was not an isolated incident was shown in the case of another
Elder who was charged in the Urban Court with using insulting
language in public. One day a group of Elders were drinking
beer together in one of the shelters at the Beer Hall. An old man
came over to join them, and put some beer in a tumbler that was
lying idle on the table. The owner of the tumbler, an Elder, had
gone away for a moment, and when he returned started to upbraid the old man for having taken his tumbler. 'Do you not know
that I am a Chief?' he demanded. 'Do you not know that even at
the Boma I am recognized as a Chief?' The Elder was severely
admonished by the Urban Court, and warned that his 'chieftaincy'
operated only within the shelter where the Elders heard cases.

I was unable to observe any election for the office of Elder. But
it is clear from the responses of interviewees in the sample survey
undertaken in Mikomfwa that a royal connection was regarded
by many as an important attribute of Eldership. The following
were fairly typical responses. A Lunda from the Mwinilunga
District, aged 37 and employed as a labourer, said that he did not
know how his Elder was elected—it was before he arrived in
Luanshya—but he considered that he was the right kind of man,
because he was related to the Chief at home. A similar point of
view was expressed by a Bemba, aged 44, who had lived more
or less continuously in Luanshya since 1928, and who was employed as a bricklayer.

'I do not know much about Mwamba [i.e. the Elder]. I hear that he
is related to a Chief, and if that is true then he is fit to be a Tribal Elder.
It is those Elders who are not related to Chiefs who bring troubles. . . .
I mean troubles like those which occurred on the mine compound. In
the mine compound, Tribal Representatives took themselves to be as
important as Chiefs at home and wanted people to respect them as they
would their Chiefs. But the people would not do this. Because of this
trouble Puta was sent to prison. The Union was quite right to do away
with Tribal Representatives because they were going to bring more

troubles. The only mistake the Union made was that it did away with even those Tribal Representatives who were related to Chiefs. What the Union should do is to ask the Chiefs at home to send their representatives to all compounds.' [1]

A second important attribute of Eldership frequently stressed both by Elders and by interviewees was length of residence in the town. The Elders must be men who had had the opportunity to become widely known throughout the community. When I discussed the matter once with the Bemba Elder, he quoted to me the Bemba proverb *Ku cibolya takubula mukaya*, 'even in the case of a deserted village there is always an old native of the place', a *mukaya*, who knows what happened there. Table 3, which sets out the length of time spent by the Elders in the urban areas, shows that in the main they are the *bakaya* (plural) *par excellence*. Only one—a younger man still in his thirties—had spent less than ten years in the urban areas, while nine had lived more or less continuously in Luanshya from its foundation.[2] Fifteen of them

TABLE 3

PERIOD OF RESIDENCE IN URBAN AREAS OF LOCATION
ELDERS IN MIKOMFWA (1953)

		Cumulative length of residence in Luanshya, in years				Total number of Elders
		5–9	10–14	15–19	20+	
Cumulative length of residence in all urban areas, in years:	5–9	0	0	0	0	0
	10–14	1	0	0	0	1
	15–19	0	0	7	0	7
	20+	0	1	2	12	15
Total number of Elders		1	1	9	12	23

[1] The trouble to which my informant referred was the abolition of Tribal Representatives in mine compounds in March, 1953. I discuss this in the succeeding chapter.

[2] In the social survey of the Luanshya Municipal Board Location undertaken by the Rhodes-Livingstone Institute in 1951, Mitchell found that 65 in a sample of 510 (12·7 per cent) had been resident in the town for more than 15 years. This sample included both men and women. See J. C. Mitchell, 'A Note on the Urbanization of Africans on the Copperbelt', *Rhodes-Livingstone Journal*, xii (1951), p. 21.

had served as Elders for more than ten years, and at least five for close on twenty years.

While the Elders had thus spent many of their adult years in an urban environment, it does not follow that they formed a highly 'urbanized' category, if by that term we mean that their norms of behaviour and scheme of values had been modified fundamentally by living in town. Without exception the location Elders had been born in the tribal areas, and their childhood spent in a world that was still largely bounded by the village. Though many years had passed since some of them had last visited their rural homes, it was still the idiom of village life which punctuated their conversation and dominated their thought. Once I visited the Elder of the Mambwe tribe of the Abercorn District in the Northern Province. This Elder had not visited his village since 1936. In the course of conversation he told me that his daughter had just become engaged to a young man from the Fort Rosebery District. I expressed my surprise that he had consented to an inter-tribal marriage of this kind, particularly as there were considerable differences of custom between the two peoples. The Elder replied that he would have objected to the marriage if the young man had been a Lozi, or a Lenje, or had come from the Fort Jameson area, because these places were all far away. But Fort Rosebery and Abercorn were quite near to one another, he said. He could do the journey in a few days on a bicycle!

Connection with a Chief and long residence in the town were thus two of the most important social characteristics of the Elders. But, at the same time, no one could successfully carry out his duties as an Elder unless he possessed the necessary personal qualities. Many discussions which I had on this point, both with the Elders themselves and with others, showed that there was a high degree of consensus on what these qualities were. An Elder must be intelligent, and skilled in the arts of a judge, so that in the hearing of a case he would not be deceived by a too-ready tongue, but would cut quickly through to the heart of the matter. More frequently stressed were the moral qualities which an Elder should display—patience (*ubufuke*), a proper humility (*kuicefya*), and due respect for oneself and for others (*mucinshi*). The Luvale Elder once summed it up for me in the Bemba saying *Kupetama ne chikuku e chikusha mushi,* 'it is uprightnessness and generosity which make a village grow'.

Tribal Elders of course did not always achieve these high standards, but flagrant departures from the norm were soon known and widely discussed. During my stay in Luanshya the Bemba Elder became involved in a series of actions before the Urban Court. Long after the cases had finished, I continued to hear criticism of his quarrelsome temperament. One Bemba, a very old man who had spent many years in Luanshya, said that the *bakalamba* or 'big men' were now looking for someone to replace their Elder. He declared that if all behaved as that Elder did, there would be no reason for having Tribal Elders. Then the old man went on in an interesting aside to say that as a result of the Elder's bad behaviour his daughter was no longer living in Luanshya. The parents themselves knew that they were 'no good' and that if she stayed in the town she might never get married.

We shall see shortly that the functions of the Elders on the mine were always more comprehensive in character than those of the location Elders. But one of the primary functions of Elders, both on the mine and in the location, has always been the hearing and settling of disputes. In following one of these cases in the *nsaka* or shelter of the location Elders, we will be able to gain a clearer idea of the rôle of the Elders in the community, and observe in particular how that rôle was conceived by the Elders themselves.

The shelter itself consisted of a high thatched roof perched on timber supports. In appearance it resembled a large barn. There were long forms on which Elders,[1] litigants and others could sit, but many squatted on the ground, with their legs crossed, as they would in some remote tribal court. As it was evening, and as darkness here falls fast, a hurricane lamp flickered fitfully in the middle of the shelter. The case I am going to describe was brought by the Senior Clerk in the Location Superintendent's office, Phillip Sinyinza.

The hearing commenced when the plaintiff, Sinyinza, took his place on a small stool before the Elders. He was addressed by one of them who advised him that he was in the court of the Elders,

---

[1] When a case was reported to the Location Superintendent, he normally summoned the Elders of the respective tribes involved in the dispute. These were usually joined by a number of Elders of other tribes. Whenever I attended the shelter I generally found about four or five Elders present, hearing the cases together.

that they were authorized to look after the people in the location, and that he must tell his story honestly, and according to what he himself had seen. The plaintiff stated his case:

'It was on Saturday morning. While I was at the office I gave Sunday two shillings to go and get me some eggs.

'At last we stopped work. I went home, and after a time I went off to the Beer Hall. I spent some time there quite pleasantly, then I bought four bottles of Castle Beer [1] and a bottle of wine and I set off home. On the way I suddenly remembered about the eggs, and I called in at Sunday's house. Sunday himself was not at home, but his wife told me that he had already taken the eggs round to my house. Then I called at Samson's place. There they welcomed me, and I found that they had a small calabash of beer. Glancing at the calabash I found they had finished the beer, so I suggested that they have some Castle. Samson's wife brought some glasses. Those in the house were Samson and his wife, and a brother-in-law of Samson's wife. We were all sitting together enjoying a pleasant chat. There were no arguments, and I was not drunk. It was all very happy. Then the brother-in-law of Samson's wife heard a noise outside, as if somebody had been moving the bicycles. He went outside to hear what it was, and found a young man there. He asked the young man what he was doing with the bicycles, but the young man replied: "No, I just came to the house and called out *Oti* [2] but you did not answer me." Then I went outside and asked what it was all about. The brother-in-law wanted to tie up both bicycles together, saying that there were too many thieves about. Then suddenly this young man, Bwalya, attacked me. He struck me a blow on the forearm, then on the eye. He tried to seize me and butt me with his head. But he missed, and as I slipped to one side he fell backwards and hit his head on the cement. He was completely drunk and did not know what he was doing. But I did not throw him down. He injured his head himself. Just then his wife came along and began screaming that we had killed her husband. I was very surprised to hear such words for I am *mukalamba*, a "big man" in the location and everybody knows me. How could it be said that I had killed a person? I told Bwalya's wife that it was her husband himself who had injured his head by falling on the cement. She took her husband away, and then we went back into the house and carried on drinking.

'After a time two constables called at the house and told us that they

---

[1] Castle Beer is one of the standard 'European' beers. It is now sold in the African Beer Halls.

[2] This is the customary greeting sung out on approaching a house to advise the owner that one is calling upon him. It indicates that one comes as a friend.

had heard a man had been killed and they took us all to the Charge Office. There we explained the case, and after everybody had talked a lot, they said that there was no case at all, and that we were all drunk. They told us to go back to the location. On the way Samson's wife began arguing with Muyai, the elder brother of the injured man Bwalya. The Police came and took us back to the Charge Office, and we had more explaining to do. At last we went away leaving Samson and Muyai at the Charge Office. Next morning I heard rumours going about the location that Sinyinza had drawn a knife on a man. This has annoyed me very much. I am the senior clerk here and one of the leading men in Luanshya. I am well known to the Location Superintendent, to the District Commissioner, and to the location Tribal Elders. All of those people trust me. So I find it is very bad that my name should be ruined like this. That is why I have brought this case before the Elders.'

The plaintiff was immediately followed by the defendant, Bwalya.

'I had been drinking with my elder brother. After a time I left saying that I was going to look for beer elsewhere. As I passed by Samson's house I heard a great noise, and thinking there must be beer there I cried out *Oti*. They did not hear. After a little while a man came out and asked me what I was doing. Was I trying to steal their bicycles? Then Sinyinza too came out and asked me the same question. He came over and struck me a blow on the arm. I was very surprised that he should do this for I had done nothing wrong. I tried to hit back, but the brother-in-law of Samson caught me round the shoulders. I don't know what they hit me with, whether it was a bottle or whether it was a knife. They hit me on the head and I fell unconscious to the ground. That is all I saw.'

There was here an obvious clash of testimony which the Elders had to resolve if they were to establish what had really happened outside Samson's house. All the available witnesses were called, and the Court listened to their evidence. None added much that was fresh to the picture which emerged from the evidence of plaintiff and defendant. At last, all the witnesses had had their say, and the Elders were able to question them. The wife of the defendant was recalled.

Elder: 'Were you with your husband when he was drinking?'— *Witness:* 'Yes.'
Elder: 'And had you been drinking yourself?' —*Witness:* 'Yes.'

Elder: 'Do you follow your husband everywhere when he goes drinking?'—*Witness:* 'Yes.'

Elder: 'So you follow him about like a dog. When they were fighting outside Samson's house were you there?'—*Witness:* 'No, I just heard the noise they were making.'

2nd Elder: 'We are just troubling this woman. It is quite clear that she is just repeating what her husband has told her to say. Do you think that a man who has been hit over the head with a piece of wood could escape? I remember the case of Mikaeli which was heard in Luanshya some time ago. We were all standing talking to Mikaeli and he was telling us how he had been in a fight with a fellow. Then suddenly this fellow himself appeared and struck him over the head with the handle of an axe. He died. So I know that if they had hit Bwalya as he claims to have been hit he would not be alive.'

Elder: 'How did you know that they had wounded your husband with a knife?'—*Witness:* 'I know because I was there when they threw him to the ground. What I don't know is how they beat him on the head.'

A third Elder now intervened. He explained to the witness that her story differed from that which she had told earlier on. Now she said that she was there when they started to fight. At first she said she had stayed behind. Did she think the Elders just listened to people talking without paying attention to what they said? Did she think the Elders would forget what had happened at the beginning of the case, and that she could confuse them by now saying something different? The witness was caught, and tried to wriggle out of it by pleading that she had not understood clearly one of the Elder's questions as he was speaking in Nyanja, a language she did not know very well. The Elders recalled the defendant's elder brother for a moment.

Elder: 'Is it good that the stories of the witness should differ?'— *Witness:* 'It is good so far as you Elders are concerned, but for myself it is not good.'

Elder: 'Who then is in the wrong?'—*Witness:* 'It is the woman.'

Elder: 'How can a man escape from a case? Is it not through having a proper witness?'—*Witness:* 'Yes.'

Elder: 'So, your case is settled.'

The Elders rose and left the shelter for a while to discuss the matter between themselves. At length they returned and their spokesman addressed the defendant:

'We Elders do not wish to charge any man unjustly. But you,

Bwalya, our child, have done wrong. First of all one should not go wandering about the location at night on one's own. When that happens you may possibly get stabbed, and then you go and blame somebody who had nothing to do with the case. Secondly, you went to another man's house at night and found they were drinking. But they were drinking Castle Beer, and that beer was their own which they had bought with their own money. It is not like a [tribal] beer-drink to which anyone may come. But today you are lucky. Normally, if a case of this sort comes before us we order compensation to be paid. But Sinyinza has brought this case because he wishes us to teach you properly. Sinyinza is a senior man here. He helps to look after the people, and after us, the Elders. We have been authorized by the Location Superintendent and by the people themselves to hear these cases, and we find that it is not proper that a man like Sinyinza should be defamed in this way. So we are not making you pay anything, but we are instructing you that you should learn to live properly. You have escaped this time, but if in future you have any more cases remember that we have the power to turn you out of this location. We suggest that you stop living with your elder brother, and try to find a house of your own as quickly as possible.

'And now you, Samson, you are a senior constable here. It is your job to look after the people. How can you do this when you are drunk? If a man like Sinyinza comes to your house it should be your job to see that he gets home properly or to give him a place to sleep. But how can you do this if you are so drunk that you have cast away your wits?'

In conclusion, Sinyinza thanked the Elders for the way in which they had heard the case, and for instructing the defendant how to behave himself. The case was over, the parties rose, and moved off into the night.

From a legal point of view, the case was perfectly straightforward. The law governing the matter in dispute was clear, and the issue resolved itself into a simple question of credibility—which of the stories produced before the Court was the more worthy of Credit. Through its questioning of one of the witnesses, the court was able to show that her evidence was inconsistent. Indeed, the contradiction was so patent that even the elder brother of the defendant had no choice but to admit it. The way in which the Elders heard the case was indeed typical of much African Court procedure. The atmosphere was completely informal, and though due deference was shown to the Elders, nobody had the slightest hesitation in presenting his case, or giving evidence. Each party was given every opportunity to say what was in his mind, free of interruption. In cases of a minor character, where witness after witness will recite the same testimony, sometimes in almost identical terms, this mode of procedure may appear cumbersome and tedious, but there is little doubt that in the main it is effective, and that it gives general satisfaction to the litigants themselves.[1]

The interest of the case for the present discussion lies not in its legal, but in its sociological, aspects. The case was brought by a man who was a leading figure in the African community. He was mature and educated, and he held a responsible post as Senior African Clerk in the office of the Location Superintendent. His claim to be widely known and respected was not unjustified. So the rumours going around the location that he had drawn a knife and stabbed a man represented a serious blemish on his reputation. In the normal way, he could have claimed heavy damages before the Urban Court for having been defamed. All that he was seeking was a public pronouncement re-affirming his high social standing and integrity; although in other circumstances, as an educated man, he might have had little time for the Elders, it is interesting to note that in the present situation he found it convenient to bring the matter before them. Apart from establishing the facts of the matter, the case presented no real difficulty to the Elders. It was not proper that a man of Sinyinza's status should be defamed in that way, and their judgment marked an attempt to re-establish his position as *mukalamba*, a responsible member of the community.

The Elders see themselves as the 'fathers of the location' and all the people in it as their children. It is their task to uphold the established order of society by teaching those who depart from its norms how to live properly. In the exercise of their judicial functions they do not see themselves as forming a court which operates by punishing the people. Rather do they see themselves as guardians of law and morals whose function it is, through instruction and advice, to re-affirm the moral values of society. The work of the Elders is *kulamununa*, to restore and maintain harmony in social relationships: and they do this by giving *mafunde*, moral instruction. It is through the giving of *mafunde* that the Elders distinguished themselves from the members of the Urban Court who, they used to claim, did not give proper

---

[1] For further discussion of this question see below, ch. VI.

mafunde, but only heavily fined and imprisoned the people. One of the Elders once expressed it thus:

'Nowadays the people on the mine just live like animals in the bush. They have no big leaders [*ntungulushi bakalamba*]. If a man and his wife are having a tiff in the house, all they can do is go to the Compound Office, and there they are given a letter to take to the Boma. There they have to leave much money, for at the Boma [i.e. the Urban Court], there is no charity, *uluse*. The Court Members just work on a ticket basis, not like ourselves who work for *ubuteko*, for the sake of governing just as we do in the villages, without receiving any pay. When a man comes before us, and we find that he has wronged his fellow, we give him the law [*ifunde*—pl. *amafunde*]; if he is not satisfied we tell him to take the matter to the Boma, where they will make him pay much money. If he agrees then we ask him to take five shillings and give it to his fellow so that they may be eating together, and that there may be understanding between them. . . . But if he went to the Urban Court we would say, "You see, we gave you *mafunde*, but you didn't want to listen. Now you have been made to pay heavily. We follow the law as it is in the village, but there at the Court they work for the salary they get every month. They do not follow the law of government as we know it at home." '

Tribal Elders, both on the mine and in the location, possessed fewer legal powers than the Urban Court. Their jurisdiction rested mainly in the voluntary submission of the parties to their arbitration. They had no power to grant divorces, to award compensation in cases of adultery, or to impose fines in criminal offences. Nevertheless, they claimed higher moral authority than the Members of the Urban Court. The claim rested upon two grounds. To begin with, they were unpaid. 'We work for the soil [*tubombela fye mushili*]', they would tell me, 'just as we would as *bakalamba* in the villages.' Again, it was they, the Elders, and not the Urban Court Members, who represented the true spirit of customary law through which they were still able to express the deepest values of tribal society. To some extent these claims were justified, for in the main I found that Tribal Elders in the location were held in wide respect. The sample survey showed very few people who did not know who their Elder was; and when we asked people to state who was regarded as the most respected African in Luanshya many replied in some such terms as : 'It is hard to say. Every Tribal Elder is important to his people'; or, 'I can't be sure about this. The Bemba say their Elder is the most important man, the Ngoni say their Elder is, and so on.' In the early days, according to one informant, Tribal Elders were as important as Chiefs, and people used to bring them regular gifts of beer as tribute. And this practice of buying beer for the Elders continues even today, though possibly on a smaller scale. Once when my Research Assistant visited the Beer Hall he found the Bemba Elder sitting together with a number of *bakalamba* and a group of young men from the areas of the Bemba Chiefs Muce-leka and Mwamba. Seeing them drinking beer, he asked the Elder jokingly how they came to be sitting with bottles of beer when it was nearly the end of the month. The Elder replied that even though he came to the Beer Hall with only a 'tickey' (i.e. a threepenny piece) in his pocket, still he had money—he had his 'children'. 'Do you think', he asked, 'that every time you see us drinking beer that the money has come from our pockets? No, that beer was bought for us by the young men. They are our children. For we brought them up, and now that we are old, can they neglect us?'

II

I must repeat here that this analysis of the Elder system is based upon my observations of its operation during 1953. Nevertheless, I feel that it is safe to assert that, in the main, the features which emerge from the analysis were equally characteristic of Tribal Elders in the forties. As a body, the Elders have always operated as a conservative influence. Like their fellows in the location, most of the mine Elders about whom I have information also claimed a fairly close relationship to a chiefly family. This did not mean that they were accredited representatives or delegates of the Chiefs, but it did indicate the persistence of traditional political values in an urban milieu. In settling disputes amongst the people, the Elders followed modes of procedure that were long established and well known in tribal law, and gave recognition to claims that were based in ancient customs and usage. Such prestige and authority as they had among the people derived therefore from the respect accorded to them as upholders of a traditional moral and political order.

But as I have already pointed out, there were certain important differences between the Elders on the mine and in the location. The most noticeable of these, for the purpose of the present discussion, was that by this time the mine Elders had come to acquire representative functions of a kind for which the traditional order offered no precedent.

In 1940, a strike of European miners at Mufulira and Nkana was followed almost at once by a strike of Africans, which was accompanied by serious disturbances. A Commission of Inquiry, known as the Forster Commission, was at once set up to investigate the causes of the disturbances, which had again resulted in the death of many Africans and much damage to property. I shall say something about the nature of these disturbances in a later chapter. Here it is sufficient to record that among the recommendations considered by the Commission for easing the recurrent industrial unrest on the Copperbelt was one for the formation of African trade unions. The Commission held that by their lack of education, and their very recent introduction to industrialism, the Africans were 'clearly not ready' for this step. At the same time the Commission considered it was necessary to devise some scheme to make articulate mass grievances, and to ensure that such grievances were properly brought to the notice of the mine managements. Casting around for some such scheme, the members of the Commission of Inquiry appear to have been much impressed by the system of Tribal Elders operating at the Mufulira mine. This system was rather similar to the one which had been introduced at Roan, and appears to have worked there with equal success. At any rate, the Commission of Inquiry was attracted by 'its many merits' and considered it worth encouraging. 'It may not be too much to expect', the Report explains, 'that the Tribal Elders of the various groups will tend to combine for the discussion of questions of major importance. . . . It seems to us that the developments to which we have referred may yet prove to be the seed from which will spring the African trades unions of the future.'[1]

Hitherto, Tribal Elders had not existed at all mines. Now, following the recommendations of the Forster Commission, the system was re-organized and introduced in the whole of the

---

[1] *Report of the Commission appointed to inquire into the Disturbances on the Copperbelt, Northern Rhodesia*, Government Printer, Lusaka, 1940, paras. 175–80.

F

Copperbelt under the name of Tribal Representatives. The establishment of Tribal Representatives on a more formal basis led to some doubts about their exact position vis-à-vis the Government, the Mine Managements, and the African mine employees. At the beginning of 1942, the Secretary of Native Affairs issued a circular minute [1] which sought to clarify this position and set out Government policy with regard to the Tribal Representatives. The cornerstone of this policy was to avoid the premature formation of Native Workers' Associations by developing, as soon as possible, the Tribal Representatives as an embryonic organization for collective bargaining, under the guidance of the Labour Department.

In line with this policy the major function of the Tribal Representatives was now stated to be 'to keep in touch with all native workers and to present to the Management on their behalf any grievances there might be in regard to working conditions'. They were to be responsible to, and elected by, the native workers only; it was important, the circular minute declared, that they should not feel themselves beholden either to the Government or to the Mine Managements. It was further envisaged that the system would develop under the guidance of Government Labour Officers, who had also recently been appointed to the Copperbelt following the recommendations of the Forster Commission.[2] Labour Officers were charged with the task of educating the Tribal Representatives to become familiar with all problems connected with native labour. Thus the Tribal Representatives were to be regarded primarily as a 'labour body'. District Commissioners were not to be prevented from attending meetings of the Tribal Representatives if they wished to do so, but the Secretary of Native Affairs considered that Administrative Officers could still maintain their contact with the African miners without the assistance of the Tribal Representatives. Similarly, it was considered undesirable that they be used by District Commissioners to disseminate news to the mine employees. 'The Tribal Representatives should be regarded by the workers as their people, and not in any sense as the instrument of Government or the mines.'

---

[1] Circular minute No. 6-MIN/C of 11/2/1942.
[2] *Report of the Commission of Inquiry*, 1940, para. 190.

Towards the end of 1942 Boss Boys' Committees also made their appearance on the Copperbelt. The term 'boss boy' is used on the Copperbelt to describe an African who has been placed in charge of a gang of African labourers. The gang, usually composed of about 10–15 men, is the unit of labour, and the boss boy acts as intermediary between the men of his gang and the immediate European supervisor. Following a meeting between Government Officials and the Chamber of Mines toward the end of 1942, it was agreed that Compound Managers would meet the boss boys, both surface and underground, to discuss with them grievances or other matters relating to their particular employment. The Committee at Roan was usually composed of about twenty of the senior boss boys, and met regularly once a month together with the Compound Manager and the Labour Officer. The Committee was able to raise complaints, and at the same time was informed of any changes to be made in working conditions. For example, at one meeting of the Roan Boss Boys' Committee early in 1943, among the points raised were:

(1) If a man is assaulted by a European he goes at once to the nearest official to complain, either shift boss or mine captain. He is thereupon assaulted again for complaining.

(2) Why is the complainant in an assault case laid off while the European accused still continues to work and draw pay? The Compound Manager replied that he had agreed to give work in the compound at full pay pending the Court decision.

(3) The deplorable lack of manners and respect between Africans underground, and more particularly the insufficient respect paid to boss boys by their gangs. 'As this is so how can we expect the Europeans to show good manners? Surely we should set them an example.' [1]

Labour Officers also submitted reports to the Labour Department on their meetings with the Tribal Representatives. One such meeting which was held at the Roan in July, 1944, is reported as follows:

(1) Tribal Representatives considered that their yearly Christmas present (from the Management) was not enough, as it only amounted to 1s. 8d. a month.

(2) A request that electric lights be installed in the houses of the Tribal Representatives. The Compound Manager explained that there were no materials available.

---

[1] From the Labour Officer's report, filed at the Rhodes-Livingstone Institute.

(3) The wives of Tribal Representatives were finding difficulty in drawing the extra rations to which they were entitled. The Compound Manager said that he would look into the matter.

(4) There were no lights in some of the latrines. The Compound Manager agreed to fix lights as soon as possible.

(5) Would the Compound Manager build another *nsaka* [that is, a shelter in which law cases are heard] for the Tribal Representatives as soon as possible? This will be done.

(6) The Tribal Representatives wished to object to the hookworm treatment being done every six months. It was decided to ask the Senior Medical Officer to meet the Tribal Representatives and discuss the matter.[1]

Thus together the Boss Boys' Committee and the Tribal Representatives provided the two avenues of approach to the Compound Manager, which were available to the African worker. The former represented the more specific interests of the boss boys alone, although when it raised the question of assaults by Europeans on Africans, it was discussing a matter of some moment to the ordinary labourers who made up the mass of the African labour force. The Tribal Representatives were supposed to act as spokesmen for the remainder of the people, though the Labour Officer's report quoted above suggests a body more concerned with maintaining and extending its own privileges. In complaining about the size of their Christmas present they showed clearly that they regarded it not so much as a gift, but as a payment in return for services rendered to the Management. Indeed, the Assistant Labour Commissioner commented on the Labour Officer's report of the meeting that the complaint of the Tribal Representatives that they should be paid for their services was an old one. 'I still feel', he remarked, 'that in view of the fact that direct payment results in the Tribal Representatives being more the spies of the Compound Manager than the spokesmen of their people we cannot make any representations to the Company.'

In the disturbances which took place in 1935 the authority of the Tribal Elders at the Roan mine was rejected by the people because they suspected the Elders of collusion with the European

---

[1] It is not clear from the record of the meeting whether the Tribal Representatives considered that the injections for hookworm, which were compulsory for all mine employees, were too frequent or too infrequent. At the next meeting of the Tribal Representatives the Compound Manager announced that in future treatment would be given every six months and not once a year.

authorities. As we saw in the previous chapter, the position of the Elders was an extremely difficult one because they occupied an intercalary position within the authority structure of the mine. Like the village headman [1] or the tribal chief in relation to Colonial Government,[2] the Tribal Elders found themselves caught up in contradiction: in one set of relations they were themselves workers, and shared the interests of their fellow-workers whom they represented to Management; in another set of relations they were at the bottom of the hierarchy of mine authority, and represented Management to the people. The nature of the contradiction, and its implications, emerged again quite clearly in the events which took place at Mufulira in the 1940 disturbances. It was the Elders there who first reported to the Compound Manager the possibility of a strike by African miners. Later, when the strike broke out, it became clear that the Elders had lost the confidence of their people, who accused them of having agreed to accept the 2s. 6d. a ticket offered by the companies, instead of pressing for an increase of wages to ten shillings a day, which the Africans now demanded. On the advice of the District Commissioner, the workers appointed a Committee of 17 who acted as strike leaders until the conclusion of the strike. The strike leaders appear to have fulfilled their rôle with great success. When threats were uttered against the person and property of the African Compound clerk, the strike leaders were made responsible for his safety and nothing came of the threats. The Committee was also induced to undertake that intimidation should cease, and the days passed quietly until the strike came to an end.

I have no information about the composition of the Committee of 17, but its emergence in the strike situation at Mufulira, and the discipline it was then able to exercise amongst the people, provides

---

[1] M. Gluckman, J. C. Mitchell, and J. A. Barnes, 'The Village Headman in British Central Africa', *Africa*, xix, 2 (April, 1949).

[2] See, for example, E. Colson, 'Modern Political Organization of the Plateau Tonga', *African Studies*, vii (1948), pp. 85–98, and J. A. Barnes, 'Some Aspects of Political Development among the Fort Jameson Ngoni', ibid., pp. 99–109; and J. C. Mitchell, 'The Political Organization of the Yao of Southern Nyasaland', ibid., pp. 141–59. Cf. M. Gluckman, 'The Zulu of South-East Africa' in *African Political Systems* (1940); and Lloyd Fallers, 'The Predicament of the Modern African Chief: an Instance from Uganda', *American Anthropologist*, lvii (N.S.) (1955), pp. 290–305.

Fitz Memorial Library

Endicott College

Beverly, Massachusetts 01915

one of the first indications of the growth of an urban leadership within the mining compounds themselves. At the same time, representation on matters affecting wages and working conditions was only one of the many functions carried out by Tribal Elders, and it was presumably their success in these other matters which led to the reinstatement of the Elders at Mufulira. It is in the Urban Advisory Councils that we find the clearest expression of the struggle begun between the Tribal Elders and the new, rising, urban leaders who, through the Welfare Societies, were now claiming to speak for the people in the towns.

Urban Advisory Councils were introduced on the Copperbelt towards the end of 1941. The Urban Advisory Council at Luanshya was built upon the foundations of the earlier Advisory Committee. Like the latter, it operated as a link between Government, in the person of the District Commissioner, and the Africans of the Mine and Government Townships. Appointment to the Advisory Council at this time was by nomination,[1] and the members of the Council were drawn almost exclusively from the ranks of the Tribal Representatives on the mine, and the Tribal Elders in the location (see Table 4). The Council met at irregular intervals, and discussed with the District Commissioner matters of general interest to people in the town. Among the items I have culled from the minutes were: complaints about the treatment of patients by African hospital orderlies; discussions on the cost of living and the rise in prices because of the war; the desirability of having a separate sub-Beer Hall in the Mine Compound because of the distance between the mine and the main Beer Hall (see sketch map of Luanshya).

About this time, there appears to have been a revival of interest in the Welfare Societies. As already indicated,[2] the Welfare Societies were an early feature of African urban life. But their history seems to have been one of fluctuation, of sudden bursts of energy and activity, succeeded by periods of apathy when the societies often existed only in name, and sometimes not at all. Lewin reports that in 1940 the Native Welfare Associations were almost defunct.[3] A few years later flourishing societies existed at Nkana and Luanshya, and possibly elsewhere too.

---

[1] See below, p. 70.   [2] See above, p. 47.
[3] Lewin, *The Colour Bar in the Copperbelt* (1941), p. 17.

The Luanshya African Welfare and Recreational Society developed out of a Library Committee which was run by a European, the Rev. G. Fraser of the United Mission to the Copperbelt.[1] At one of the meetings of this committee held in October, 1942, it was decided that there was a need for a body serving a more general purpose. The functions of the new Society were laid down in the constitution that was drawn up shortly afterwards:

(1) To co-operate with the Government of Northern Rhodesia with a view to the continuance of the good government of Africans living there.

(2) To co-operate with the District Commissioner, the Luanshya Management Board, and the Native Welfare Committee in the development of good lines of African living in the District, and with a view to their mental, moral, and physical improvement, and generally to do any work calculated to improve the general welfare of Africans, to promote their contentment, and to make representations on their behalf.

(3) To form sub-committees and organize various activities falling within the sphere of welfare and recreational work.

The membership of the Welfare Society included a number of the Tribal Elders who were also members of the Urban Advisory Council; but in the main the appeal of the Society was to, and its more active members drawn from, a small group of relatively well-educated men who were beginning to take an active interest in the affairs of the local community. The first chairman of the Society, and one of its leading figures, was Mr. Dauti Yamba, at that time the Headmaster of the African School. He later became a leading figure in the African National Congress, and a member of the Territorial and Federal Legislatures. Other members, too, were to become at a later date prominent figures in African political affairs within the Territory.

Unlike the Urban Advisory Council, the Society was not in any sense an 'official' body, and could make no claim to represent the community. Moreover, it was avowedly non-political in its

---

[1] The rôle of the various churches and religious societies in the social and political life of the towns raises many complex problems which I was unable to study adequately in Luanshya, but which I hope to examine in the course of further field research.

aims. Nevertheless, the Society rapidly acquired a position of some influence within the political structure of the town. Through its President, the Rev. G. Fraser, who was a member of the Native Welfare Committee, the Society had a strong link with the Management Board. On one occasion, for example, it was able to protest effectively against the poor quality of the mealie (maize) meal being sold in the stores in the Township. Then a direct link was established with the Urban Advisory Council when Mr. Yamba, who for some time had acted as interpreter to the Council, was nominated to represent the Welfare Society. But the Society's greatest practical achievement at this time lay in persuading the Mining Company to agree to make a road between the location and the Mine Township. When the Chairman presented his first Annual Report, he was able to state that part of the road had already been finished, and that he hoped the remainder would not take long to complete.

In the same report Mr. Yamba had referred to the support given the Society by the Urban Advisory Council. Yet it was already becoming plain that the Society was assuming representative functions which official opinion regarded as vested in the Urban Advisory Council. Although the Society had been formed in the Government Township, leading members were drawn from both sections of the town. Meetings were usually held at the Central School, which lay mid-way between the location and the African Mine Township. In its discussions, the Society dealt with matters of concern to the whole town. During the earlier part of 1944, considerable time was devoted to the question of the large-scale dismissal of African mine employees. At one meeting it was agreed that the matter should be referred to the Advisory Council, asking for full information on the discharges. Shortly afterwards, the Society discussed the question further at a meeting with the Labour Officer, who explained that the discharges followed on a request by the United Kingdom Government to reduce the production of copper. At the following meeting of the Society it was noted that the question had been investigated by the Urban Advisory Council, which found that the reports of the dismissals had been greatly exaggerated. The minute of this meeting continues: 'As the Society is becoming more popular, if a person who is maltreated by his master or company tells the Society of anything happening the Chairman or the Secretary should take this man before the District Commissioner and make a written statement.'

Thus while members of the Welfare Society continued to give due acknowledgment to the position of the Urban Advisory Council as the body officially representing African opinion in the town, the expansion of the Society's functions and the members' awareness of their own growing influence, made inevitably for tension in the relationship between the two bodies. By 1944 the conflict between the two had become sufficiently open for the District Commissioner, Luanshya, to ask what notice Administrative Officers were to take of the activities of the Welfare Society. In a letter to the Provincial Commissioner at Ndola, he referred to the danger that the Advisory Council 'might easily find itself taking second place to the Welfare Society'. Shortly afterwards the Welfare Society called a special meeting to arrange subjects for a forthcoming African Regional Council. This was really a matter for the Urban Advisory Council, and when the Welfare Society forwarded the minutes of its meeting to the District Commissioner he commented, somewhat ruefully: 'The trouble is that the Urban Advisory Council is not a go-ahead body, and the unofficial Society is.'

When the next Conference of Provincial Commissioners was held in the following year, Sir Stewart Gore-Browne, who was present as the Nominated Representative of African Interests in the Legislative Council, submitted a note for discussion on the relationship between the Welfare Society and the Urban Advisory Councils. This relationship, he said, was not entirely satisfactory.

'Theoretically a Welfare Society should concern itself with welfare (as opposed to "politics") and should make use of its representatives on the Urban Advisory Council (which is a political body) in order to bring its recommendations to the notice of Government through the District Commissioner, or through the African Provincial Council on which representatives of the Urban Advisory Council sit. In practice the Welfare Societies are not infrequently more energetic and efficient bodies than the Urban Advisory Councils, the line between welfare and politics is difficult to draw, and in some townships at any rate a visitor desirous of sounding native opinion on any matter would be better advised to consult the Welfare Society than the Urban Advisory Council. At best there is considerable duplication of work, at worst the Welfare Societies suffer from a sense of frustration.'

Sir Stewart felt that the reasons for the superior vitality of the Welfare Societies lay in the fact that when the District Commissioners nominated the members of the Advisory Councils, they were bound to select representatives from all the main sections in the community, whereas the Welfare Societies, which generally had no formal constitution, merely attracted the most progressive and energetic individuals in the local community. He considered, too, that there had been cases when the Urban Advisory Council had been too much dominated by the personality of the District Commissioner, and so tended to be a less valuable body than the more independent Welfare Society. He suggested, in conclusion, that the two bodies might be combined into one, to be known simply as, for example, the Luanshya African Council. The membership, he argued, should not be too strictly limited, and should be by election as far as possible; but the District Commissioner should be responsible for using his right of nomination when necessary in order to ensure adequate representation of all important sections of the African community.

These views were not generally acceptable to the Conference, and the Provincial Commissioners opposed the combination of the Welfare Societies with the Urban Advisory Councils. They felt that the Welfare Societies consisted predominantly of the more advanced and educated Africans, 'who represented no one but themselves'. Furthermore, the Societies were already represented on the Advisory Councils. They pointed out, finally, that African Civil Servants could become members of the Welfare Societies, but there were objections to their sitting as members of an Urban Advisory Council.

Yet while the views expressed in the Gore-Browne memorandum were rejected by the Conference of Provincial Commissioners, the memorandum itself did serve to draw attention to the whole question of the composition of the Advisory Councils. An analysis of the composition of the Council at Luanshya at this time would have revealed a variety of principles, all operating simultaneously within the major principle of 'nomination' by the Provincial Commissioner. The mine compound representatives were elected by the Tribal Representatives, 'recommended' by the Compound Manager, and finally 'nominated' by the Provincial Commissioner. In the location, the members appear to have been elected by and from the body of Tribal Elders. The Welfare

Society now had its own representatives on the Council. Finally, representation was also on a tribal, and even national, basis. When the Lunda people of the Mwinilunga District living in Luanshya approached the District Commissioner and expressed their desire to be represented on the Council, the Council itself agreed that there was a need for a Lunda representative. The Nyasalanders, too, had their own special representative, though his election was strongly opposed by a group of Elders on the mine who objected to allowing 'a foreigner to have a full right in the deciding of cases about the country'. A short time later, yet a further principle was introduced when the Provincial Commissioner told the Council at one of its meetings that representation would now be on a vocational and occupational basis. The idea of trade-group representation in the township was quickly agreed to by the Council, and it was suggested that representatives should be elected to represent the shop assistants, domestic servants, employees of the Management Board, and contractors' employees and independent contractors. The Provincial Commissioner informed the meeting that Government was looking for ways and means to give the public townships a more democratic form of representation. 'Eventually,' he said, 'a system of nominations and ballot boxes may be evolved.'

In the meantime, the Advisory Council at Luanshya continued to decline, while the Welfare Society waxed in strength. In addition to holding regular meetings for the discussion of current issues, the Society organized dances and sports-days for the children. When visiting Chiefs came to Luanshya it was the members of the Society who would prepare the address of welcome, and make the arrangements for their entertainment. The Society also helped in campaigns to raise money for various purposes associated with the war effort, and at one point even managed to produce a penny broadsheet giving items of local news. During 1946 the various Welfare Societies throughout the Territory came together to form a Federation of Welfare Societies. Their Conference at Lusaka represented a considerable landmark, since it was the first time an unofficial body of Africans had met together to discuss their problems at a territorial level.

The chairman of the Luanshya Society, who had played a leading part in the formation of the Federation of Welfare Societies, continued to speak of co-operation with the Urban Advisory

Council, but it was now clear that the Advisory Council was completely moribund. On a number of occasions the Welfare Society had come forward with criticisms concerning the management of the Ndola African Hospital, which also served Luanshya. On each occasion the Society was reminded by the District Commissioner that the proper channel for raising such complaints lay through the Advisory Council. At length, according to an official minute, the 'quiescent Council had to be galvanized into activity' by the District Commissioner to give consideration to the criticisms raised by the Welfare Society. By 1947 the situation had reached a point where the African Secretary of the Advisory Council was himself led to move a motion that in view of the unsatisfactory work done by most of the members, and their failure to attend meetings, drastic steps should be taken to reconstitute the Council, and elect a body of more active and interested members.

But by this time the Urban Advisory Councils had acquired a new and most important function. With the introduction of the African Representative Council for the Territory, the Urban Advisory Councils took their place in the hierarchy of African political representation as electoral colleges to the Provincial Councils, the African Representative Council, and ultimately to the Northern Rhodesia Legislative Council itself. So, when the next election for the Legislative Council fell due, the existing Urban Advisory Councils were dissolved and reconstituted.

III

The membership of the new Council, which came into being in 1949, was made up as follows:

African Mine Township	10 members
Luanshya Management Board Location . . .	4 ,,
The Welfare Society	2 ,,
Peri-urban settlements	1 member
Township workers	1 ,,
Fisenge African Township	1 ,,
	19

The total membership of nineteen represented a substantial increase in numbers over previous Councils. But the mode of election showed no fundamental departure from practice followed in the past. The Secretary of Native Affairs had declared that the elections should be conducted, as far as possible, in accordance with normal democratic principles; but he felt it was too soon to lay down hard-and-fast rules, and the actual arrangements for holding the elections were left to the local District Commissioner. The District Commissioner at Luanshya recommended that the Tribal Representatives of the location and the mine compound should ballot for their representatives. He argued that since the Tribal Representatives had already been elected by the people, it was unnecessary to conduct a popular ballot, even if such a step were practicable. This procedure was followed and on the mine the Tribal Representatives first nominated people to a grand total of twenty, from whom they then selected ten to represent the mine compound. In the small African Township of Fisenge,[1] whose total population at that time numbered less than 300, and in the contractors' compounds, a ballot was conducted of all residents. It is not certain how the occupational group members were appointed. According to Heath,[2] it appears that influential clerks, at that time engaged in organizing contractors' labour into a trade union, held individual meetings and then submitted nominations which were accepted as the two duly elected representatives of the township workers and the contractors' employees living in the peri-urban settlements.

Representation in the Advisory Council thus still rested on the fourfold principles of tribe, occupation, membership of an association, and residence in a ward (Fisenge). Nevertheless, I consider that the accompanying tables (Tables 4 and 5) show that there was now a significant change of character in the composition of the Council, particularly in the case of the mine representatives. Whereas in 1944 the Council was composed almost entirely of

---

[1] Fisenge lies about four miles from Luanshya, and just off the main Ndola-Luanshya road. It forms one of a small class of Townships designed for self-employed Africans working in or near the towns. Africans may build their own houses in the Township, the affairs of which are run by a Board consisting of residents of the Township itself under the general supervision of a Township Officer. For a short account see L. D. Conyngham, 'African Towns in Northern Rhodesia', *Journal of African Administration*, iii (1951), pp. 113–17.

[2] 'The Growth of African Councils on the Copperbelt of Northern Rhodesia', p. 127.

TABLE 4

COMPOSITION OF THE LUANSHYA URBAN ADVISORY COUNCIL
DECEMBER, 1944

Name	Tribe	Representing	Age in 1953	Occupation in 1944	Membership in other groups, or other social position
A. Chungu . . .	Mukulu	Govt. Location	55	Capitao in Indian store	Tribal Elder
R. Tembu★ . . .	Tumbuka (Nya)	,, ,,	55	,, ,,	Tribal Elder; Member of Welfare Society
A. Njovu . . .	Nsenga	,, ,,	60	Shop Assistant	Tribal Elder
S. Jere . . .	Ngoni	,, ,,	49	Piece-work Tailor	,, ,,
Ndungu Kasoka★ .	Luvale	Lunda-Luvale peoples	—	Capitao of Night-Soil Gang in the Location	,, ,,
D. Yamba★ . . .	Tabwa	Welfare Society	41	Headmaster	Chairman of Welfare Society; Chairman of Parent-Teachers Association
J. Kambatika . .	Chewa	Mine Township	57	Mine Clerk	Tribal Representative
D. Tengeneshya .	Ushi	,, ,,	d. 1952	Compound Capitao	,, ,,
W. Mushumba . .	Lozi	,, ,,	,,	Clerk in Time Office	,, ,,
W. Mulimba★ . .	Nkoya (Barotse)	,, ,,	—	Boss Boy U'ground	,, ,,
G. Mutwali★ . .	Henga	Nyasalanders	48	Hospital Orderly	,, ,,

★ Has since left Luanshya. Nya = Nyasalander.
N.B. There was one other Member whom I was unable to trace.

TABLE 5

COMPOSITION OF THE LUANSHYA URBAN ADVISORY COUNCIL
DECEMBER, 1949

Name	Tribe	Representing	Age in 1953	Occupation in 1949	Membership in other groups, or other social position
J. Chitanda	Lenje	Govt. Township (Location)	38	Store Capitao	Tribal Elder; now a Committee Member Shop Assistants' Union
D. Chikombola	Mukulu	"	41		Tribal Elder
T. Chatupa*	Ushi	"	48		" "
A. Ngulube*	Nsenga	"	40	Piecework Tailor	" "
R. Banda	Tonga (Nya)	Township Workers	33	Clerk to Contractor	Formerly Secretary of Luanshya Branch of General Workers' Union
A. Chunga*	Chewa	Welfare Society	30	Clerk to Contractor	Former Secretary of Welfare Society
L. Ngambi*	Henga	"	36	Headmaster	Member of Welfare Society; Sometime Chairman Roan Branch of Mine Workers' Union
T. Mzumara	Henga	"	38	Hospital Orderly	—
G. Musumbulwa	Ushi-Bemba	Mine Township	38	Clerk in Silicosis Department	Former Secretary of Welfare Society; Committee Member Roan Co-operative Society
A. Chambeshi	Lala	"	38	Clerk in Time Office	Member of Welfare Society; Treasurer Roan Branch of Mine Workers' Union
C. Mhone	Tumbuka	"	37	Clerk in Silicosis Department	Founder Member of Nyasaland African National Congress Branch at Roan. Elder in Free Church
S. Banda	Tonga (Nya)	"	53	Hospital Clerk	Tribal Representative
T. Nsama*	Ushi	"	45	Medical Attendant (First Aid Surface)	" "
R. Chikwanda	Bemba	"	35	Bossboy U'ground	" "
J. Kambatika	Chewa	"	57	Mine Clerk—Grain Store	" "
J. Milonga	Nsenga	"	—	Teacher Mine Sch.	—

* Has since left Luanshya.   Nya = Nyasalander.

Note: There were three other members, one representing Fisenge African Township, whom I was unable to trace.

men of the Tribal Elder class, now there were a number of younger men of the kind who were attracted into the Welfare Society. In 1944, in a discussion on its own internal organization, the Council had decided that the choice of representatives in future Councils should be based upon educated Africans. Mindful of this, perhaps, the Tribal Representatives on the mine sought their nominees from all departments of the mine, and not merely from among their own ranks. The result was that five of the mine representatives were mine clerks. The contractors' two representatives were also young clerks, though one resigned almost immediately when he left his employment. The Welfare Society was directly represented by one of the teachers from the African school, and by a medical orderly from the African mine hospital. Thus compared with previous Councils, the new body had a high proportion of literate and English-speaking members.

The new Council began in a flush of enthusiasm. At a special meeting called immediately after the re-constitution of the Council, the African Deputy-Chairman, Mr. Musumbulwa, read an address of welcome to the Senior Provincial Commissioner. The address expressed the sincere thanks of the Africans to His Majesty's Government for providing channels through which complaints and suggestions could be expressed. High tribute was also paid to the Senior Provincial Commissioner himself, whose aim it was, in accordance with the policy of His Majesty's Government, to find rapid means and well-founded avenues for their progress. The address referred to the wider and deeper interest in the affairs of the colonial peoples which the British Government had shown in recent years. The Africans now enjoyed greater opportunities for self-expression through Trade Unions and the Co-operative Societies, and through direct representation on various Boards and Councils on which previously only Europeans had sat. The address concluded: 'We hope to be careful and wise in using these chances.'

The general tone of the address is itself quite interesting. While it has to be understood in the context and nature of the occasion, I believe that Musumbulwa's remarks were a genuine expression of African hopes and aspirations at this time. (Fulsome expressions of praise and gratitude towards the Government were soon to become increasingly rare among African leaders, and it is interesting to note that it was Musumbulwa himself who was to declare shortly afterwards in the Western Province African Provincial

Council[1] that he no longer regarded the British Government as the trustee of the interests of the African peoples.) The new councillors, such as Musumbulwa, who had also been for a time secretary of the Welfare Society, were not merely better educated than their predecessors, they also belonged to a younger generation whose vision and values were no longer confined within the narrow limits of tribal politics. Unlike the Tribal Representatives, whose prestige and authority derived from an ancient order, these leaders drew their strength from the new order that was arising. They were the early product of a new industrial society, and looked forward to taking what they considered to be their rightful place within it.

Significantly, one of the first acts of the new Council was to call for an investigation into the work of the Luanshya Urban Court. At a meeting specially called by the members themselves, reference was made to the discontent among the African public about the work of the Urban Court, and it was resolved to lay a general complaint against the Members of the Court before the District Commissioner. A memorandum was prepared setting out the Council's charges against the Urban Court, and it was considered at a later meeting of the Urban Advisory Council at which the District Commissioner took the chair. The Advisory Council alleged, *inter alia*, that the Court Members received bribes, and allowed their decisions to be influenced by such extraneous considerations as the tribal affiliation or social standing of the litigants. It was also claimed that the Court Members' mode of handling cases was cumbersome, involved too many irrelevancies, and was prejudicial to a fair hearing. Little evidence appears to have been adduced in support of these charges and, after dealing with each allegation in turn, the District Commissioner concluded by inviting the members to tell him of anyone who was prepared to come forward and make a sworn statement regarding the allegations against the Urban Court. If no one was prepared to do this, he said, it could only be assumed that the charges were based on loose talk. Later, in an official minute on the subject, the District Commissioner commented that he suspected the criticisms represented only the views of the 'disgruntled intelligentsia', and not those of

---

[1] *Record of the First Meeting of the Western Province African Provincial Council*, Government Printer, Lusaka, 1950, p. 13.

G

the masses, who generally accepted without question the decisions of the Court.[1]

In my earlier study of the Urban Courts, I attempted to examine in some detail these and other kindred charges sometimes levelled by Africans against the Courts. I argued there [2] that although there was some substance in many of the complaints, the roots of the matter really lay very much deeper. The complaints were in fact an index of political hostility, rather than an expression of concern about the administration of justice as such. A younger and better-educated set of leaders had gained a foothold in the Urban Advisory Council at the expense of the Tribal Elders. In attacking the Urban Courts they were expressing their opposition to what they considered a further 'intrusion of tribal government' into the urban areas.

The forces underlying the charges levelled against the Urban Courts emerged quite clearly at the first meeting of the Western Province African Provincial Council in March, 1950,[3] at which the urban members were delegates from the Urban Advisory Councils of Ndola and the Copperbelt. At this meeting Mr. Kazunga, a well-known storekeeper at Ndola and Secretary for many years of the Ndola African Traders' Association, moved that the Members of the Urban Court should be chosen from persons residing in the urban areas. He pointed out that Africans appreciated the existence of Urban Courts in each town, but he argued that the present system of having Court Members appointed by Native Authorities in the tribal areas created many difficulties. He complained that Court Members from the reserves had little experience of the urban way of life, and little sympathy with the more educated element growing up in the towns. 'Whenever an accused reads a statement, he is regarded as cheeky, and [the Court Members] say he is proud because he is educated and can speak English.' Mr. Kazunga and the other urban spokesmen were careful to explain that the motion did not mean that people in the urban areas were trying to cut themselves off from the Native Authorities. But the implications of the motion were not lost upon the rural delegates—among them a number of Chiefs—who voted

---

[1] Quoted in full in my report, *The Administration of Justice and the Urban African*, p. 42.
[2] Ibid., pp. 41–3.   [3] *Record*, pp. 75–82.

solidly against it. Their position was summed up by Mr. Pupe, representing the rural District of Solwezi: 'I am very sad to hear these things brought before us in this Council,' he said. 'They are all sad news to our Chiefs. Our Chiefs sent us here because we are the only people who know the customs of the tribe. . . . We are dealt with by the Chief, therefore the Chief sends his representatives to the Copperbelt to do exactly the same as the Chief does in his court. It is surprising to us to hear that the urban people say they should have the right to choose their own assessors [i.e. Court Members] here. Why is this? Is it that they have enough knowledge and are civilized? Education does not matter, to despise what the Chiefs do is not right. The Chiefs will think that this matter is brought up because we want to break away from them. It is not right.'

The urban representatives were heavily outnumbered on the Provincial Council, and the motion was lost by twenty-seven votes to nine. But, irrespective of the result, the debate is most valuable in that it enables us to place in their proper perspective the events at Luanshya which I have been describing. The political structure obtaining in the mining centres was the creation of the European authorities, and within it both the Advisory Councils and the Urban Courts had their place. In the absence of an Urban Native Authority with executive, legislative, and fiscal powers, the Advisory Council provided the only African local governmental body, with the Urban Court as its judicial arm. The doctrine of the 'separation of powers' may operate differently in different political systems, but everywhere executive and judicial functions exist in close association. They both operate within the one authority system. In the present situation this was not the case. The Advisory Council was a purely urban body which claimed, particularly in its attacks on the Urban Court, to speak for the people living in the towns. Even the Tribal Elders and Tribal Representatives who continued to sit on the Luanshya Council owed their position to their election by their fellow-townsmen. By contrast, the members of the Urban Court were appointed by, and were responsible to, Native Authorities in the reserves. The establishment of Urban Courts was a recognition of the fact that the African had a rightful place in the towns, and was entitled to assume some measure of responsibility for the maintenance of law and order there. The continued association of the Urban Courts with the Native Authorities suggested that the responsibility for urban affairs, which many urban dwellers considered to be their own concern, remained vested in the Chiefs. We have seen that when the new Advisory Council came into being at Luanshya in 1949, the 'Tribal Elder' had given way to younger and more educated men. At the same time, the Elders were not completely eliminated, and it is interesting to observe that they too associated themselves with the attacks launched by their fellow-councillors on the Members of the Urban Court. In particular, they complained that the judgments of the Tribal Representatives given at the preliminary hearings of cases were frequently disregarded, and that insufficient respect was paid to the Tribal Representatives by the Members of the Urban Court. As the remarks of some of the Tribal Elders which I quoted earlier [1] indicate, there was a certain amount of tension in their relationship with the Members of the Urban Court. Tribal Elders and Court Members shared certain values in common. In handling disputes, Elders and Court Members employed the same basic concepts of law and ethics, and made appeal to the same time-honoured norms. Ultimately, too, they derived their prestige among the people from the same political values, and each claimed to be the 'true' representatives of the Chiefs in the urban areas. Thus united by common values, they were also divided by the sharp struggle for political precedence. In terms of those values, the Court Members enjoyed undoubted superiority, for not only did they possess greater legal powers than the Elders, but they were also the nominees of the most important Chiefs and Native Authorities. The Elders, on the other hand, owed their appointment to election by their fellow-tribesmen in the town, and their recognition by the Compound Manager on the mine, or the Location Superintendent. In this context the Elders appeared as spokesmen of the urban dwellers, and expressed their opposition to the Members of the Urban Court by associating themselves with their fellow-members of the Advisory Council.

It is important to stress here that in all the many criticisms directed against the Urban Courts, there was never any attempt to impugn the principle that justice should be administered to Africans in the urban areas in African Courts. As Mr. Kazunga

---

[1] See above, p. 59.

had stated in his speech before the Provincial Council, Africans appreciated the existence of the Courts. There were some, indeed, with whom I spoke who favoured the extension of the jurisdiction of the Courts so that they could entertain suits in customary law brought by Africans against Europeans. What urban Africans were objecting to, therefore, was the basis on which the Courts were at present organized. In protesting against the tribal character of the Courts, and urging the selection of Court Members from the towns, they were staking the claim of the urban community to run its own affairs. Viewed in this light, it becomes clear that the allegations levelled against the Court Members by the Luanshya Advisory Council were largely an index of a struggle for power within the existing administrative framework. This struggle had been going on within the African community with increasing intensity throughout the decade under discussion.

IV

I have referred to the present period as one of conflict and growth. Although the African labour force in the towns was still essentially migrant, the disturbances of 1940 showed plainly that the Africans were coming to regard themselves as industrial workers as well as members of different tribes. The African strike had followed immediately upon a strike of European miners, and indeed, according to the findings of the Forster Commission, resulted directly from it. Quite simply, it was a strike for higher wages to meet the rising cost of living following the outbreak of war,[1] though it appears that at Nkana and Mindola [2] mines no generally accepted demand could be ascertained at that time, nor could any recognized leaders be discovered.[3] At Mufulira, the strikers appear to have had a clearer sense of purpose, and they sent messages to their fellow-workers at Nkana to carry on with the strike until their demands for 10s. a day with food or 15s. a day without food were met. Indeed, Mufulira workers appeared

---

[1] Starting rates for Africans prior to the disturbances were 12s. 6d. per ticket for surface workers and 22s. 6d. per ticket for underground workers.

[2] The Mindola mine belongs to the Rhokana Corporation and is situated at Kitwe.

[3] *Report of the Commission of Inquiry*, 1940, p. 15. Similar statements were made to me by African informants.

to have developed sufficient sense of unity to reject the authority of the Tribal Elders there, and follow the lead of their own Strike Committee. The strike at Mufulira passed off without serious incident.

At Luanshya during the disturbances of 1935, the authority of the Elders had also been rejected, but no body of accepted leaders appears to have emerged to take their place. The appointment of the Committee of 17 at Mufulira in 1940 thus represented the first real challenge by the urban workers to the established form of authority. With the passage of time the growth of the urban community came to be marked by the increasing differentiation of its members, and associations of various kinds emerged to promote the interests of different groups. In the Mine Townships the mining companies had been persuaded by Government to recognize Boss Boys' Committees, and to arrange regular meetings with them for the discussion of issues specific to their employment. In the Government Townships the small educated core of clerks, teachers, and African ministers of religion were coming together in Welfare Societies, and were joined by the mine clerks and hospital orderlies. The clerks and hospital orderlies were amongst the most highly-paid African employees on the mine. Very commonly they occupied a position of some importance on the mine for, in the rôle of interpreter, in which they were sometimes employed, they came to act as intermediaries between the people, the Tribal Representatives, and the European Compound staff. Mine clerks did not fall into the category of Boss Boys, and, since they were thus excluded from the Boss Boys' Committees, there was a strong feeling among many of them that they had no real representation on the mine. In this way Clerks' Associations gradually emerged at a number of the mines. The Clerks' Association at Roan appears to have been formed about 1945, though it never became really firmly established. It was not welcomed by Management who saw in it a threat to the authority of the existing bodies, and the Association never succeeded in bringing any important issue before Management. It appears, too, that there were internal dissensions, and only three meetings were held by the Roan Association over a period of six months. The Boss Boys' Committees were themselves later replaced at all the mines by Works' Committees.

The Clerks' Association at Roan had been short-lived. Yet, like the Welfare Society to which many of its members also belonged, it not only showed the increasing social and economic differentiation within the community, but it also reflected the Africans' deep involvement in the industrial economy and an urban way of life. The administrative system that operated in the towns was the creation of the Europeans, and deliberately looked back to the tribal areas. Administrative policy rested fundamentally on a view of the urban Africans as migrant tribesmen, rather than town-dwellers, and Urban Court Members appointed by Native Authorities and Tribal Elders were the twin offspring of this conception. Clerks' Associations and Welfare Societies, on the other hand, were the product of urban social growth; by their very emergence they represented a challenge to the claim of Tribal Elders and Chiefs' nominees to speak for the people of the towns.[1]

The process of growth and conflict may be seen as operating in a variety of ways, each reflecting the same underlying social forces but in a different aspect. To begin with, the protracted struggle that went on throughout this period for power within the existing administrative framework can be viewed as a conflict of 'generations'. By and large, tribal society in Northern Rhodesia was gerontocratic; high status and political power were the prerogative of the aged. Knowledge of the soil, of the magic to protect oneself in high office against the machinations of one's rivals, and of the esoteric mysteries of the rituals of chieftaincy and the village, came largely with the advance of age. For knowledge itself was a function of age. *Ukanya mukulu takota*, ran the Bemba proverb: 'who heeds not the advice of the elders, does not grow old'. The attitudes of respect and reverence for the aged were deliberately cultivated, and are enshrined in innumerable proverbs and maxims. These attitudes persist and in the towns terms such as *mukalamba*, or the widely-used honorific *shikulu*, grandfather, still carry deep overtones of respect, mingled with intimacy and affection. The Tribal Elders of the towns were rarely very old, though in the main they fell within the upper age-categories of

---

[1] For example, when a society of mine clerks was formed at Nkana, it at once asked to be allowed to elect a representative to the Urban Advisory Council there. This was refused on the grounds that the mine clerks were already represented on the Council by the mine Tribal Representatives. See G. C. R. Clay, 'African Urban Advisory Councils in the Northern Rhodesia Copperbelt', *Journal of African Administration*, i (1949), pp. 33–9, at p. 35.

the urban population, and they were respected as *bakalamba*, 'big people'. They were the local repository of tribal lore, custom, and morals, and Africans with domestic or other private problems, or who were strangers in the town, turned to them for guidance in the customary fashion. But as the urban communities themselves took root, new problems arose for which the traditional wisdom of the Elders provided no solution, and of which they were sometimes unaware. The need for new roads in the town, the need to seek avenues of employment for African women, the need in the towns for hostels for old people, the problem of discharged mine employees—these were some of the problems facing the new urban communities. They were drawing the attention of the younger and better-educated men in the Advisory Councils: they aroused little response among the 'Elders'.

The Africans who were led to join the Welfare Societies were of a younger generation, and were better educated. They were more conscious of the problems of urban life, and of the rapidly developing pattern of relations between the races. Significantly, the discussions of the Welfare Societies were conducted, and the minutes of their meetings recorded, in English. A District Commissioner had once sneered at the Welfare Societies as debating societies where the educated native had the opportunity to get up before his fellows and air his English. The District Commissioner did not appreciate that in using English at their meetings, the Africans were learning to handle one of the most important tools of the new culture. When Africans conversed together in English, they showed that they had interests in common which cut across tribal divisions. Furthermore, in the handling of novel concepts they were broadening their intellectual horizons, and making possible closer contact and acquaintance with the world outside. But more than this, in their professions of schoolteacher, of Christian minister of religion, and of clerk, they were actively engaged in pushing forward into a new form of society where clan affiliation or attachment to village headman and chief were no longer mechanisms of primary significance in ordering social relations. Through such organizations as the Welfare Societies, these people were beginning to stake out their claim to full membership in the new industrial society that was growing up around the mines.

Conflict and growth in the urban community were expressed

in the opposition of the 'generations', and of literate and illiterate. But these oppositions were themselves only a reflection of a wider conflict of values. As I have already indicated, the system of Tribal Elders and of Urban Courts operating in the towns was rooted in the view, held by many European officials, and Africans too, that the Copperbelt was a place of temporary sojourn whence the worker would return after one or two years to resume the more even tenor of tribal life. For the migrant labourer, the presence of Tribal Elders in the compounds, and Chiefs' nominees in the Urban Courts, served as a reminder that although his home lay many hundreds of miles away, his strongest links were still with kinsfolk in the distant villages, and in allegiance to his Chief, all cemented by a body of customs and values which divided him sharply from the other people of other tribes with whom he lived and worked in the towns. But there were now new leaders in the towns who were also bidding for his support, and claimed to be his spokesmen. Like the Elders, they were mostly of rural origin: but unlike the Elders, they had committed themselves to the new industrial and multi-racial society of the towns. The period of the forties was one of protracted struggle in which the emergence of the urban community was marked by the gradual weakening of the authority of the Tribal Elders in the wider sphere of political representation. In their selection of a number of mine clerks to sit on the Urban Advisory Council, the Elders themselves gave tacit recognition to the decline of their authority. Their final defeat and abolition on the mines came with the emergence of the African Mine Workers' Union.

CHAPTER IV

TRADE UNIONISM AND SOCIAL COHESION
(1950-4)

I

IN previous chapters I have spoken of the growth of the urban community in terms of the increasing social and economic differentiation of its members. African town-dwellers were now linked and divided not only by tribal ties. The urban community included those who had come to accept an urban way of life, and those for whom 'home' would always be a small village in the tribal areas. It included the vast majority whose formal education had been negligible, and a small minority who were distinguished by their ability to converse with Europeans and their fellow-Africans in English. There were wide differences in standards of living, which were sometimes associated with these factors, and with differences in occupation. On the mines, some earned their living by operating drills and handling explosives far below the surface of the ground, in the first stages of extracting the raw material; others spent their days in the less grimy tasks of administration. In the Government Townships, similar processes were also at work. In addition to the mass of unskilled labourers, there was an increasing number of African bricklayers, carpenters, plumbers, and the like, as well as private traders.

Politically, this process of growth is shown in the emergence of a number of bodies, both 'official' and unofficial. On the mines there were Boss Boys' Committees and later Clerks' Associations. The Welfare Society at Luanshya had originated in the location, though some of its leading members were also drawn from the mine. In this way the Society could claim to represent the town as a whole: as an unofficial body it was structurally equivalent, but opposed, to the official Urban Advisory Council. Thus the trend of development tended to follow the dichotomy in the social structure of the town, and this has been continued to a marked degree in the more recent emergence of African trade unions and the African National Congress. The unions and the National Congress are alike the product of similar social forces, and are closely related. But their emergence has to be explained within a wider politico-economic system than the one which I have taken as my unit of study. Moreover, they arise from different sets of political and economic relations. For convenience of exposition, therefore, I confine myself for the present to a discussion of the African trade union movement, leaving the analysis of the inter-relations of these various bodies within the urban community until the following chapter.

There was an indirect reference to the possible formation of African trade unions in the evidence of the District Commissioner, Ndola (Mr. Keith), given before the Commission of Inquiry of 1935. Keith pointed out that under the Employment of Natives Ordinance, which governed the relations between employers and African employees, the Africans could not strike legally—they were liable to criminal prosecution if they broke their contracts by not going to work. He said that all that the Africans had lacked in the strike was some organization by which they could elect their own representatives to put the objects of the strike before the mine or Government. Sooner or later the Africans would have to have some means of representing their grievances, and of striking legitimately if they wished to do so. He thought that some such sort of organization should be introduced, and given legal recognition.[1] The Commission of Inquiry referred to the possibility of further industrial unrest on the Copperbelt, but did not take up the question of African trade unions; and it was not until after the disturbances of 1940 that the suggestion of forming trade unions seems to have been put forward seriously.

The African strike of 1940 followed immediately upon a strike of European miners. The Africans were aware that the European strike had been undertaken in order to secure a general increase in wages to meet the rise in the cost of living for all Europeans employed on the mines. Therefore, according to the Forster Commission, the Africans took the view that if by strike action those objects could be attained by the Europeans, a strike must be the appropriate and, indeed, necessary means to obtain similar benefits for themselves.

The strike [2] itself had begun quite peaceably, and the actual

---

[1] *Evidence*, i, p. 158.
[2] For an account of one meeting of African miners which preceded the strike see R. J. B. Moore, op. cit., pp. 78–80. One source of grievance, to which the

disturbances only broke out at Nkana on the sixth day when a crowd of 3,000 strikers tried to prevent a queue of 150 men, who had remained at work, from drawing their pay at the mine Compound Office. Police and troops tried to push the crowd back, and tear-gas bombs were used, though without effect. The crowd, infuriated, made an attack on the Compound Office, where many of the Europeans had sought shelter. It was driven off by rifle fire. Looting in the compound occurred on quite a large scale. According to my own informants, one group of people attacked a tea-room. They took meal, nuts, sugar, and other foodstuffs, and threw these outside where people picked them up as they could. Others attacked the houses of domestic servants, clerks, and police-boys. Everything that was to hand was seized and burned. Petrol, paraffin, and benzine were all thrown on the houses of these persons, and personal belongings such as suitcases, bicycles, and 'even chickens', were all burnt. Police-boys could not appear in the compound, and they were all sheltered behind wire fences to protect them from the people. Europeans, too, came in for some attention from the rioters, and stones were thrown at passing cars. Apart from the widespread damage, the riot had resulted in the death of seventeen Africans, while more than sixty were injured in the firing.

The Report of the Forster Commission drew attention to a wide variety of grievances on the part of Africans, in addition to those relating to their rates of pay, although it noted that these had not been raised previously with the mine managements. Indeed, one of the most serious problems to which the Report referred was the lack of an adequate channel of communication for presenting these grievances. This was particularly the case at Nkana, where no system of Tribal Elders, such as operated at Mufulira or Luanshya, had been introduced.

Among those who gave evidence before the Commission of Inquiry was Mr. Julius Lewin, a lecturer in Native Administration

---

Forster Commission does not appear to have referred, but which is mentioned by Moore and which was repeated to me by my own informants, was the question of tax. The rate of tax for Africans was 15s. p.a. on the line of rail in 1940. Rural areas paid a lower tax graded by distance from the line of rail. Since basic starting rates for surface and underground workers were 12s. 6d. and 22s. 6d. respectively for a ticket of 30 shifts, this meant in effect that many Africans were paying an annual tax roughly equivalent to their monthly wage.

at the University of the Witwatersrand. Shortly before, there had been formed in Johannesburg the South African Committee on Industrial Relations. This Committee decided to present to the Commission through Mr. Lewin evidence on the general position of Africans in modern industry, and on methods of preventing similar disturbances in the future.[1] Mr. Lewin's most important recommendation, directed towards this end, was for the formation of African trade unions. Referring to the strong possibility of the extension of an industrial colour bar to Northern Rhodesia, he pointed out that in this complex situation the Africans themselves were unable to exercise any direct influence: 'At present they have no organization or other means adequately to protect their interests in this or any other matter.' But, as we have already seen, the Commission considered that the Africans were not yet sufficiently advanced to take a responsible rôle in organizing themselves in trade unions, and suggested the development of the system of Tribal Representatives as an interim measure.

The Tribal Elders, where they already existed, were now re-organized, and re-appeared as Tribal Representatives. The significance of this change was that the Tribal Representatives were to work in closer contact with the Government Labour Officers, who were charged with the task of educating the Tribal Representatives to 'become intelligently familiar with all matters relating to Native labour', and to teach them to present to Management or the Government 'any case the Native workers may have for the adjustment of labour conditions in a reasonable manner'.[2] Later, as I described in the previous chapter, Boss Boys' Committees and Clerks' Associations appeared for a short time. Then in 1946 it was decided to supplement the work of the Tribal Representatives by the introduction of Works Committees. The Works Committee at each mine was made up of African representatives from each of the mine departments. The Works Committees represented another interim measure, for while they could discuss such matters as the distribution of working-hours, the provision of canteens, safety measures, and other day-to-day

---

[1] None of the evidence submitted to the Forster Commission was published, but Lewin set out his views shortly afterwards in the pamphlet, *The Colour Bar in the Copperbelt*, quoted above.

[2] Government Circular Minute No. 6-MIN/C of 1942.

problems, they did not usually negotiate on wages or conditions of service. This was the position when, in 1947, under the policy enunciated by the British Labour Party for the post-war period, Mr. W. Comrie was sent to Northern Rhodesia by the Colonial Office to help organize the African trade union movement.

In spite of the institutional instability of African urban life, the 'leadership core' itself was fairly constant. Indeed, there was a good deal of overlapping of leadership positions among the various bodies existing at this time. Leading persons in one body were likely to be found in similar positions of leadership in different, and possibly opposed, groups. At Luanshya certain of the Tribal Representatives became members of the Boss Boys' Committee, and later of the Works Committee. Members of the Clerks' Association held office in the Welfare Society, and later also sat on the Works Committee, and so forth. Thus it was through a very small leadership group or élite that Mr. Comrie made his first approaches to the African workers. Indeed, one of his first introductions took place at a 'Brains Trust', an inter-racial meeting at which Europeans and Africans 'took the ring' in answering questions from the audience. Gradually he gathered around him a small team of men who came to be known among Africans as 'the Disciples', and through whom the gospel of trade unionism was spread about the Copperbelt.

Curiously enough, the mine workers were among the last to become organized within a trade union. The shop assistants, who at that time appear to have enjoyed high prestige among their fellow-Africans, were the first to form a union. The mine workers, apparently considered by other African workers as too barbaric ever to understand the principles of trade unionism, followed in the wake of the general workers and the railway workers. The mine workers had in fact a number of serious obstacles to overcome. Among the rank and file there was a certain amount of suspicion of Mr. Comrie himself. After all, he too was a White man, and they did not understand why he was keen to start a trade union which would benefit their interests when they considered that his 'brothers' aimed only at their subjection and domination. There was opposition, too, from some of the most influential Africans at each mine. Some of the mine clerks talked from the very beginning of the formation of a Salaried Staff Association, while others were keen to give priority to the co-operative movement, or considered that Africans were not sufficiently advanced to be able to run a trade union.

The possibility of a strong and independent trade union movement among the African mine workers was viewed by the European miners as at once representing a serious threat to their own position. Mr. Brian Goodwin, the President of the [European] Mine Workers' Union, who some time previously had said of the formation of African trade unions, that one could not stop a mass movement,[1] began to make overtures to the Africans, whom he addressed at a number of meetings. He sought to persuade them to drop the idea of forming a separate union, and instead to enter the existing Mine Workers' Union. He argued that the African union would be weak and ineffective since, being sponsored by Government, the Africans would not be accorded the right to strike. He pointed out further that such a move would strengthen the position of the mining companies by causing a division in the ranks of labour. However, these advances were rejected by the African leaders. Why was it, they asked, that no such proposal had been made in all the years that had passed since the [European] Mine Workers' Union came into existence, until the Africans appeared to be about to have their own union? The African leaders claimed, too, that if, raw and completely inexperienced in trade union affairs, they went in with the European miners, all executive control and power to conduct negotiations would vest in the Whites. Moreover, it was at this time that the political atmosphere began to be stirred by renewed discussions of Responsible Government and Northern Rhodesia's constitutional development. The Africans asked how, if they were not to have responsibility in running their own trade union, they would be given the opportunity of showing that they were capable of shouldering responsibility in the wider political sphere. Those African union leaders with whom I discussed the question made it clear that they were not thereby rejecting out of hand a merger with the Mine Workers' Union; they were postponing it until they considered they had achieved a strong enough bargaining position. So, at length, the first branch of the African Mine Workers' Union came into being at Nkana in February, 1948.

---

[1] Quoted in J. W. Davidson, *The Northern Rhodesia Legislative Council* (1948), p. 88.

One of the first tasks of the new branch was to elect a committee. The elections for office were keenly contested, and there were many nominations for each post. Mr. Godwin Lewanika (who was later to play an important part in founding the Congress movement as well as the African Salaried Staff Association at Nkana) and Mr. Lawrence Katilungu contested for the office of chairman; and Messrs. Kaluwa, Chapoloko, and Simamba for that of secretary. With the exception of Kaluwa, who was an underground first aid attendant, all of them were mine clerks or hospital orderlies. There was some protest that the first election was not properly conducted, and a second election was held immediately under the supervision of the Labour Officer, the District Commissioner, and Mr. Comrie, who had previously instructed the Africans in the use of the secret ballot. Messrs. Katilungu and Kaluwa were returned. Katilungu had not played an important rôle in the early meetings with Comrie, but he enjoyed great influence among the Bemba people.[1] Indeed, he had once been elected by them as a Tribal Representative but, as he himself once expressed it to me, he refused the appointment because as a young man he was more interested in dancing and having a good time than in listening to people's cases. His job gave him a position of some importance, and made him widely known, for all those joining the mine had to pass through his hands. One man, who is himself a Bemba, and a prominent figure in the Union, summed the election up in this way: 'Katilungu was an old employee, and a clerk. He knew how to write, and he understood English. At that time there were very few Bemba clerks, and we few Bemba took him as "the big man" for all of us. All the clerks were Nyasa, and they liked to favour their home people. But the Bemba people were very numerous on the mine. So, when it came to having a leader they took it on a tribal basis.

[1] Katilungu is a grandchild of the Bemba minor chief Chipalo. However, he is commonly regarded by Africans on the Copperbelt as being closely related to the Bemba Royal House, and there is no doubt that he is able to exercise considerable influence on Chitimukulu, the Bemba Paramount Chief. At a later date, his political opponents came to refer to him as the 'Paramount Chief of the Bemba Trade Union'. For a time Katilungu had been a teacher at a Mission school in Bemba country. He joined the Nkana mine in 1936, and at the time of the 1940 disturbances was employed as an underground worker. Later he became a recruiting clerk, whose task it was to issue passes to all new recruits so that they could proceed for hospital examination, etc.

Each tribe decided that it must have one of its own people as chairman.'

From Nkana the movement extended. Committee members of the Nkana branch toured the Copperbelt, seeking to make African converts to trade unionism. Their task was no light one. Sometimes they were unable to get the permission of Compound Managers to hold meetings within the compound, sometimes the meetings themselves were poorly attended. Recalling this period in its history, an article in *The African Miner*, the official bulletin of the Union, speaks glowingly of those men, 'the first inspired, who did not mind where and how they slept, nor what and how they ate, wherever they went'. Within a short time unions had been formed at all mines on the Copperbelt, and at Broken Hill where zinc and vanadium are mined. In March, 1949, these unions amalgamated to form the present African Mine Workers' Union.

Shortly afterwards the Union submitted to the Chamber of Mines claims for increases in wages for all African employees of the copper-mining companies on the Copperbelt. The companies insisted that first there should be an agreed method of procedure for dealing with points raised by the Union. After some negotiation, the agreement was signed which now regulates the relations between the Union and the mining companies. Further meetings took place on the wages issue in accordance with the terms of the agreement. Following lengthy but unsuccessful negotiations between the parties themselves, agreement was finally reached at formal conciliation meetings under a conciliator appointed by the Governor-in-Council. The Union obtained wage increases, although these were substantially lower than its claims.

During 1950 there was a major industrial dispute, following on the Union's demand for a profit-sharing scheme for the Africans identical in kind to that enjoyed by the European employees, and for a general wage revision. Negotiations extended into 1951, and agreement was ultimately reached after the Union had taken a strike ballot. Then in March a strike was called at Nchanga on the grounds of the alleged wrongful dismissal of a member of the Union. The Union claimed that the member was discharged not for inefficiency in his duties, but simply because he happened to be treasurer of the local branch and that the Management was seeking merely to test the power of the Union. A number of

H

meetings followed, at which the Labour Department was represented, but no agreement was reached. The Union gave notice that if the member was not reinstated it would call a strike. At this point the Company sought to persuade the Tribal Representatives to use their influence to induce the people to go to work. The strike continued for fourteen days, but in the end failed to achieve its object.

The strike itself passed off peacefully and without incident and, although it failed to reinstate the dismissed member, it did serve to draw the attention of the Union to the position of the Tribal Representatives as a rival source of authority and influence. Accordingly, at the next Annual Conference of the Supreme Council of the Union held at Broken Hill in 1952, a resolution was passed demanding the abolition of the system of Tribal Representatives.

But while the discussion was still in progress in the Union, a more important issue developed. Following the Annual Conference, the Union presented demands for a general increase of 2s. 8d. per shift. During the negotiations which followed the mining companies made a number of counter-offers which included improvement in the wages of certain categories of African mine workers, a shift differential payment for afternoon and night shifts, increased payment for Sunday work, and certain other proposals concerning cost-of-living allowances. When these counter-offers were rejected by the Union, the companies stressed that they would be willing to withdraw their counter-offers and allow the dispute to be settled by arbitration. The Union declined to agree to arbitration, and, after a secret ballot of its members gave a strong mandate, the Union called a strike on October 20, 1952. On this occasion the strike covered the whole of the Copperbelt, and lasted three weeks, during which production was totally halted. Throughout the whole of this period order was maintained, and there were no disturbances or incidents. A short article by F. M. N. Heath,[1] the District Commissioner at Luanshya, provides an interesting account of the situation there at the time of the strike:

The strike began on Monday. Throughout the weekend people in

---

[1] F. M. N. Heath, 'No Smoke from the Smelter', *Corona* (April, 1953), p. 149.

the African Mine Townships behaved as if nothing was impending. Men and women put on their Sunday clothes. Tribal dances were organized and soon the familiar sound of numerous drums drew crowds to the flagged enclosure where competing teams of dancers formed a focus for gay, friendly crowds of African sightseers. People greeted one another, children scampered about, and all over the township well-dressed miners and their families were visiting one another, while the young men and maidens chatted gaily on the roads. The weather was hot and as Sunday evening drew on the hustle of the day subsided into the throb of a moonlit African night. Gradually the drumming ceased and by midnight the people had dispersed and were abed.

Next morning no one came to work except a handful of essential service workers. The mine had stopped. The wheels at the shaft-heads no longer turned and the only sign of activity came from the power plant and the sprays of water from the cooling reservoir. At the entrance to the African Mine Township African picket men stood on guard but there were no passers-by to attract their attention. As you drove past the rows of huts where the strikers lived there was hardly a sign of life. Not even the children, who normally would be playing in the yards and along the roadsides, were to be seen. There was no one moving about. The Mine Offices were deserted. It was incredible that 30,000 people should have been so much in evidence the day before and that twelve hours later there should be only a deserted town. Throughout the day the atmosphere remained unchanged as if human activity had ceased. Only a few seemed interested in buying food through the Government ticket system while some women with baskets were making their way up the hill to the Indian-owned shops. There was no excitement and no crowds gathered at street corners. No one seemed interested in the mine lying silent across the valley.

Next day it was the same and soon a week had gone by. Gradually the unfamiliar sight of Europeans off-loading coal from railway trucks and wielding pick and shovel passed without comment. The Company had already announced that Europeans would be kept at work as far as possible but that only a third of their normal monthly earnings could be guaranteed. Some took leave and left for the South; others busied themselves around their houses or went visiting other mining camps. But few spent money. Notices appeared outside garages stating that repairs to motor-cars could only be effected for cash payment. Shop-keepers looked anxiously at their large stock of Christmas goods ordered in readiness for the seasonal rush which begins with the receipt of the October pay cheques.

Here was a clear demonstration, if demonstration were needed, of the vital position occupied by the Africans in the economic structure of the Territory. The strike suddenly brought home to the European section of the community what a speaker in the Legislative Council debate on the Artisans' strike of 1946 had earlier pointed out, that 'without the African worker there would be no profit for the shareholders, no wages for the [European] mine workers, and no living for the rest of the community'. Yet after all, there was nothing novel in this point. The dependence of the industry on African labour had always been perfectly patent. What was novel in the situation, and gave rise to so much concern among the Europeans, was the evidence of the emergence of an organized African labour movement. Almost a week had elapsed between the announcement that strike action was proposed and the actual shut-down; during this period details of the essential services to be maintained were worked out in accordance with the terms of the Union's agreement with the mining companies. The companies had also announced that men not at work would not be fed, yet throughout the strike no one complained openly of hunger and the demand for food tickets—a system immediately introduced by Government to enable the strikers to buy food for themselves and their families through the companies' feeding system—remained small. Each day the strikers and their womenfolk would go off *en masse* to cultivate their gardens,[1] or to reap the crops they had already sown. From time to time the Union leaders called public meetings. Then, to quote Heath, vast crowds in their thousands would begin to assemble as if from nowhere and the Mine Township spring into life. 'It was as if a concourse of ants were converging on the carcase of some animal. But as soon as the business of the meeting was ended, the crowds dispersed in good order and the uncanny stillness returned.'

Thus it was the success with which the Union leaders had organized the strike that aroused the wrath and anxiety of the Europeans —feelings which were at once reflected in the local Press. An editorial in the *Central African Post*,[2] after remarking that the Africans had now learnt all the tricks of the modern strike, pointed out that

---

[1] These gardens are smaller and less significant than those described by Wilson at Broken Hill, where he considered they had a stabilizing effect (*Economics of Detribalization*, Part 1, p. 22). The women choose a small plot on vacant mine land: there is no control by the Company.

[2] October 23, 1952.

people who refused arbitration earned the displeasure of the rest of the community:

> We learn with dismay that there will be practically no mining while the Africans remain out. Is it not about time that our Copper Companies remedied this state of affairs by introducing Europeans who can keep the mines going? The fact that a strike of Africans can put a stop to active mining puts them in a very strong position and the companies and country in a very weak one.

In mid-November the Union asked that the dispute be settled by arbitration on condition that the tribunal consisted of an Arbitrator chosen from the United Kingdom, and two assessors of whom one should be nominated by each party. This was agreed to by the companies. The Union claimed before the Arbitration Tribunal that the African workers were suffering from a deep-seated feeling of frustration. While it was true, the Union agreed, that the companies provided scales of remuneration which enabled a certain number of their African employees to maintain a standard of living that afforded some margin above the barest necessities of life, this did not help the vast majority—74 per cent of the total—who were in the three lowest grades. The counter-offers of the employers were described as an illusory gesture, and the Union argued that it was necessary to get away completely from the existing levels: therein lay the justification of the claim for a flat-rate increase of 2s. 8d. per shift. This claim was based largely on the lowness of the cash wage,[1] particularly for the unskilled workers in Groups 1, 2, and 3. The starting rate at that time for Group 1 (surface) was 45s. per ticket of 30 working days, and the worker could reach a maximum of 67s. 6d. per ticket in just over five years of continuous service, if he did not in the meantime gain promotion to a higher group. Group 1 indeed was of particular importance, for it composed more than 50 per cent of the total African labour force. The Union contended that the spendable margin when spread over the period of a ticket—usually about

---

[1] It should be noted however that the cash wage did not make up the total cash earnings. There was also a cost-of-living allowance and a Christmas bonus, together with other bonuses of varying amounts for which a proportion of the workers could qualify. The real wage was much higher, since it included housing, hospital facilities, welfare, and other services provided by the mining companies.

34 days—did not allow of a decent existence judged by the rising standards of the Copperbelt mining communities. The companies by their counter-offer had recognized that there was a case for an increase of basic wages, but while the Arbitrator (Guillebaud) found that these proposals did not go far enough, he considered that a sudden rise in the basic wage of the magnitude involved in the Union's claim would have very undesirable results for all the parties concerned, including the mine workers themselves, as well as those in other industries. He considered, too, that to recognize the Union's full claim would lead to discontent on the part of those in the higher groups whose customary differentials would have been drastically disturbed. So, while the final award provided for substantial increases amongst all groups of the African labour force, it fell short of the Union's original demands.[1]

In presenting their case before the Forster Commission of 1940 the Africans had evidently relied upon the Bemba proverb, *ulu-lombe nkwale ku mwaiche ukubalilapo ku ikanga*, 'if you wish to beg a partridge from a child you must first ask for a guinea-fowl'. It is not unlikely that a similar principle was invoked on this occasion. At all events, the Union claimed a victory, and the measure of its popular support among the workers was immediately manifested in the abolition of the Tribal Representatives.

This issue had now come to a head dramatically in the case of Robinson Puta, who was at that time chairman of the Nchanga branch, and later Vice-General President of the Union. By this time it had become apparent to the Union leaders that the mining companies were going to throw the full weight of their support on the side of the Tribal Representatives in an effort to offset the influence of the Union with the mass of workers. A meeting of Tribal Representatives—the first of its kind involving the whole Copperbelt—was called under the chairmanship of Mr. Scrivener, the African Personnel Manager at Nkana mine. At this meeting the mining companies were said to have agreed that, in return for the closer collaboration of the Tribal Representatives, they were prepared to provide superior accommodation and domestic facilities in the compounds for the Tribal Representatives, and to present them with gowns of office.

---

[1] Wage rates before and after the Guillebaud award are set out in an Appendix.

A number of the Tribal Representatives were also committee members of the local branches of the Union, to which they at once carried word of the new proposals. The Supreme Council of the Union responded immediately by instructing all branches to hold meetings with the local Tribal Representatives in order to learn exactly what had taken place at the meeting. The Puta case[1] arose out of such a meeting called at Nchanga, where Puta was alleged to have threatened the Tribal Representatives with violence if they did not return their gowns of office. The Tribal Representatives were asked to explain the meaning of the gowns issued by the mining company, and Puta demanded that these be returned immediately. One of the Tribal Representatives refused, and was at once asked whether he considered he enjoyed the power and status of a Chief because he wore a gown. Some of the others replied that they had been given the gowns in order that they should appear as tribal Chiefs, and said that they had the same powers as tribal Chiefs at home because they were called after their names. It was at this point, according to the Magistrate hearing the case, that the meeting almost got out of hand. The Tribal Representatives began to squabble among themselves, for some of them, hearing now the views of their fellows that they were themselves akin to Chiefs, felt that they were committing the dread offence of *misula*, disrespect for a Chief, and began to feel qualms about the propriety of wearing the gowns. Puta was alleged to have told the Tribal Representatives that they were on the side of the Europeans, and that they were not true representatives of their own people. He told them that he had just been to Kenya, and had heard that people there were killing one another because of 'misunderstandings'; if they did not all act and work together there might be similar 'misunderstandings' in Northern Rhodesia. Puta was found guilty of the charge, and was sentenced to imprisonment for three months.

I have examined in a previous chapter the difficulties which confronted the Tribal Representatives in the mine compounds.[2] I argued there that the prestige which Tribal Representatives enjoyed related only to certain situations of African social life on the mine; it did not apply over the total field of social relations in

---

[1] Reported in *Central African Post*, February 20, 1953
[2] See above, pp. 45, 65.

which the Africans were involved. In particular, it did not apply in those situations where Africans were involved as workers rather than as tribesmen. The tribal values were irrelevant here, because such situations as a dispute over wages involved a different set of relations, and a different set of interests. The ties which linked Africans in these situations cut across those very divisions in which the system of tribal representation was rooted. The difficulties of the Tribal Representatives thus stemmed in part from a confusion about their social rôle; but these difficulties were also exacerbated by the intercalary position of the Tribal Representatives within the authority structure of the mine. It was the contradictions implicit in their position itself which underlay the charges repeatedly levelled against them that they were working in league with the Europeans, and brought them into immediate conflict with the newly-founded African Union.

Although there were some Tribal Representatives who served on Union branch committees, the relationship of the two bodies from the beginning was mainly one of opposition. Shortly after the formation of the Union, it was reported that there had been differences of opinion between the Union executive and the Tribal Representatives about the division of their respective spheres of work.[1] These squabbles continued, and, after the events of the strike at Nchanga referred to above, the Union decided to press for the abolition of tribal representation. At length the Chamber of Mines was persuaded to allow a ballot to be held under Government supervision to ascertain the wishes of their African employees on the question of tribal representation in the African Mine Townships. The Chamber of Mines insisted on a vote of 40 per cent in favour, before it would accept the abolition

TABLE 6

SUMMARY OF VOTING ON TRIBAL REPRESENTATION ON THE
COPPERBELT—MARCH, 1953

	%
Votes cast of the total labour force (35,000)	84·8
Votes cast for retention based on total votes cast	3·1
Votes cast against retention based on total votes cast . . .	96·9
Votes cast for retention based on the total mine strength . .	2·6
Votes cast against retention based on the total mine strength . .	82·2

[1] *Annual Report on African Affairs* (*Western Provinces*) *1950*, Government Printer, Lusaka.

of the system. It is evident from Table 6 that the result was in fact a landslide.

II

The appointment of the Arbitration Tribunal marked an important point in the growth of the African Mine Workers' Union; but the report of the Arbitrator, Mr. C. G. Guillebaud, also contained some indications of the developments which were to follow. In the final sentences of his report he recorded his conviction that satisfactory and harmonious industrial relations would not be obtained on the Copperbelt unless or until effective steps had been taken to enable the African workers to advance to positions of greater responsibility than those which were now open to them. This question had been the subject of a Commission of Inquiry in 1948, and its report, known as the *Dalgleish Report*, made certain important recommendations.[1] Mr. Guillebaud now referred to the failure to implement the recommendations of the *Dalgleish Report*, and observed that the fundamental issues which led to the appointment of the Dalgleish Commission remained unresolved. 'Throughout this arbitration,' he said, 'I have been conscious of them hanging like a dark cloud in the background.'

Fundamentally, what is known as the problem of the advancement of Africans in industry may be stated fairly simply. It is the struggle of two sections of a single community, which are separated by vast differences of wealth, experience, custom, and economic opportunity. As we saw at the outset, when the copper industry of Northern Rhodesia was developed the native inhabitants of the country had at that time a technology backward by modern standards, and were industrially equipped only for the most menial tasks. But the local Africans showed a capacity for adjusting themselves to the conditions of the new society. At first, local labour was so inefficient that at the Roan, for example, it was found more expedient to engage Nyasalanders and others who had gained their experience in the mines of Southern Rhodesia and the Witwatersrand. But within a few years the 'alien' curve on the labour graph was dropping, while the 'local'

---

[1] *Report of the Commission appointed to inquire into the Advancement of Africans in Industry*. Government Printer, Lusaka (1948). For further discussion of the Report see below, p. 104.

curve was going up. To some extent this situation was affected by Government regulations, for certain restrictions had been introduced to discourage alien Africans from entering the Territory. Yet it was not only the Government restrictions which made it necessary for the mines to employ larger numbers of indigenous Africans. For as Spearpoint [1] observes, there had been a remarkable improvement in the efficiency of these peoples, and they were becoming good workmen as the result of their closer association with the trained aliens. Indeed, by 1936 they had advanced so far that they were undertaking certain semi-skilled jobs which, on the mines of the Union of South Africa, were reserved to the Europeans. It was this situation which underlay the visit in that year to the Copperbelt of Mr. Charlie Harris, a leading European trade unionist on the Witwatersrand, and led shortly afterwards to the formation of the Northern Rhodesia [European] Mine Workers' Union.

The Europeans, for their part, represented a small group of technicians, artisans, and others employed in supervisory duties. To attract them to a country such as Northern Rhodesia, the companies had to offer high wages, to build modern houses for them, and to offer generous leave provisions and other facilities. And although African earnings have risen through the years, the great disparity of wealth as between Europeans and Africans, which was perhaps inevitable in the days of the industry's infancy, has continued to be maintained. Guillebaud himself records that in 1952, before his own award was made, approximately 40,000 Africans earned a total of £3,490,000 (including rations and bonuses), while about 6,000 Europeans earned £8,359,000 (including bonuses).[2] Guillebaud added that the European standards of wealth in Northern Rhodesia were highly artificial judged even by the standards of South Africa and Southern Rhodesia. The situation was once summed up for me in the comment of one European who had close links with the labour movement in England: 'Here,' he said, 'they [the White miners] turn up for Union meetings in Hudsons, Cadillacs, and the like, whereas in England they'd be lucky if they could turn up on a bicycle.'

---

[1] Op. cit., p. 52.

[2] *The Northern News*, Ndola, May 26, 1954. This was an article reprinted by special arrangement with *The Times*.

The obvious clash of interests, economic and political, which is inherent in this situation has been at the root, in one way or another, of every official inquiry into industrial relationships within the Territory. The Report of the Forster Commission (para. 195) had this to say:

We have formed the view that the African is so advancing in efficiency that the time cannot be long before the number of European supervisors can be reduced. . . . This might cause some resentment by the [European] mine workers, but if the attitude of the European is favourable to this course it would be necessary to settle a separate wage standard which would secure to the Africans a fair wage.

We recognize that the advancement of the Africans towards a higher standard might result in the first instance in a lower working cost to the mining companies, but this result of an attempt to satisfy to some extent the Africans' aspirations towards a higher standard it would be obviously unfair to ascribe to managerial self-interest.

This pronouncement was not welcomed by the European mine-workers. They saw in the Commission's suggestions for advancing the Africans not some possibility of the 'exploitation of the Africans' of which they spoke, but a distinct threat to their own standards. In point of fact, unskilled Africans were seldom in competition with skilled Europeans. The area of competition, as Lewin [1] had observed, was in the intermediate sphere of labour, that is in the semi-skilled occupations. The real fear of the Europeans was of replacement in these positions by Africans able and willing to perform the job for considerably lower rates of pay. Advancement of the Africans would have meant in fact their taking over European jobs at lower wages. But the bargaining position of the European Union was strong at the time, and the mines were under pressure to avoid industrial disputes at all costs.[2] The mining companies were compelled to accept with reluctance first the principle of the 'closed shop', and later a clause in the agreement with the Union touching on the dilution

---

[1] Op. cit., p. 6.
[2] See the address given by Mr. R. L. Prain at a joint meeting of the Royal African Society and the Royal Empire Society, printed in *African Affairs*, liii (1954), pp. 91–103. Mr. Prain is Chairman of the Rhodesian Selection Trust, which controls the mines at Luanshya (Roan Antelope) and Mufulira.

of labour. Immediately after the war this clause, no. 42, was amended to read:

The Company agrees that work of the class or grade that is being performed or job that is being filled by an employee at the time of the signing of this agreement, shall not be given to persons to whom the terms and conditions of this agreement do not apply.

Since the terms of the agreement applied only to daily-paid European employees, this meant in effect that no job performed by a European in 1945, when the agreement was made, would be given thereafter to an African.

The Forster Commission had recommended that the mining companies and representatives of the Government and the Mine Workers' Union should meet together, to discuss the question of African advancement. But Government had felt that the position was complicated by the situation created by the war, and the recommendation was not in fact taken up until 1947, when a conference was called to re-examine the question. The conference achieved nothing, and later in the year Government announced that it would set up a Commission of Inquiry (the Dalgleish Commission). It was to this Commission that Guillebaud had referred in his report.

The Commission arrived in Northern Rhodesia in September, 1947, and suffered an immediate rebuff. The European Mine Workers' Union objected to the personnel of the Commission,[1] and to the fact that the Commission's terms of reference did not contain a direct reference to 'equal pay for equal work': it refused to co-operate. The Commission's terms of reference extended to all industries in Northern Rhodesia, but as it found that in all of the lesser industries there was no opportunity for the Africans to advance to any higher post except after a long period of training and with improved education, most of its recommendations were confined to the copper-mining industry. These included the listing of certain posts (3 underground and 24 on the surface) not then occupied by Africans, which they would be capable of filling immediately; others that they would be capable of undertaking in the comparatively near future; and yet others to which

---

[1] The Chairman, Mr. Andrew Dalgleish, had been a member of the earlier Forster Commission which made the original suggestion for African advancement.

Africans might advance after a period of training. The Report of the Commission also carried recommendations on training facilities, an inclusive wage, and improved housing conditions; but there was also one important qualification, that no European should be discharged in order to make way for an African. The African should only be promoted when a European ceased to be employed, or was himself promoted.

There, in the main, the matter rested until 1950, when there was a meeting between the Mine Workers' Union and the newly formed African Union. The Europeans stated that they were prepared to accept the principle of African advancement to posts which up to that time had been filled by Europeans, provided that the Africans for their part would accept the principle of 'equal pay for equal work'. In this context the expression 'equal pay' was interpreted to include similar conditions of work, and the other facilities available to European miners. Thus the concession made by the European Union was wholly illusory, since it was perfectly obvious that Africans would no be employed on these terms. I am not at all clear, therefore, why the Africans should have agreed to the Europeans' proposals. From my discussions of the point with a number of African leaders, it seems that some felt that they ought to accept a principle which was, after all, a basic tenet of trade union doctrine. Others considered that as new jobs were created on the mines it would be necessary to discuss the conditions attaching to them through negotiation, and that from such negotiations the Europeans would be excluded. However, as Guillebaud observes in the article quoted above, both sides appear to have let the agreement fall into the background almost at once. At all events, the European Union took no steps to cancel clause 42 of their agreement with the companies which was the effective bar to the implementation of the *Dalgleish Report*.

It was the *Guillebaud Report*, in combination with the situation created by the discussions on Federation, now advanced, which once more focused attention on the recommendations of the *Dalgleish Report*. In May, 1953, the two mining groups—the Anglo-American Corporation (controlling Nkana and Nchanga) and the Rhodesian Selection Trust (controlling Roan Antelope and Mufulira)—wrote to the [European] Mine Workers' Union. The letters referred to the distrust shown by Africans of the Central African Federation proposals, and suggested that 'some effective step, taken at this juncture, by the European employees and management acting together, should go some way to re-assure Africans regarding the good faith of Europeans'. They went on to propose discussions to find to what extent 'the maintenance of the principle and spirit of the above clause [clause 42] can be reconciled with some voluntary and agreed concessions to the aspirations towards advancement amongst the African employees'.

Shortly afterwards the Central African Federation was established, and preparations were soon made for holding the first Federal elections. A number of political parties were formed, and for the first time in the history of Northern Rhodesia an election to a Legislative Assembly was contested along party lines. The details of the election campaign waged by the different parties do not concern us here, and it is sufficient to notice that it was the issue of 'native policy' which provided the major source of cleavage between the parties, and, indeed, the keynote of the whole election. Invariably, the candidates took as the theme of their election addresses the question of race relations, and the position of the Africans within the wider community. Not a few of the candidates stated their position on the *Dalgleish Report*, and on the recommendations it contained for African advancement in industry. At one meeting the Confederate Party Parliamentary candidate for Kitwe-Chingola referred to the *Dalgleish Report* as a dangerous policy to implement on the mines. A few days before, the chairman of the Nkana branch of the Confederate Party said in a Press interview:

'Although we are prepared to let the African advance, it must not be to the ruin of the economic structure of Northern Rhodesia, which is what the Dalgleish Report would do. It means putting a tremendous amount of power into the hands of the African through giving him an economic advantage before he is ready for it.'

Federal Party candidates also expressed their opposition to the *Dalgleish Report*. The party leader, Sir Roy Welensky, said in a speech at Kitwe: 'I feel that the Dalgleish Report is completely dead and it should be allowed to be buried peacefully.'

These remarks evoked an immediate response from the African Union leaders. At the Annual Delegate Conference held at Luanshya in September, 1953, one of the main topics of discussion had been the means of implementing the Report's recommendations. Now, they declared, if the *Dalgleish Report* were dead, it would be given a violent burial. A similar resolution was carried at a meeting of the African T.U.C., into which the eight African trade unions in the Territory had organized themselves.[1]

The correspondence between the mining companies and the European Mine Workers' Union, published in May, 1953, had revealed some divergence of policy between the two mining groups. Now this was suddenly emphasized in an address given by Mr. R. L. Prain, the Chairman of the Rhodesian Selection Trust, before a joint meeting of the Royal African Society and the Royal Empire Society in London in November. Referring to the colour bar in industry, he declared that the present situation was untenable both in practice and in principle, and the failure to deal with it in the past had made it even more difficult and dangerous. Now there was danger in action or inaction, he said. Positive action would cause trouble from the European employees. But if they accepted inaction, what about the Africans, now organized into a very powerful union, with a membership of 40,000 as against 6,000 Europeans? Stated shortly, the new policy of the Rhodesian Selection Trust was to break the colour bar before the Africans decided to take matters into their own hands, and try to break it themselves.

The same question was once discussed briefly at one of the Management courses on 'Training Within Industry', which I had been invited to attend. The lecturer, an official of the mining company, pointed out that it was not so much a question of advancement, as of the opportunity for advancement. Where an African showed that he was capable, then some means had to be found to open his way to more responsible posts. Then if, as most members on the course considered, the African showed himself incapable of doing a more responsible job, they could turn to him and say that it was his own fault. But if they did not provide this outlet, the lecturer concluded, then there was going to be trouble.

If there was any suggestion in Mr. Prain's remarks of unilateral

---

[1] At a Congress rally in Lusaka earlier in the year, the White Paper containing the proposals for Central African Federation was publicly burned as an expression of African opposition to Federation. The resolution of the T.U.C. now declared that if the *Dalgleish Report* were dead, then it was as dead as the Federal White Paper which Mr. Harry Nkumbula [the Congress President] had burned. See below, p. 161.

action on the part of the mining companies to break the industrial colour bar, it was immediately repudiated by Sir Ernest Oppenheimer, Chairman of the Anglo-American Corporation. In a public statement he re-affirmed that the companies had no intention of breaking or denouncing their agreement with the European Union. 'We recognize', he said, 'that whatever progress can be made along the lines we have in mind, could only be achieved in co-operation and agreement with the Union.' His statement concluded with an assurance to the African employees that the companies had their interests constantly under consideration; to which Mr. Nkoloma, the General Secretary of the African Union, replied that they had been given similar assurances for the past eight years. 'The Union wants more evidence than mere statements that this matter is being dealt with in an active and practical manner,' he declared.

The General Council of the African Trade Union Congress met again at the beginning of January, 1954, and decided on action to support the economic advancement of all Africans in trade, industry, and Government. But the plans were to be kept secret so that their action, when taken, would be more effective. Although *The African Miner* in its November, 1953, number had asked members not to think that the *Dalgleish Report* had been forgotten, there had been up to this time little discussion of advancement at local branch meetings. Now, following the meeting of the T.U.C., the rank-and-file membership was apprised of pending developments. A mass meeting of the Roan Branch heard one of their leaders narrate the fable of the Hare, the Elephant, and the Hippopotamus. The Hare had made a wager with the Elephant that despite his own small size he could defeat the Elephant in a tug-o'-war. The Elephant, amazed at the challenge from such a puny creature, scornfully accepted. Thereupon the Hare approached the Hippopotamus, and made a similar proposal. On the appointed day the Hare arrived with a long rope, one end of which he gave to the Elephant, telling him that when he received the signal he should start pulling. The other end the wily Hare gave to the Hippopotamus with similar instructions. But the rope was so long that the Elephant and the Hippopotamus could not see one another and so, at the signal to start, they began to pull against one another. They tugged and tugged until they grew so tired that each in his turn approached the Hare and acknowledged his superior strength. In this matter, the speaker declared, the Africans resembled the wily Hare, standing in the middle while the companies and the European miners pulled against one another. Welensky had said that the *Dalgleish Report* was dead. Well, they would see. The Union had secret plans, and he urged all members to stand together so that their aims would be soon achieved.

Shortly after this it was suggested that the African Mine Workers' Union should be invited to take part in discussions on advancement together with the Chamber of Mines, the Mine Workers' Union, and the European Salaried Staff Association; and when Sir Will Lawther, President of the British [United Kingdom] National Union of Mineworkers, visited the Copperbelt in March, the mass of the African workers were filled with the wildest expectations. Some began to speak in terms of wages of £60 per ticket for casual labourers; others thought that if the principle of 'equal pay for equal work' were applied they should get even higher wages than the Europeans, for the 'Europeans were very lazy fellows. After a short time, they had to sit down and have a cup of tea.' One African who had got into a dispute with a bus conductor was overheard to remark that it didn't matter, for soon they would not need the buses, as they would all have their own cars.

Sir Will Lawther had come out to Northern Rhodesia at the invitation of the two Unions, and before returning to England he claimed that his visit had been marked by a big achievement in that he had been able to bring the two Unions closer together on the question of advancement. No doubt he was referring to the resolution adopted at a joint meeting held under his chairmanship. This resolution had declared:

That the validity of the aspirations of the African Mine Workers' Union for advancement is recognized, and that both Unions pledge to strive unceasingly, with all effort, to realize this just demand; that it is in the interests of maintenance and improvement of the living standards of all mine workers that the principle of equal pay for equal work and responsibility must apply within the mining industry of Northern Rhodesia; and that there should be officially constituted a joint consultative committee to examine any matter submitted by either of the two mining organizations affecting any section of, or all, the miners within the industry.

I

The most casual perusal of the resolution shows that in fact it marked no very real advance. It did not clarify in any way the attitude of the African Union itself towards the formula of equal pay for equal work. And the further the talks between the various parties proceeded, the clearer it became that the African Union itself was deeply divided on the formula. On the one hand there was the view of the General President, Mr. Katilungu, that advancement should take place on two levels. The first would involve the relatively small number of Africans who were able to prove themselves capable of doing work now performed exclusively by Europeans. Where such Africans did take over certain of the lower categories of European work, it would be done on the basis of equal pay for equal work. While negotiations necessary to advancement of this type were going on, the Union would also work for advancement at a second level. This would consist in a complete re-assessment of the work done by Africans and Europeans on the mines; and on the basis of such an assessment, considerable numbers of Africans who were judged to be doing jobs of some responsibility should have those jobs re-graded. In this way Katilungu was looking towards the creation of certain new categories of mine labour which would carry a higher rate of pay than under the existing system of labour classification.

But there was also a strong and influential body of opinion within the Union leadership which, while it accepted the formula of 'equal pay for equal work' as a valid and even fundamental principle of trade unionism, at the same time considered it inapplicable to the conditions of Northern Rhodesia. The members of this faction argued that if, indeed, opportunities for advancement were to be made available on these terms, very few Africans would profit immediately, if ever, from the acceptance of the equal pay principle. They were afraid that to accept this formula would be to accentuate the gap which was already growing up between the mass of the workers, and the few Africans who were already earning relatively high wages. One Union leader with whom I discussed this question told me that once, in a meeting with the Chamber of Mines, the Europeans had referred to them as a bunch of clerks, who did not represent the workers. If they accepted the formula of 'equal pay for equal work' that charge would have been justified, because the mass of the people, the ordinary labourers, who saw no improvement in their lot, would turn away from the Union and its leaders, as men who had betrayed them. There was a further danger, too, in the equal pay formula. Some of those who were in highly paid groups were already beginning to speak of themselves as African Officials of the mining companies. The Union's position would be further threatened by the defection of these men, some of whom were Union officials, to form an African Salaried Staff Association. It was argued that the members of such an Association, by virtue of their higher pay, their social position, and their smallness of numbers, would be more ready to co-operate with the companies; they would be, in fact, to quote one informant and the current Copperbelt slang, 'company stooges'. Members of the opposing faction felt that in this way the whole cause of African advancement would be seriously retarded, not only within the mining industry, but also within the wider sphere of social and political development. They themselves had not yet been able to formulate any clear alternative policy; but so far as I was able to ascertain, they appeared to be thinking in terms of a complete re-classification of all labour on the mines, and of general wage increases for all grades of African labour.

This then was the position in broad measure when I completed my field-work in Luanshya in May, 1954. Clearly, the whole question of African advancement raises many very complex problems, with which I am not competent to deal and which, in any case, lie outside the scope of this study. In this section I have been concerned simply to set out the facts which I consider necessary to an understanding of the internal relations of the Roan branch of the African Mine Workers' Union, and of its rôle in the local community.

III

According to the terms of its constitution, membership of the Union is open to all African workers employed in the industry regardless of race or sex. As used here the term 'race' is misleading, and presumably it is 'tribe' or 'ethnic group' which is intended. Women may become members of the Union, but opportunities for their employment on the mine are still few, and when I undertook a survey of Union membership at Roan in mid-1954 there were no paid-up women members in the branch. But this does not mean that women are unaware of, or uninterested in, the activities of the Union. Meetings of the branch are regularly attended by women, and there is some evidence to suggest that they are sometimes able to bring pressure to bear on their back-sliding husbands. For example, one case that I heard of concerned a young Ngoni clerk at Nkana who had left the Union and joined the newly established Salaried Staff Association there. After a short while he returned to the Union. He said that his wife kept nagging him for not attending the Union meetings, and at last forced him to go back because all her friends mocked her, and said her husband was 'an informer'.

The Union has not yet succeeded in getting the mining com-panies to concede the principle of the 'closed shop'. Consequently, the Union remains a voluntary association, and its membership strength is subject to considerable fluctuation. Initially, the col-lection of dues operated on the Stop Order principle. Monthly deductions of 6*d*. from the pay of each man registered as a member of the Union were made by the Mine Management, and the amounts thus deducted were handed over to the Union. The Chairman of the Roan branch told me that membership strength during this period varied between 70 and 80 per cent of the total labour force, a claim which was supported by the Government Labour Officer. Towards the end of 1953 the Union decided to raise the monthly contributions from 6*d*. to 2*s*. 6*d*. The mining companies considered that, in view of the larger sums involved, and their own obligations to their African employees, they were unable to continue the collection of dues, and gave notice to the Union that it would have to make its own arrangements for collecting members' subscriptions. In March, 1954, a few months after the Union had begun the collection of its own dues, the registered paid-up membership of the Roan branch of the Union was 6,182. When I conducted a survey of Union membership later in the year, membership strength had fallen to 2,224, or 22 per cent of the total African labour force on the mine at that time.

These figures, and the survey itself, require a preliminary word of explanation. Originally I had intended to study the composition and membership of the Union using the methods of the sample survey. Subsequently, this course turned out to be impracticable. However, with the co-operation of the Union leaders, my research assistant was able to spend a period of 13 weeks [1] between May and September working in the Branch Secretary's Office. Throughout this period each member appearing at the office to pay his dues was interviewed briefly in terms of a simple schedule. For some months past, four-party talks between the Mining Companies, the European Mine Workers' Union, the European Salaried Staff Association, and the African Mine Workers' Union, had been taking place on the question of African advancement, to which I have previously referred. In the earlier part of the survey my assistant was able to interview steadily, sometimes at the rate of about 80 members per day. During this period, the expectations of African workers, particularly of those in the lower labour groups, were high; people looked forward eagerly to the announcement of the results of the talks. But gradually members grew restive and, as the Union leadership remained silent, the numbers of those appearing at the office to pay their dues began to fall away rapidly, and became a mere trickle. There was a temporary recovery when the branch leaders announced that the General President, Mr. Katilungu, would address them on the results of the talks. It seems, however, that when Katilungu did appear, he had little to say on the question of advancement, and large numbers left the meeting before he had finished speaking. Simultaneously, a local branch of the African Salaried Staff Association was formed, and enrolled many members. These factors have to be borne in mind in assessing the significance of the figures I produce below. I will attempt this assessment at a later stage of the analysis.

Table 7 sets out membership strength of the Roan branch at the time of the study in terms of major tribal groupings. [2] The grouping of tribes adopted here is to some extent arbitrary

---

[1] This period was chosen because members whose dues are more than three months in arrears cease to be entitled to benefits.

[2] These are made up as follows:

(a) *Bemba*—Bemba, Bisa, Chishinga, Lunda (Kazembe), Lungu, Ngumbo, Tabwa, Unga, and Aushi;

(b) *Nyasaland*—Henga, Nkhonde, Nyanja, Tonga, Tumbuka, and Yao;

(c) *Eastern Tribes*—Chewa, Kunda, Ngoni, and Nsenga;

(d) *Western Tribes*—Chokwe, Lunda (Mwinilunga), Luchazi, Luvale, Mbunda, and Mbwela;

(e) *Central Tribes*—Lima, Lala, Lamba, Lenje, Sala, Soli, and Swaka.

TABLE 7

MEMBERS OF ROAN BRANCH, A.M.W.T.U., BY TRIBAL GROUPINGS,
MAY TO SEPTEMBER, 1954

Tribal Grouping	Number of members	Total number in employment	Percentage membership
Bemba	880	3,868	23
Nyasaland	334	868	38
Eastern Tribes	347	1,214	28
Western Tribes	111	523	21
Central Tribes	211	1,640	12
Nyakyusa (Tanganyika) . .	170	1,031	16
Miscellaneous	171	766	22
Total	2,224	9,910	22

but in the main does correspond with broad linguistic, cultural,
and territorial divisions. It is worth recording here that in the
course of the inquiry we found some members who resented

TABLE 8

MEMBERS OF ROAN BRANCH, A.M.W.T.U., IN LOWER (1–4) AND UPPER
(5–SPECIAL GROUP) LABOUR GROUPS, MAY TO SEPTEMBER, 1954

Labour Groups	Union membership	Total number employed per labour group	Percentage membership
1	800	5,214	15
2	191	748	24
3	288	1,180	24
4	345	1,264	27
Sub-total . .	1,624	8,406	19
5	320	895	35
6	175	350	50
7	64	142	45
8	29	89	33
Special Group	12	28	43
Sub-total . .	600	1,504	40
Grand Total .	2,224	9,910	22

being asked to state their tribe on the grounds that there was no room for tribalism within the Union, and we had therefore to be content with the district of origin. It is interesting, therefore, to find what appear at first sight to be significant differences in the extent to which members of various tribal groupings joined the Union.

But even when a connection is established between tribal grouping and Union membership, it does not follow that it is a causal connection. It may simply reflect, or be related to, a number of other and possibly more significant factors. In Table 8, therefore, I have looked at Union membership in terms of the labour groups into which all African labour on the mines is classified. As explained earlier, Groups 1–3 are made up of unskilled manual labourers. The higher groups include the more skilled and experienced workers, manual, supervisory, and clerical, so that the higher the labour group the higher the wage. Table 8 shows that the percentage of Union members in Group 1, which is by far the largest single group, accounting in itself for more than 50 per cent of the total labour force, falls below the mean of the total. But the percentage of those in Groups 5 and above is consistently above the mean of the total. In short, the table appears to suggest that the higher the group, and therefore the wage, the stronger the tendency to support the Union, at least in terms of payment of dues. This impression is strengthened if one compares Union membership in Groups 1–4 and in Groups 6 to Special Group. In Groups 1–4, which make up about 85 per cent of the labour force, Union membership was 19 per cent; in Groups 6 to Special Group, which form only 6 per cent of the labour force, Union membership was 46 per cent.

How does this conclusion square with the implication contained in Table 7 that tribal factors are relevant to the question of Union membership? Clearly, a satisfactory answer to this question can only lie in contrasting the number of Union members in each tribal grouping with the total number of people of such tribal groupings in each labour group. Unfortunately, I was unable to get the figures necessary for such a breakdown. The closest approximation I can make is to relate members of the Union who are in Labour Group 6 and above to their tribal groupings. The result this procedure gives is set out in Table 9.

Table 7 brought out clearly that the proportion of workers who

TABLE 9

MEMBERS OF ROAN BRANCH, A.M.W.T.U., IN LABOUR GROUPS 6 AND
ABOVE BY TRIBAL GROUPINGS, MAY TO SEPTEMBER, 1954

Tribal Grouping	Number of Union members Group 6 and above	Total Union membership	%
Bemba	107	880	12
Nyasaland	71	334	21
Eastern Tribes . . .	50	347	14
Western Tribes . . .	9	111	8
Central Tribes . . .	25	211	12
Nyakyusa	2	170	1
Miscellaneous . . .	16	171	10
Total	280	2,224	13

were Union members was higher for Nyasalanders than for any
other of the tribal groupings. From Table 9 we see that Nyasaland Union members also have a higher proportion in the upper
labour groups than have the other tribal groupings. Taken in
conjunction with Table 8, these facts suggest that in comparison
with the other tribal groupings, a higher proportion of Nyasalanders is to be found in the more highly paid jobs, and that the
Nyakyusa and Western tribesmen are to be found in the lowest.
The Bemba-speaking people, who are numerically dominant,
occupy a middle position. Since the necessary statistics are not
available to me, I am not able to affirm positively that this is so,
but it does appear to be supported by what we know of the growth
of the labour force, to which I referred in an earlier chapter.[1]

When one considers the paid-up membership of the Union
in terms of formal education a similar picture emerges. In Table
10 I compare Union membership in different tribal groupings in
terms of those who have reached Standard 4 or higher. Here
again, the proportion of Nyasaland members who are educated
is much higher than in any other tribal grouping. The tribes of
the Eastern Province are just above the mean percentage. The
remainder are below, but no differences emerge between the
Bemba and the Central and Western tribes. The Nyakyusa have
the smallest proportion of educated members.

[1] See above, p. 6.

TABLE 10

MEMBERS OF ROAN BRANCH, A.M.W.T.U., BY FORMAL EDUCATION,
MAY TO SEPTEMBER, 1954

Tribal Grouping	Union members who have Standard 4 education and above	Total Union members	%
Bemba	97	880	11
Nyasaland	102	334	30
Eastern Tribes	54	347	15
Western Tribes . . .	11	111	10
Central Tribes	21	211	10
Nyakyusa	2	170	1
Miscellaneous	16	171	9
Total	303	2,224	14

But here too, in the absence of figures giving details for the total labour force, one has to be cautious in interpreting these results. For example, we can say that nearly 40 per cent of the Nyasalanders on the mine are paid-up members of the Union, and of these 30 per cent have achieved Standard 4 education or over. But we do not know the proportion of educated to uneducated in the remaining 60 per cent. It may be, as indeed I suspect, that the proportions are in fact the same. In other words, we cannot argue from the table that there is a correlation between Union membership and formal education. The higher proportion of Nyasaland Union members in the upper educational categories may simply be a function of the fact that the Nyasaland group as a whole contained a higher proportion of educated men.

Before proceeding further, it might be useful to sum up at this point by bringing these tables together in one table. Table 11, therefore, shows Union membership by tribal grouping, by Labour Groups 6 and above, and by formal education. In each case the Nyasalanders and the Nyakyusa are found consistently and respectively above and below the mean. The Bemba are more or less evenly distributed around the mean, while there is some fluctuation in the Central and Western tribes, but always below the mean. However, it is necessary to repeat that while these regularities may be set out in terms of tribal groupings, this does not mean that they are explained by such groupings. A more satisfactory hypothesis is that they merely reflect in different ways the

TABLE 11

MEMBERS OF ROAN BRANCH, A.M.W.T.U., BY TRIBAL GROUPINGS, LABOUR
GROUPS (6 AND ABOVE), AND EDUCATION (STANDARD 4 AND ABOVE),
MAY TO SEPTEMBER, 1954

Tribal Grouping	Percentage membership of Union of all mine employees by tribal grouping	Percentage membership of Union of those in Labour Group 6 and above	Percentage membership of Union of those of St. 4 education and above
Nyasaland	38	21	30
Eastern Tribes . .	28	14	15
Bemba	23	12	11
Western Tribes . .	21	8	10
Central Tribes . .	12	12	10
Nyakyusa	16	1	1
Mean percentage of total	22	13	14

significance of the labour group in determining Union membership. The assumption here is that the higher the labour group,
the longer will be the period of service of its members, and therefore the stronger the tendency to protect one's interests through
membership of some collective body. There is some evidence for
this view in the fact that the highest rate of labour turnover is
in Groups 1 and 2, and it is in these groups that we find the lowest
proportions of Union members. Again it appears from Table 12

TABLE 12

MEMBERS OF ROAN BRANCH, A.M.W.T.U., BY LENGTH OF SERVICE IN
'TICKETS', MAY TO SEPTEMBER, 1954

Number of tickets worked	Total mine strength	Union membership	%
0–24	4,590	655	14·3
25–49	2,150	543	25·2
50–74	1,408	380	26·9
75–99	681	239	35·0
100–124	438	157	35·8
125–149	214	97	45·3
150–174	115	47	40·8
175–199	90	45	50·0
200 plus	155	61	39·3

that Union membership increases in relation to the period of continuous employment on the mine.

If the general argument is valid one would then expect to find, for example, a greater proportion of Nyasalanders in high labour groups, and that they would have had longer periods of continuous employment than had members of the other tribal groupings, and so forth. The differences between the various tribal groupings would then be explained in terms of the historical circumstances by which they were brought into the European economy. Unfortunately, I do not have the material either to substantiate or disprove this hypothesis.

Yet even if the proportionate membership of the Union is consistently higher in the upper labour groups, the fact remains that it is the membership in the lower labour groups which is numerically preponderant. Although only 18 per cent of those in Groups 1–3 are paid-up members of the Union, together they account for 60 per cent of the total membership. It is the workers in these groups, therefore, upon whom the Union primarily relies for financial support, to whom it addresses its appeals for co-operation, and for whom it claims to fight.[1]

Leaders and ordinary members alike see the primary function of the Union as the raising of wages and the improvement of working conditions by collective bargaining through the formal machinery of negotiation and, where necessary, by concerted strike action. As one old Nsenga underground boss boy once put it: 'Before we had the Union whenever we wanted to ask the Company to increase our pay they refused, and we had to throw stones as we did in 1935. But now we have the Union we strike peacefully and we get what we want.' In this context the Union stands as a body in opposition to the Management, and purports to represent the unity of all workers against the employers. But in fact wage claims and strikes are spasmodic and relatively infrequent events, and the internal organization of the Union is maintained through its day-to-day activities, through the ancillary functions which it comes to acquire, and through the personal contact which members have with their leaders.

Each branch of the Union has its own Committee, the membership of which—like the membership of the Works Committees

---

[1] See above, p. 97.

which the Union superseded—is drawn from the various departments of the mine in proportion to their numerical strength.
The Committee at Roan consists of 46 members, of whom 17
represent the Underground Department, which is the largest on the
mine. The latter form the largest single bloc on the Committee.
The African Personnel and Administration Departments have
between them 14 representatives. The Smelter, Concentrator, and
Engineering Departments all have much smaller representation.
The Committee meets regularly at least once a month. It hears
reports from the various departments, and discusses questions of
Union and local policy. It is here, according to my informants,
that the Branch Chairman meets 'left wings', an expression on
the Copperbelt which has come to stand for any form of open
opposition. Unfortunately, I have no evidence to show what form
alignments take within the Committee, and whether they coincide
with departmental divisions. When agreement is reached the
matter is ready for presentation to members at a public meeting.

Public meetings of the branch are usually held at least once a
month. News of the meeting soon disseminates round the compound; and as the appointed hour approaches, large crowds of
Africans may be seen converging on the Welfare Centre, where
they gather in a large enclosed space, rather like an amphi-
theatre. It is difficult to get accurate figures of attendance at
meetings, though newspaper reports have sometimes put the
figure as high as 8,000.

The meeting itself is conducted from a high, raised platform
where the branch leaders sit, and all points on the agenda are introduced by one or other of the Executive Committee, which is
composed of the office-bearers. I am told that where some point
of policy is expected to meet with public opposition, each office-
bearer of the branch will speak on the matter in turn, with the
chairman speaking last, to emphasize his approval of the policy
being advocated. The participation of the public at these meetings
is not purely passive. Speakers, whether from the platform or the
floor, whose views do not command popular support, may be
howled down. In other cases the public may express its dis-
approval of a speaker by leaving the meeting, as it has done on a
number of occasions when addressed by the General President
of the Union.

From my own brief observations, and from accounts of meetings I have received from others, it is clear that rank-and-file members are free to participate, and in fact frequently do participate, in the discussions, although a criticism sometimes levelled at the Union by some Africans is that too often the views of the ordinary members are not given a proper hearing. Individuals raise questions, offer advice to the leaders and to their fellow-members, and may seek to rally opinion in opposition to some measure which has the approval of the Executive Committee. For example, when the Company once sought to make fencing of houses compulsory by all occupants, it first approached the Union. But although members of the Committee argued in favour of the measure, their view was rejected by the public meeting. Labour was unstable, the members argued, and workers were always being discharged, so that the benefits of their labour would be enjoyed by subsequent occupants of the houses. This view was taken back to Management, and it was finally agreed that fencing should be purely voluntary.

The vast gathering is in itself a striking symbol of the Union as a vital entity, and the freedom of all to participate in the discussions an expression of identity of leaders and people in their common purpose. In this way, the regular mass public meetings have a very significant function in maintaining the internal cohesion of the Union.

In the main, the public meeting confines itself to the discussion of broad, general issues of Union policy. The complaints and problems of individuals are handled, at least initially, by the Branch Office. The Branch Office is a small building set aside by the Company for the use of the Union. The office is in the hands of a full-time paid Secretary. Unlike the other members of the Committee, who are all employees of the Company, the Branch Secretary is an employee of the Union. Because of increasing pressure of work, due largely to the fact that the Union now has to collect its own dues, the Secretary also has the assistance of a full-time clerk. Between them they handle the questions, complaints, and problems that are brought before them every day. By way of illustration I record the following cases which were brought to the Branch Office one day in quick succession:

(1) A man sought the assistance of the Union in securing his promotion from Group 6 to Special Group. He said that he worked in a mine store, and that his job involved dealing with books and

keeping records. It was a job which demanded intelligence, and there were even some Europeans who had failed to do it. But whenever he asked the European foreman about promotion to a higher group he was always put off, and told to wait. Now he was tired of waiting, and had decided to bring the matter to the Union. The Secretary commented later that such cases were common, and many of them had been taken up successfully by the Union.

(2) An underground worker had been discharged for being drunk on shift. He agreed that he had been drunk. The Branch Secretary pointed out that it was a difficult case because being drunk on shift was a breach of the mining regulations. However, because he was a fully paid-up member, the Union would do its best to help him. He was advised to attend the meeting of the Executive Committee later that evening, when his case would be discussed further.

(3) A man complained that he had not yet been given a house, although he had already been in employment for some months. The Secretary drafted a letter to the African Personnel Manager, asking him to provide accommodation for the bearer. The Secretary said that if the man were not given a house then he would go round and see the Personnel Manager himself and discuss the matter with him.

(4) There was some discussion of a case involving a claim for Workman's Compensation by a man who had been injured while on duty, and subsequently discharged. The Secretary felt that he had insufficient knowledge of the law relating to Workman's Compensation, and referred the case to the Head Office of the Union at Kitwe. He said the question of the man's discharge would be taken up when that of compensation had been settled.

In these cases, coming up day after day, we see the Union dealing with problems important to every African living on the mine. Loss of job, lack of accommodation, accidents, and promotion—these are all vital issues, and it is to the Union that the African miner now looks for assistance when such problems arise. But the cases have a further significance; they are part of a continuous process of creating ties, which radiate from the Branch Office, and link together within a common organization large numbers of individuals from every department of the mine. In all this there is little that is peculiar to the Mine Workers' Union. What is significant is the way in which the organization of the Union parallels the organization of the mine itself where it touches on African affairs. The Branch Office of the Union stands just behind the African Personnel Department Block and, in sociological terms, is structurally equivalent to it.[1] Again, as already noted, the composition of the Executive Committee follows the departmental divisions of the mine. Even the collection of dues is geared to some extent to the mine pay system. All dues are paid at the Branch Office, and on pay-days the Branch Secretary or his clerk is always present to 'catch' people as they leave the pay line. Finally, as we have observed, Union meetings are held at the Mine Welfare Centre, and for this reason non-members cannot be excluded from attending. Thus at every point Union organization appears to be geared in with that of the mine itself.

It is important to bear in mind what I may term the 'unitary' structure of the mine. As I have already explained, the mine is a self-contained industrial, residential, and administrative unit. Every employee is housed by the mine, and no African who is a mine employee may live off the mine premises. Moreover, until recently, every African was fed by the Company, and the vast majority of the employees continue to draw weekly rations from the Company's Feeding Store. A butchery and a number of other stores enable those who wish to supplement their rations to do so without making a trip to town or the Second Class Trading Area. It is the mine which provides the hospital, and employs the doctors and nurses who care for the sick; and it is the mine, again, which provides for the recreational needs of its employees. The African miner writes his letters at the Mine Welfare Centre, he drinks with his friends at the sub-Beer Hall on the mine, he prays in the church of his own denomination on mine property, he sends his children to school on the mine. In the work situation he has an allotted place within the structure of the mine. He has a job within a department, works together with the members of his gang under an African boss boy, who is in turn responsible to a European supervisor, and so on. In short, the mine impinges on his life at every point, a state of affairs which is epitomized in the office of the African Personnel Manager, who

---

[1] Dr. Mitchell has drawn my attention to the fact that the Branch Office of the European Mine Workers' Union stands opposite the Mine General Offices (see Map 2). I do not know if this is the position at other mines.

is ultimately responsible for almost all matters arising within the African Mine Township.[1]

The Union itself has grown up within the framework provided by the organization of the mine, and has been able to build upon that framework. At the same time, developing within a 'unitary' structure, the Union itself has tended to take on certain 'unitary' characteristics. The Union is confined by the terms of its agreement with the mining companies to matters relating to the wages and working conditions of the African mine employees. But Africans rarely conceive the functions of the Union as being limited in this way. On the contrary, they look to the Union for assistance in many situations which are usually regarded as falling outside the scope of trade unionism.

Two cases may be cited briefly in support of this statement. For some time a pass system had operated at the African Mine Hospital. All those wishing to visit their relatives and friends in the hospital had to obtain passes at the gate, and only two passes were available for each patient. The system gave rise to much complaint. Some objected to the need to queue up outside the gates, while others found that when they eventually reached the orderly giving out the passes, the two passes allocated to each patient had already been distributed. The matter was reported to a number of the departmental representatives of the Union, and was later discussed at one of the Union's public meetings. The Union decided to take action to have the system of passes abolished. Accordingly, on the appointed day, many people mustered at the gate of the hospital and, led by the Branch Secretary and other Union officials, filed inside without passes, and gathered in small groups about the patients, irrespective of whether they were relatives, friends, or complete strangers. Discussion followed between the Union officials and the hospital authorities, and it was agreed that the practice of issuing passes should be discontinued.

The second incident emerged in course of a conversation with an underground worker who was anxious to know when the next Union meeting was to be held, so that they would all learn the results of the advancement talks. He added that at this meeting he was going to move that the Union conduct a boycott of the

---

[1] As noted earlier (p. 17), responsibility for policing the compound has now largely been taken over by the Northern Rhodesia Police.

Beer Hall. He explained that many women were now being arrested for being in illicit possession of beer, and were being heavily fined, or sent to prison in default. There was one woman, he said, who had been fined £20 for having brewed illicitly 2½ forty-four-gallon drums of beer. He blamed the authorities who were doing all in their power to discourage the brewing of beer because they did not want to see African women making money. He argued that this state of affairs could only be remedied by getting the Union to conduct a boycott of the Beer Hall. Indeed, they would have the Beer Hall closed altogether unless Government and the Mining Company agreed to allow the women to brew freely. He thought his motion would have the support of many members, especially those who were themselves *bacakolwa*, great drinkers. So far as I am aware the motion never in fact came up before a Union meeting, but the incident is worth recalling as indicating the rôle ascribed to the Union by those living on the mine.

Both these cases involved situations where it was hoped to bring pressure to bear on the Company, and effect a change of policy. More significant in the present context, therefore, is the way in which Union leaders have also taken over certain of the functions formerly exercised by the Tribal Representatives, where no such pressure is demanded by the situation. The passing of the Tribal Representatives has brought about certain difficulties. From time to time one heard complaints that whereas formerly minor disputes could be settled easily by the Tribal Representatives, now one had to go to the Urban Court where there was a strong likelihood that one would be heavily fined. Formerly, too, an important task of the Tribal Representatives was to care for new arrivals at the mine until they had been able to contact their relatives. One Union member once explained that when his younger brother arrived recently at the mine he had to spend three nights sleeping at the market place until my informant's wife accidentally found him there. In the old days, he said, they would have found one another much sooner through the Tribal Representatives. Yet while the passing of the Tribal Representatives has posed these problems, I never once heard the suggestion that tribal representation should be re-introduced. On the contrary, the general attitude appears to be that since these difficulties exist, it is for the Union to find a solution to them.

K

In some situations the attitudes, and the behaviour associated with them, adopted towards Tribal Representatives in the past have been transferred to the Union leaders. Formerly, it was the custom for a Tribal Representative to be given 'tribute' in the form of beer, which he distributed amongst the members of his 'court'. Now it is the Trade Union leader who holds 'court' in the Beer Hall. Men and women bring him bottles of beer, which are then distributed amongst the members of his retinue. In other situations the Union leaders appear to have taken over functions once exercised by Tribal Representatives, which related to purely tribal affairs. When I was in Luanshya Mr. Chambeshi, then chairman of the Roan branch, received an invitation from the Portuguese West African Chieftainess, Nyakatolo, to pay a visit to her capital. According to a note in *The African Miner*, when the Chieftainess visited Luanshya earlier in the year the members of the Branch Committee had worked very hard to make her visit a success. On another occasion we received word in Luanshya of the death of the minor Bemba Chief Muceleka, and a number of leading Bemba met together to discuss how they should conduct the mourning ceremony. Shortly afterwards I visited Kitwe where I met a number of Bemba elders who had gathered at Mr. Katilungu's house to welcome him on his return from a journey to Southern Rhodesia. In the course of conversation I asked if any arrangements had been made at Kitwe for holding the wake for the dead Chief. The elders replied that no arrangements had been made, but now that Katilungu had returned they would be able to discuss it. Katilungu is himself a leading Bemba in the town, though in terms of tribal status he is by no means the senior. Nevertheless, his status as a Union leader is carried over into many other situations which lie outside the scope of trade unionism. On this occasion people looked to him for a lead in arranging the mourning ceremony, rather than to a more senior Bemba in the town.

Thus the province of Union activity and influence is not confined, as the stereotyped responses of members sometimes suggested, simply to the issues of wages and working conditions. On the contrary, it is to a large extent co-extensive with life on the mine itself, and a whole range of human problems associated with it. Within the 'unitary' structure of the mine, Union and Management, represented by the African Personnel Department, occupy positions which are, in a sense, structurally equivalent though opposed. For, just as the African Personnel Manager epitomizes the unity of the African Mine Township viewed from the standpoint of the employer, so the Union has come to express a similar unity viewed from the standpoint of the employee. Similarly, just as the African Personnel Manager has a general authority in all matters affecting the welfare of the African employees on the mine, so the Union leaders are regarded as having a direct concern in all similar matters, even though they may not fall within the usually accepted scope of trade unionism.

IV

Initially, in discussing the composition of the Union, I showed that there were differences in the degree to which the various sections of the mine population were paid-up members of the Union, and I suggested there that the labour group appeared to be the significant factor in determining membership. I have now been arguing that since almost any problem arising within the Mine Township may be regarded by the Africans as falling within the province of the Union, the Union's position within the structure of mine society has to be seen as equivalent to the African Personnel Department to which, however, it stands in opposition. Looked at from this point of view, the Union represents the unity of the workers in opposition to the Company. Yet in fact less than 20 per cent of those in Labour Groups 1–3 are paid-up members of the Union. On the face of it the two hypotheses advanced here are plainly contradictory, and it would seem that one or the other must be discarded. However, closer examination will show, I think, that this is not the case. We have seen now how the Union was able to bring copper production at all mines to a complete standstill when it organized the strike of 1952; and we have seen, too, how the Union was able to achieve the abolition of the Tribal Representatives. Later, I will show how the attitudes of members also had an important bearing on the voting in the elections for the Urban Advisory Council in 1954. In all this, the Union appears as a factor making for social cohesion, binding together within the framework of its organization large numbers of individuals who have been brought together through the chance of common employment. At the same time, we have seen that it is no longer possible to view the population of an African Mine Township as an undifferentiated mass. It includes the casual labourer and the relatively skilled worker; the migrant labourer and the urban dweller who was born and brought up in the towns; the illiterate and the highly sophisticated, and so forth. The population of the Township is held together by common interests created in the joint productive task, and its unity is expressed politically through the local branch of the Union. But since the population is also divided by cleavages which correspond to the separate interests of its different sections, these cleavages too must find their expression within the Union. It is precisely because the Union claims to speak for all sections of African mine opinion that it must contain within itself the conflicts of interest which operate within the mine community at large. I suggest that the data on Union membership set out in Tables 7–12 have in fact to be seen as an index of such conflict.

It will be recalled that shortly before I began the survey of Union membership, the number of registered paid-up members of the branch was 6,182. When the survey was completed the total stood at 2,224, a decline of close on 4,000 members. Thus, in the space of about six months, Union membership had fallen from over 60 per cent of the total labour force to little more than 20 per cent. Now if it be assumed for the moment that when the Union membership stood at around 6,000 there was 100 per cent paid-up membership amongst Labour Groups 5–Special Group, their numbers could not have exceeded 1,500 which was the total number in those groups employed by the mine. At the time of the survey there were 600 paid-up members in these groups, so that the decline in membership in the upper labour groups could not have exceeded 900. In other words the decline in Union membership by a further 3,000 must have taken place in the lower Labour Groups 1–4. The lower labour groups in fact must have contributed at least 4,500 members or 55 per cent of the total numbers employed by the mines in those groups. I say 'at least' advisedly, because the further the Union membership in the upper labour groups falls short of 100 per cent, the higher must be the proportion of members in the lower groups. Thus if membership in Labour Groups 5 to Special Group had stood in March at the still fairly high figure of 75 per cent, the corresponding proportion for the lower groups would have been 60 per cent. That is to say, the greater decline in Union membership would have been in Groups 1–4 (i.e. a decline of 40 per cent as against 35 per cent in the upper groups). The point emerges with greater force, perhaps, if we present it in tabular form, showing the actual decline in Union membership as between the upper and lower labour groups, again on the assumption that in March there was 75 per cent Union membership in the upper groups.

TABLE 13

DECLINE IN UNION MEMBERSHIP IN UPPER AND LOWER LABOUR GROUPS
BETWEEN MARCH AND SEPTEMBER, 1954, ON THE ASSUMPTION OF A 75
PER CENT PAID-UP MEMBERSHIP IN GROUPS 5 TO SPECIAL GROUP IN MARCH

	Union membership in March	Union membership in September	Percentage decline on previous membership
Labour Groups 1–4	5,054	1,624	67·8
Labour Groups 5–Special . .	1,128	600	46·8

Since the Union does not itself keep the necessary statistics, it is of course impossible to say what the proportion was of Union members in the various labour groups before the survey was undertaken, and therefore the precise degree of decline as between these groups. Nevertheless, if the present argument is correct, it does appear likely that the greater decline in Union membership took place in the lower groups. Conversely, while we must assume that there was also a considerable falling away of members in the upper groups, a higher proportion of these retained their attachment to the Union. The original hypothesis that those in higher labour groups tended to become members of the Union to a greater extent than those in the lower has thus to be reformulated. We can restate it in this way: that given a general decline in the membership of the Union, the tendency was for those in the lowest labour groups to drift away from the Union more quickly than those in higher groups.

Why was this? There are a number of possible explanations. One is that institutional instability in African urban life to which I have already referred. Another is that after the Mining Company had ceased to collect Union dues, the Union had been unable to devise some effective alternative system for collecting subscriptions. There may be an element of truth in these explanations, but I consider that they are not by themselves adequate. The system of collecting dues had been working effectively until May, when I undertook the membership survey. In the early stages of the survey, members continued to pay their dues at the Branch Office as they had become accustomed to do since November, 1953, when the Management brought the earlier arrangement to an end.[1] Thereafter the decline in numbers of those paying their contributions was most rapid.

A third explanation is that the decline may be related to the failure of the talks then in progress on African advancement. As we saw in the previous section,[2] many members had been living for some time in the expectation that the result of these talks would be the raising of wages to a point almost on a par with the European wage-scale. When these hopes failed to materialize large numbers turned away from the Union in disappointment. But here again the explanation is not sufficient: it does not explain the stronger drift away from the Union among the lowest paid workers as compared with the higher. The hypothesis which I wish to consider in the remainder of this section is that certain cleavages had been developing within the Union for some time, but had remained obscured until the discussions on African advancement brought them into the open. I shall argue that the men who had hitherto provided the Union with its leaders were now regarded by their followers as having a different kind of interest in the industry, and that this difference of interest was reflected in the Union leaders' acceptance of the principle of 'equal pay for equal work'.

Throughout the history of the Copperbelt there runs one persistent thread. In each of the urban communities, it is the mine, the office of the District Commissioner, and the Management or Municipal Board, that provide between them the fixed and enduring points of the political structure. But about them there is constant change in the actual relations of power, change which is marked by a continuous struggle for power within the African section of the community. Arising out of the total situation created by the opening of the mines, new groups and

---

[1] At a public meeting of the Roan branch held in mid-January, 1954, the branch officials were able to announce that subscriptions had just reached £1,000.

[2] See above, p. 109.

associations emerge in opposition to existing groups and associations. This struggle goes on through time, and ends in the defeat and death of the older group. The functions of the victorious group proliferate as it takes over those of the group it has supplanted, and for a time a new unity is created. But during the period of struggle the cleavages within its own ranks are obscured. Gradually, however, the separate and conflicting interests operating within the new group appear; and since there are no mechanisms and no common body of norms by reference to which these tensions may be resolved and group unity re-affirmed, fission takes place, and yet another new group emerges.

We have seen something of the way in which this process works in our earlier study of tribal representation. Compelled to devise some instrument of administration to deal with a large and highly mobile African population of many tribes, the Mine Management, and later the local government body, created the system of Tribal Elders. And although the position of the Elders within the mine community was clearly reflected in situations of crisis such as the disturbances of 1935 and 1940, the Elders otherwise appear to have fulfilled their functions to the general satisfaction of the African mine employees. Thus it is significant that although the authority of the Tribal Elders was rejected during the strike at Mufulira in 1940, at the election of the new Tribal Representatives shortly afterwards all the old Elders were reinstated. At this time, then, what leadership there was, was provided by men whose very presence on the mine as Elders symbolized the political and social values of the tribal societies from which most of the workers had so recently come. Yet, as the events at Mufulira showed, new forces were also at work. Inevitably, with their background and vested interest in the past, the Elders saw the Copperbelt in terms of a breakdown of society; and they saw the increasing laxity of the marriage tie, the rise of prostitution, and the decline of parental discipline, as the symptoms of this breakdown, and the major problems confronting them. From their point of view, they could not see that while marriages were breaking up, and parental discipline declining, new types of ties between husband and wife, and parents and children, were also being formed. Perplexed by many of these phenomena, they missed the indices of an emerging new society, made up not only of many tribes, but also of many races.

As the urban communities took root, new problems arose out of urban living, of which the Elders were often unaware and which they were not equipped to handle. Gradually there emerged the Welfare Societies, new groups with new leaders, whose vision was no longer confined within the framework of an ancient social order, and who were themselves actively interested in what a new order offered. At first limited in scope to matters falling within the sphere of social welfare, the new associations rapidly expanded their functions. When Chiefs on one occasion visited Luanshya on their return from a training course at the Government Jeanes Teachers centre at Chalimbana, it was the local Welfare Society which made the preparations for their reception, and organized the tribal dances conducted in their honour. Soon, as we saw at Luanshya, these associations began to take on more directly political functions, until they were in a position to challenge the Tribal Elders who dominated the Urban Advisory Councils of that time. A similar struggle was going on within the organization of the mine, and was reflected in the efforts of certain leaders in the Welfare Society to form a Clerks' Association at Roan in opposition to the Tribal Representatives and the Boss Boys' Committee.

Thus it is fallacious to dismiss or explain away the new leadership, as has often been done by officials,[1] as made up of a disgruntled intelligentsia representing no one but themselves. It is of course true that they were representing their own interests; but at the same time, by arranging for the entertainment of Chiefs, by pressing for the building of new roads within the township, or by raising complaints about the conditions at the hospital and clinic, they were speaking for all the people living in the urban areas. And the election by the Tribal Representatives in 1949 of a number of senior mine clerks to sit on the Luanshya Urban Advisory Council was a tacit recognition of this state of affairs.

In considering the rise of the new urban leadership two points may be noted. Firstly, although there had been serious disturbances on the Copperbelt in 1935, and again in 1940, in neither instance had the Africans attempted any damage to the power-houses or other vital mine plant.[2] Conceivably, the Africans might have

---

[1] For example, see above, p. 70.

[2] *Report of the Commission of Inquiry, 1935*, para. 133. The members of the Commission noted: 'When it is borne in mind that at the outbreak of the

taken to smashing the machinery as an expression of resentment against the new system, just as the Luddites had done at a corresponding period of the Industrial Revolution in England.[1]

Significantly, they did not do this. By their behaviour on these occasions they showed that they were not protesting against an industrial system as such; they were complaining of the position accorded to them within that system. Secondly, given this acceptance of an industrial system, and given, too, the sharp division of society into Black and White groups, where wealth and skill, and the means of acquiring them, appeared almost as a natural monopoly of the Europeans, the clerks and other educated Africans had a particularly important rôle to play. Through their increasing use of the English language they were learning not only to master one of the most important tools of the new culture, but they were also helping to build a bridge between tribes and between Europeans and Africans. By their example they demonstrated to their fellow-Africans that the gulf between Black and White was not in fact determined in the nature of things. Only

---

disturbances the whole of the immensely valuable plant and workings of the mines, and the houses, shops, and other premises in the townships, were at the disposal of the strikers, it must be considered remarkable that they did not take advantage of the position. The amount of damage done was very slight.'

[1] See, for example, G. D. H. Cole, *A Short History of the British Working-Class Movement* (1948), pp. 4–5. Cole sums up the early period of the Industrial Revolution in England as follows: 'During this phase the [Labour] movement was looking backwards, and kicking in vain against the pricks of a new system to which it felt an instinctive hostility. . . . The [wage-earner] responded most readily to leaders who . . . had their hearts in the country rather than in the town. . . . The revolts of the Luddites, the strikes and machine-breakings of 1818, the Reform agitation . . . were all deeply penetrated with the hatred of the new industrialism.'

It should perhaps be noted here, as an important difference between the Industrial Revolution in England and the modern industrial revolution in Central Africa, that whereas in Africa the revolution came to a people following a traditional subsistence economy, in England there was a long history of industrialization before the Industrial Revolution. As Bronowski remarks, the Revolution came to an England whose wealth was made in cottages, and it moved the sources of wealth to factories (J. Bronowski, *William Blake: A Man without a Mask* (1954), pp. 35–8). It was the change from a society of money to one of capital which led to the later struggle of the workmen 'for the maintenance or the revival of customs and laws, from which the employers wish to be free'. For a discussion of the Luddite Riots from this point of view, see J. L. and Barbara Hammond, *The Rise of Modern Industry* (1937), pp. 104–9.

K*

in this way can we account satisfactorily for the very high prestige which clerks and hospital orderlies on the mines came to enjoy among their less literate fellows. They provided the nucleus of the new leadership because, in the emerging society of the Copperbelt, it was they who pointed the way forward to the new social order.

Accordingly, when trade unionism was introduced to Africans in Northern Rhodesia, we find that the leadership was predominantly recruited from the core of clerks and other relatively well-educated men who had been leading figures in the Welfare Associations. Hence, too, many of the early Union leaders were of Nyasaland and Lozi origins, for both of these areas had had much longer experience of missions and mission schools than the other tribal areas of the Territory. The right of this small educated group to lead was accorded triumphant recognition when more than 80 per cent of the total labour force of all the mines on the Copperbelt turned out to vote for the abolition of the Tribal Representatives.

Just as the Welfare Societies had expanded their functions at the expense of the Tribal Elders, so now there was a proliferation of the functions of the Union. Through the Union a new unity was established. Yet, in the course of time and by a kind of paradox, the very factors which had brought the Union leaders into their position of power were now tending to divide them from the people who had supported them. By virtue of their education, they are to be found in the highest paid jobs on the mine. They have a higher standard of living, and can enjoy forms of conspicuous consumption which are still denied to the mass of African mine-workers. Again, in earlier years their ability to speak English was regarded by the rank-and-file not only as a mark of prestige, but as an indispensable asset in conducting negotiations with the mining companies. Nowadays fluency in English is sometimes seen by others as another wedge dividing the educated leaders and the ordinary members of the Union. Such leaders are more able to interact socially with Europeans, and in some cases are suspected of having moved into the 'enemy camp'. They are accused by the rank-and-file of a lack of militancy. They are afraid of strikes, it is said, because they are afraid to lose their jobs. Their policy is described as one of appeasement. In order to document these cleavages developing within the Union, and to provide material for the further analysis of my hypothesis, I describe here the election which took place at Luanshya in February, 1954, for the office of Branch Chairman of the Roan branch of the African Mine Workers' Union.

As we have seen already, the leadership group of the local branch is made up of the office-bearers, and the members of the Committee, who are drawn from all departments of the mine. In past years the Chairman of the branch had been elected by the Committee from among its own members, but this method was now criticized by the Branch Secretary as being undemocratic. He argued that the Chairman should be elected by popular ballot. His suggestion, which was acted on, was that each department of the mine should be asked to nominate any member of the Union to stand for election. Committee members then addressed departmental meetings, and the following four candidates were nominated:

(1) Chambeshi
(2) Nkoma
(3) Mzumara
(4) Chapolani

Chambeshi was the retiring Chairman. He was Lala by tribe and a grandchild of the Lala Chief Mboloma. After taking his Teacher's Certificate at Mapanza, a secondary school run by the Anglican Mission, he took up a post as teacher at a school in his own tribal area. In 1936 he came to Roan, where he was employed as a clerk and interpreter. In time he played a leading rôle in forming the Clerks' Association, and was a member of the Works Committee when that body was introduced. He became the first treasurer when a branch of the Union was founded at Roan. In 1949 he was elected to the Urban Advisory Council. Recently he had been promoted to Group 7 as a mine labour capitao.

Nkoma was a Committee member representing the underground department. He had been born in Lamba country, of a Lamba mother and a Nyasaland father who was working on the mine. Through his father he claimed chiefly connection, and his paternal uncle had in fact been the Tribal Representative for the Manganja people (Nyasaland). He had no formal education, but had a slight command of English. He was now employed as an underground boss boy (Group 8), and had indeed spent the whole of his 24 years' service on the mine as an underground worker. In his youth he had been a fine footballer, and was now Chairman of the Roan Football Club.

Like Nkoma, *Mzumara* was also the offspring of an inter-tribal marriage. His father, a Nyasalander, had married a daughter of the Bemba Paramount Chief when he was employed at Kasama. Mzumara regarded himself as a Nyasalander, and had earlier helped to found a local branch of the Nyasaland National Congress. He was an educated man, and had travelled widely in the Rhodesias and other parts of Africa. He had been employed for many years as a senior orderly in the African Hospital. At one time he had been Chairman of the Roan branch of the Union, and a member of the Urban Advisory Council, where he represented the Luanshya Welfare Society.

The fourth candidate, *Chapolani*, was a much younger man than the others. An Nsenga of commoner stock, he had come to Roan in 1946. After a year's teaching at the Roan School, he joined the mine as a clerk in the African Personnel Department.

At the next public meeting of the branch, the names of the candidates were read out, and the procedure of the election explained to the public. The election was to be by secret ballot. Each candidate was to have his own box coloured as follows: Chambeshi, white; Mzumara, black; Nkoma, red; and Chapolani, green. Each voter would get his voting papers at the Union office, and polling would take place at a booth set up at the Welfare Centre.

The account of what follows is based upon material collected by my Research Assistant, Mr. Nyirenda, who was invited by the Union to act as Returning Officer. His task was to ensure that each voter was a paid-up member of the Union, and therefore qualified to vote, and to see that voters fully understood the procedure and carried it out properly. In this way he was able to record the spontaneous comments of members as they entered the booth to cast their votes.[1]

---

[1] I have used the proper names of people throughout the study since it seems to me that attempts at 'disguise' rarely defeat those who have a close personal acquaintance with the area in which the research has been carried out, and who are interested in such details. I would emphasize, therefore, that the various

The new mode of election appeared to win general approval. One underground labourer with fifteen years' service, who was an early voter, remarked: 'This year we are given the opportunity of choosing a man who can lead us well. In past years we have had cowards, useless men who were elected by the Committee. This year a person like Mzumara or Chambeshi cannot be elected. These men fear the Europeans. We want people like Nkoma and Chapolani who do not fear Europeans. They are not afraid of losing their jobs. The only thing about Chapolani is that he is young, and looks small.'

An old man, coming in shortly afterwards, supported these views, and when Nyirenda explained to him the meaning of the different coloured boxes, he added: 'The one who painted these boxes is very wise. His painting has good meaning. Mzumara's box is painted black because he is dead, he has no brains; Chambeshi is white because he is a Christian, he wants peace all the time; Nkoma's is painted red—yes, because he is a strong man who is as hot as fire. He fears nothing and nobody. He is always prepared for a strike or for "Korea";[1] Chapolani's is painted green because he is as young as the green leaves. Since I am a man who does not fear strikes I shall vote for Nkoma.'

Some time later a member of the African Welfare Staff came along to vote. When he was told the names of the candidates he said: 'Well, I'm sorry, sir, but I will not vote because Musumbulwa is not standing. I can't vote for any of these others for there is none who has as much sense as Musumbulwa. None of these others is fit for they are uneducated, and their powers of reasoning are limited.' Musumbulwa had for long been a leading personality on the mine. He had been at one time secretary of the Welfare Society. Later he became Vice-Chairman of the Urban Advisory Council and a member of the African Representative Council. With Chambeshi and others he had founded the Clerks' Association at the Roan. Like Chambeshi, too, he had once been a

---

statements about the personal character and qualities of particular individuals made during the course of the election, and quoted in my account, must not be taken to mean that they are true as to their content. Such statements are the expression of social attitudes: they are cited here only in so far as they are relevant to the analysis of certain sets of social relations, and express lines of cleavage within those sets of relations.

[1] 'Korea' is a Copperbelt slang expression, meaning warfare or strife.

schoolteacher, and the two had been school friends together at Mapanza.[1] For some time he was an active member of the Executive Committee of the Union, and he had recently been re-nominated as representative of the African Personnel Department. But he had withdrawn his nomination in a letter to the branch, without stating any reason.

During the morning the majority of those voting were under-ground workers. By feeling the weight of the ballot boxes it was easy to tell that most of them had voted for Nkoma. But shortly after noon, a large number of the mine clerks began to come along. One of them said to Mr. Nyirenda: 'I know that at this election people will make a mistake, they will elect a man like Nkoma to be Chairman. They will elect him because he talks much at meetings. He talks emotionally, and people agree with him. He does not know English, and how do you think he can present a case to the employers? He is a man who likes using physical power. He gets angry in meetings and wants to fight anyone who disagrees with his suggestions. The only ones are Chambeshi and Mzumara who can express themselves in English, and have some idea how to conduct meetings because they are educated.' Another clerk supported this view: 'Nkoma and Chapolani are the ones who have spoiled the Football Club because they are always insulting people or wanting to fight them,' he said. 'Nkoma is Chairman of the Football Club but he does not run it properly, so how much more likely is he to spoil the Union?'

By about 1.30 p.m. Chambeshi and Nkoma had established a long lead over the others, and were now running neck and neck. But in the early afternoon most of the voters were miners. As they entered the booth many of them asked to be shown Nkoma's box. They said that this year Nkoma should be Chairman. He would make a good leader, for in 1953, when he had once acted for Chambeshi, he had fought successfully for many things which Chambeshi had been unable to achieve. 'Nkoma is the only fit man,' said one, 'because he does not fear the Europeans. Mr. Cook [the Assistant African Personnel Manager] and others fear him very much. He talks to them with his hands in his pockets, a cigarette drooping from the side of his lips, and his hat turned down covering half of his face. All the Europeans underground

---

[1] See above, p. 135.

and on the surface fear him. He is also the only man here in Luanshya who does not fear the people at Head Office. He nearly beat the President [of the Union] last time he was here when the President used insulting language towards the people.'

Towards evening many more clerks came along and voted. The ballot closed for the day about seven o'clock. There was some doubt about where the ballot boxes should be kept overnight. A suggestion that they be kept in the Union Office was quickly rejected. It was finally agreed to keep them at an African Minister's house for 'being a Christian, he could not cheat'.

On the following morning Nyirenda collected the boxes, and as he moved towards the Welfare Centre he was followed by a crowd of voters crying out: 'Bring the boxes quickly so that we put our papers in Nkoma's.' One voter to whom Nyirenda was explaining the meaning of the boxes demanded: 'Why is Mzumara's name here? Nobody will vote for him. He was the Chairman some time ago and we passed a vote of no confidence in him. He was afraid to go and meet the employers at a meeting in Kitwe to which all branch chairmen were invited. He didn't go because he thought he would be discharged from his job. A good leader should not worry about losing his job. Chambeshi, too, is useless. He has done nothing since he was elected. He has only fought for his own promotion. He is now a compound boss boy and is in Special Group. He has fought for no one's promotion but his own. He is a selfish man; a good leader fights first for the people. Now Nkoma is a good man. We underground people are getting a lot of overtime because of him. No European can now call an African "monkey", for if Nkoma hears of it he will come and beat that European. This year we want Nkoma.'

A young clerk who had come along to give his vote to Chambeshi began to make disparaging and pointed remarks about Nkoma and his lack of education. He was promptly attacked by an older man from the power-plant. 'You are new in this Union,' the older man told the clerk, 'and you do not know what makes a good leader. It does not matter whether a chairman is educated or not, provided the secretary is educated. A chairman should be a man like Nkoma. . . . Even if he does not know English his secretary can interpret for him. . . . Educated people always fear their employers because they are afraid of dismissal. So they are not fit to be chairman. But they do very well as secretaries because they are not employed by the Europeans, so they cannot be discharged by them.' The young man walked away before the other had stopped speaking.

Shortly afterwards some women voters [1] arrived. They were nurses employed at the hospital. When they found Mzumara's name among the list of candidates they burst into laughter: 'Can such a one be chairman, one who does not respect his fellow-Africans? He calls others dogs and goats. But he fears the European sisters very much. He says "yes, sir, sister". He is not fit.' This view seems to have been popularly shared, for very few had voted for Mzumara.

The numbers coming to vote had now fallen very considerably. Among a group of casual labourers, one wanted to know why they could only vote for one man. After all, all the candidates were active members of the Union and worked together in fighting for more money for the workers: 'I shall put my paper in any box,' he said, and he voted with his eyes shut. His fellow said that since he had been on the mine he had heard no complaints about Chambeshi's leadership, and would vote for him. Both of these were fairly new arrivals on the mine.

The voting had commenced on a Monday, but by Wednesday, when the ballot was closed, the number of voters had become very small. On Thursday small clusters of Union members were standing around the Welfare Centre, and discussing the election while awaiting the result. One Committee member said he thought that Nkoma would get in, and that the General President would now have to face some stern opposition. Nkoma would not be afraid to challenge the President, for he treated him just like anybody else. Nkoma would win because as a leader he did not look upon the ordinary people as his inferiors. He mixed with everybody, important or unimportant, young or old. But people like Chambeshi and Mzumara kept themselves to themselves. As leaders they regarded themselves as Chiefs or 'lords of creation'. In another group, the Branch Secretary commended the democratic way in which the election had been conducted. He said that he had been criticized by both Chambeshi and Mzumara for

---

[1] The election took place in February, 1954. No women members were recorded in the survey of Union membership conducted later. See above, p. III.

introducing such a system. Chambeshi had accused him of introducing political methods into what was a non-political body; but
he had replied that it was not a matter of politics, but that they
were opposed to the popular ballot because they feared defeat at
the hands of Nkoma. He expressed himself as being in favour of
Nkoma who, if less educated than the others, was more straightforward, and was not afraid to state openly his opposition to the
General President. Some days later the results of the election were
publicly announced at a Union meeting. Nkoma topped the poll
with close on a 1,000 votes, followed by Chambeshi with just
under 500 votes. The other two candidates mustered between
them only 25 votes. The immediate comment, heard widely on
the mine, was that they could now look forward to many strikes,
for Nkoma was very fond of strike action.[1]

Nkoma's victory represented a radical change from the kind
of leadership which had hitherto been predominant in the Union.
At the same time it was an index of the cleavages within the
Union, which found their expression in the spontaneous comments of the voters and others. In the first place, there was the
conflict between underground and surface workers. Members
voted for Nkoma because, as they said, 'he represents us, the
underground workers'. One man, interestingly enough of the
same tribe as Chambeshi, went so far as to declare that if Nkoma
did not win they would have two unions, so that Nkoma could
be their chairman, while the surface could have its own union.
Although Nkoma himself was now in a higher group, his whole
working life, which almost corresponded with the life of the mine
itself, had been spent underground. Uneducated he might be, but
he had a long experience and deep understanding of the problems
and difficulties of underground workers. It was here that interaction between African and European was most regular and intense, here that the African had to face most frequently the violent
outbursts of some irate European supervisor. It was easier to violate
the mine regulations against assaulting an African in some dark
recess of the mine than in the surface-plant area. And because
Nkoma was a man of rugged physique and personal courage who

---

[1] This prediction proved correct, for shortly afterwards the branch called
a strike of all African employees, including essential service-men, which lasted
nearly a week.

would stand up to any European, underground workers looked up to him as their leader.

But while some of the comments thus suggested a simple dichotomy within the mine between underground and surface, it was in fact against only a section of the surface workers that criticism was levelled by the underground workers. Surface workers include the various labour categories employed at the concentrator, the smelter, the engineering and other departments, as well as those in personnel and administration. Yet it was only against the latter that the attacks were launched. It was the relatively small educated category, from which hitherto the leadership had been drawn, that alone was singled out for vilification and abuse.

It would be all too easy to see the issue simply in terms of education against illiteracy, or brain against brawn. 'Some people think that Nkoma can lead because he is powerful,' said one Committee member who was a supporter of Chambeshi. 'They do not know that Europeans do not fight with their hands, but with their brains.' The argument repeatedly urged against Nkoma by his opponents was that he was uneducated, and knew no English. How then could he sit down round a table and parley with the Europeans? Nkoma's supporters, for their part, countered by pointing out that he could always employ an interpreter, and then proceeded to castigate the clerks for being proud, for thinking of themselves as 'chiefs and lords of creation' who must hold themselves aloof from the people. One underground boss boy who had been in continuous employment at the Roan for more than fifteen years declared: 'They think we are nothing. They do not realize that there can be no Union if we underground workers withdraw our membership.'

But the basic charge against the clerks was not their education as such, nor indeed the hauteur to which it was alleged to give rise. The charge was rather that by virtue of their education they were regarded as having a different kind of interest in the industry. 'People who speak English are cowards' was an expression commonly heard through the election.[1] There are still relatively few Africans on the Copperbelt who are proficient in English, and they are generally to be found as clerks, hospital orderlies, welfare assistants, and the like. Indeed, for those with a Standard 6

---

[1] Cf. below, p. 178.

education,[1] who count as highly educated in comparison with the mass of their fellows, there are few jobs beyond these to which they can aspire. Since these jobs, which may carry a wage of £15 a month and more, are still relatively few outside the mines, there is keen competition for them. Mine clerks therefore tend to be among the most stable element in the labour force, and some that I know have been in continuous employment for more than twenty-five years. By contrast, manual labourers are easily replaceable, and correspondingly they find less difficulty in switching from one job to another. Consequently, they tend to see mine clerks and others in high labour groups as being too circumspect in their behaviour. The labourers accuse the higher grades of being dominated by the fear of losing their jobs, and being too conciliatory in their approach to the employers. Given their position, the argument runs, how can they prosecute with full vigour the cause of the mass of their fellow-workers who are unskilled labourers? Nkoma was a man who had worked with them underground, he knew how Europeans treated Africans. He did not fear 'strikes or Korea'. He had obtained concessions from the Company where Chambeshi had failed, when he had acted as Chairman for a time during the latter's absence.[2] He possessed the quality which above all they demanded in a leader—the quality of militancy which the others lacked.

Sometimes this argument was pushed even further. The educated leaders were accused not merely of a lack of militancy. They were also charged, like the Tribal Representatives in the past, with being in league with the Europeans. One man, who was himself a clerk, commented on Chambeshi's defeat: 'I know that Chambeshi has lost the vote, because people say that he is a friend of Mr. A—— [a European]. He goes to his house and drinks tea there. Moreover, Chambeshi has been given a job as Compound Supervisor which is better than the one he had. This

---

[1] It is difficult to find the exact correspondence for this standard in, for example, the English educational system. In Northern Rhodesia a boy who had reached Standard 6 would have to spend a further four and a half years before he was ready to matriculate. There is still only a very small number of Africans who have reached matriculation standard. But obviously formal education is not the sole criterion of a man's ability to do a job, nor is it a measure of intelligence.

[2] I did not discover the nature of these concessions.

means that he is on good terms with the African Personnel Manager. How can he be the Chairman if he is a good friend of Compound Officials? We know that he wants to join the Salaried Staff Association, so he is not loyal to the Union.' [1]

I have used this material on the election to show some of the cleavages that were operating within the branch, and, in particular, to show how members now saw themselves as divided from the men they had formerly accepted as their leaders by reason of their different social and economic interests. These divisions were now further exacerbated by the discussions taking place on African advancement, and on the different interpretations which Africans put upon advancement.

During 1953 discussions had taken place between Government representatives, the Chamber of Mines, the [European] Mine Officials and Salaried Staff Association, and the [European] Mine Workers' Union, in an attempt to obtain agreement for the gradual implementation of the *Dalgleish Report*. These discussions broke down because of a clause in the agreement between the Mining Companies and the [European] Mine Workers' Union, which touched on the dilution of labour.[2] As we have seen, the effect of this clause was that no job which was being carried out by a European at the end of 1945 could be given to an African. Early in 1954 the African Trade Union Congress decided on action to support the economic advancement of all Africans in trade, industry, and government. Shortly afterwards an invitation was extended by the Chamber of Mines to the African Mine Workers' Union to participate with the other interested parties

---

[1] A mines African Staff Association had been formed at Nkana in May, 1953, under the leadership of Mr. Godwin Lewanika and Mr. Simon Kaluwa, who at one time had been General Secretary of the Mine Workers' Union. The new body was conceived as an African counterpart of the European Salaried Staff Association, and confined its membership to those Africans who held 'responsible positions'. Many of the members were, indeed, Lozi and Nyasaland mine clerks who had become dissatisfied with certain aspects of the administration of the affairs of the Mine Workers' Union, and who resented the alleged tribal dominance of the Bemba within the councils of the Union. Branches of the Staff Association were formed elsewhere on the Copperbelt, though none came into being at Luanshya until September, 1954. For further discussion see below, p. 235.

[2] See above, p. 104.

in the discussions on African advancement.[1] Throughout these discussions the European Union stuck to its point that African advancement must be conditional on the African Union's acceptance of the principle, 'equal pay for equal work': and it was on this very point that the African Union was so deeply divided within itself.

Throughout this period there was widespread discussion of the question amongst Africans of all classes. In noting some of their comments here we may gain a clearer idea of the nature of this division. A Group 1 labourer who had been in employment for 16 months said: 'We only want money, and money to satisfy us all—not just those in Special Group as it was in the last strike. They got a lot, but we got only a little. It will be very bad if only those in Special Group are considered. We labourers suffer a lot, the Union should fight for labourers. At this time when our leaders go to Nkana to meetings we remain with anxiety to hear what good talks they had. If they do not achieve something, many members will not trust them at all, and they will not pay their contributions. The leaders have told us there will be a lot of money this year. They say that many people will be getting from £40–£60 a month. It will be very good if we labourers get from £15–£20. Then we shall be happy and know that our leaders promised us a true thing. Europeans should understand that we are the people who do the work. And our fellow-Africans too—like clerks, capitaos and boss boys. They only stand and watch but we sweat. In fact we should get more than they do.' On another occasion at a beer drink a man in Group 6 who had been a driver on the mine since 1942 was telling his friends that if they did not join the Union shortly they would not enjoy the privileges which members would soon have. 'We members of the Union', he said, 'will be getting a lot of money in a few months to come. We shall be getting as much as Europeans. People in Group 6 like myself will be getting about £80 which European drivers are getting per ticket. People in Special Group will be getting more than £100. Then we shall be buying motor cars, not motor bikes as some of you are buying now.' Finally,

---

[1] The invitation followed a request by the [European] Mine Workers' Union that the African Mine Workers' Union and the [European] Salaried Staff Association should be present at future discussions of the advancement of Africans.

L

one member of the Executive Committee who was a mine clerk in Group 6 said: 'We want our African workers to have the opportunity of having more responsible jobs. I myself can do some of the clerical jobs done by Europeans in the African Personnel Department, but I have no opportunity even though I am capable. Many jobs done by supervisors, clerks, typists, section Personnel Managers or their Assistants could be done by Africans. Then some of the jobs done at present by Europeans are also done by Africans but the wages are different. We want the same wages.'

The underground labourer was thinking in terms of a general wage increase. He did not see 'advancement' as the provision of facilities for Africans to advance to posts of greater skill and responsibility: 'advancement' lay in the overall improvement of wages and working conditions, especially for ordinary labourers. He foresaw that if their hopes were not fulfilled in this direction many members would leave the Union. The driver and the clerk saw 'advancement' in somewhat different terms. Once all driving jobs had been performed by Europeans, but gradually most of them were taken over by African drivers. Similarly, the clerk saw himself as qualified to carry out the administrative duties of an Assistant Personnel Officer. Indeed, as a clerk in the Administration Department, he regarded himself as a Company official, rather than a mine worker. Thus clerk and driver saw themselves as doing jobs which were being done by Europeans, and doing them at European rates.

As noted earlier, the European and African Unions had met in March, 1954, under the Chairmanship of Sir Will Lawther, and a joint resolution was passed to the effect that equal pay for equal work and responsibility must apply in the mining industry. In accepting this principle, the African leaders were well aware that there would be few Africans who would stand to benefit immediately from advancement on these terms. Some of them considered that they could then press for advancement at a second level.[1] These views were congenial to men like the driver and the clerk, whose remarks were quoted above: they were attacked by others who argued that advancement on these terms would split and destroy the Union. This view was once expressed in forceful terms to my Research Assistant by Mr. Mwalwanda.

[1] See above, p. 110.

Mwalwanda was a Nyasalander and had been employed as a mine clerk for many years. He was the first Chairman of the Roan branch and, although he later resigned because of chronic asthma, he remained a staunch supporter of the Union. He said there would probably be only about 'six' (meaning very few) Africans on the Roan who would be given the same responsibilities as Europeans and so be entitled to equal pay. They would appreciate it, but the mass of the Union members would say that 'advancement' had helped only the few, but not themselves. It would split the Union. Ultimately, those who had been advanced would either join the Europeans' Union, or form a branch of the African Salaried Staff Association. Mwalwanda's views were shared by a number of other leaders at Roan, and he said he was going to urge the Branch Secretary, who was a member of the Union's Supreme Council, to press to have the resolution withdrawn.

Eventually, the four-party talks ended in deadlock, and there was a general drift away of members from the Union. I have shown that it appears that there was almost certainly a greater decline amongst members in the lower labour groups than in the higher.[1] If this was indeed the case, part of the reason at least appears to me to be implicit in the present analysis. For, at the time the membership survey was conducted, there were those in upper groups who still foresaw the possibility of their own advancement in terms of the equal pay formula: but for the mass of uneducated and unskilled workers advancement, on these terms, could only be a hollow phrase.

V

'We are all here to earn money,' Africans commonly say of their life on the mine. Often their stay is brief, but while they are on the mine they are bound together with their fellow-workers by their common interest in the joint productive task and what they derive from it. As I have already explained, the structure of mine society is essentially 'unitary'. The African employees of the mining company are thus linked together not only through the work situation, but in almost every aspect of their daily existence

---

[1] See above, p. 129.

by a complex nexus of ties which has its basis largely in the organization of the mine itself. It was within this organization, and
utilizing the framework already created by the mining company, that the Union eventually emerged and developed.

But a 'unitary' structure does not imply a homogeneous or
undifferentiated population. Over the years there has developed
amongst Africans on the mine an increasingly complex pattern
of social differentiation which is based on such factors as differences
in their productive rôles, their standards of living, their education
and relative degree of sophistication, and so forth. In general, the
process of differentiation has been marked by the emergence of
new social groupings and associations which express the nature
of the divisions operating within the social system of the mine.
In the field I was unable to examine this process as intensively
as I should have liked, so that my account of the mine political
structure may appear to be over-simplified. Nevertheless, the
broad significance of this process in the development of the Union
should be fairly plain. Developing within a 'unitary' structure,
the Union had itself come to acquire certain 'unitary' characteristics. After the abolition of the Tribal Representatives, the local
branch of the Union was the only representative body which
could claim to speak to Management on behalf of the African
mine employees. And because the Union did claim to speak for
all employees, it also contained within its own structure those
sources of division which operated within the wider mine society.
At the Roan, the election for the office of Branch Chairman, and
the subsequent discussions on African advancement, pointed to the
existence of cleavages within the Union, and even the possibility
of a split. These cleavages reflected broadly the divergent interests
of different sections of the labour force. When I left Luanshya
early in June, 1954, the threatened split had not yet occurred.
Nevertheless, it is significant that when Africans spoke of the
possibility of such a development, they always visualized it as a
threat by certain of the mine clerks and others in high labour
groups to leave the Union and form a branch of the African
Salaried Staff Association.

Earlier in this chapter, I pointed to what appeared to be a
contradiction in my analysis. From the examination of the
functions of the Union, and the rôle ascribed to it by Africans on
the mine, I argued that the African Personnel Department and the

PLATE III

A 'Special Group' African at home with his family in the African Mine Township

local branch of the Union had to be seen as structurally equivalent, with the African Personnel Department representing the unity of the workers from the point of view of Management, and the Union representing that unity in opposition to Management. At the same time, the survey of Union membership showed that only a little more than 20 per cent of the total labour force were paid-up members. There is a contradiction here: but it resides within the organization of the Union rather than in the analysis. The contradiction arises from the Union's attempt to cater for different sections of its membership whose interests in some cases are widely opposed. The present analysis points up the dilemma now beginning to confront the Union leaders. On the one hand, it would seem that only by recognizing the major cleavage that has developed within the African labour force can the Union re-establish its claim to speak for the vast majority of the African mine workers in the lower labour groups. On the other hand, there is a strong reluctance to take a step which must inevitably weaken the effectiveness of the Union. Thus when the African Mines Salaried Staff Association made its appearance at Nkana, it was bitterly denounced by the Union leaders.[1] And, indeed, it seems clear that as the Salaried Staff Association develops and expands, it will play an increasingly important rôle in mine politics, and particularly as a 'buffer' between the African Mine Workers' Union and the mining companies.

VI

Discussion in the preceding sections has been confined almost entirely to the growth of trade unionism among the African mine workers. But trade unionism has also spread rapidly among other Africans, and there are now few industries in which the workers have not made some attempt to organize themselves within a trade union. All told, there are now about eight Unions throughout the Territory, catering for railwaymen, shop assistants, drivers, cement-workers, hotel and catering employees, and general workers. Many of these Unions are centred on the Copper-belt, but they have local branches and a membership which is

---

[1] See *The African Miner*, September, 1953, where it was claimed that certain Africans 'who had found no places in the Union' were working together with the mining companies in an attempt to destroy the Union.

scattered over the whole Territory. In contrast to the African Mine Workers' Union, however, most of them are still rather weak and poorly organized. It was clearly impracticable in the field to attempt to cover all the Unions, and I confine myself in the present section to the African General Workers' Union, of which there is a branch at Luanshya. Other Unions which had branches in Luanshya at the time of my study were the Shop Assistants, the Municipal and Management Board Workers, and the Railway Workers.

The General Workers' Union caters for bricklayers, carpenters, and labourers working for contractors, but the bulk of its membership, as in the African Mine Workers' Union, is drawn from the ranks of the ordinary labourers employed by building and other contractors. In 1946 a group of Africans had come together to form an Artisans' Association, but it was never firmly established and was unable to gain the recognition of the employers. After the arrival of Mr. Comrie, African clerks employed by the contractors were instrumental in forming a Contractors' Employees' Association. Later this association was re-organized and expanded to become the present General Workers' Union under the presidency of Mr. Wilson Shonga. In 1950 the Union met together with the [European] Master Builders' Association for the first time in a Joint Industrial Council. Recognition was now accorded to the Union, and agreement was reached on a variety of matters, including rates of pay and the introduction of trade tests for certain categories of workers. Branches of the Union were formed all over the Copperbelt, at Ndola where it had its Head Office, Broken Hill, Lusaka, and even as far afield as Fort Jameson in the Eastern Province. But although the Union could thus claim a very large membership, in fact its strength was being constantly dissipated by internal dissension. Local branches complained that they were being neglected by the Head Office, and there was much dissatisfaction with the leadership. In 1952 members called for a general election and a new set of officials was appointed. These proved to be no more satisfactory than their predecessors, and within six months Mr. Shonga had returned to the office of General President. The Union was also unfortunate in its minor officials, and a series of defalcations by branch secretaries further weakened the confidence of the rank-and-file membership.

These disputes between the Union leaders have continued. In

1951 the various African Unions came together to form a Trade Union Congress, and at one of its meetings towards the end of 1953 special attention was given to the position of the weaker unions. As we have already noted, a serious division of opinion had developed within the African Mine Workers' Union over the question of African advancement. Members of the dissident faction considered that the only way to break Mr. Katilungu's tight grip on the Union was to build up the Trade Union Congress, which hitherto had remained weak and ineffective, by seconding officials of the Mine Workers' Union to the smaller unions until they had strengthened their organization. However, at this same meeting, the Trade Union Congress had also passed a resolution calling on the General Workers to withdraw an application they had recently made for a Wage Council in the building industry. Piqued by what he considered the unwarranted interference of the Mine Workers, the General President of the General Workers called for a meeting of his Supreme Council on the very day which had been appointed for the Trade Union Congress's next conference to discuss the problems of African advancement. Delegates to the conference demanded angrily why the President should have called a meeting at Ndola when they were supposed to be present at Kitwe for the Trade Union Congress. The meeting threatened to break up in disorder when the General President and other leading officials walked out. An interim committee was immediately appointed, and it was decided to ask the Trade Union Congress to assist in arranging for another general election.

Vacillation, a weak and divided leadership, and a record showing few positive achievements, have inevitably affected the life of the branches. The rank-and-file have become discouraged and apathetic. Contributions have been allowed to lapse, so that at some places the branches would appear to have only a nominal existence. Certainly this was the situation in Luanshya at the time of my study. In the sample survey which I conducted in the Mikomfwa housing area, each interviewee was questioned about his Union affiliation, when he made his last contribution, when he attended his last Union meeting, and so on. The results of the inquiry were quite plain, and pointed to the rapid disintegration of the branch. I quote below some typical comments made by those interviewed:

'I joined the Union in 1952 and resigned this year. My reason is that when I was a member I did not get any of the benefits which the Union leaders promised us when we were being enrolled. They said that if we joined the Union it would fight for an increase in our wages and better houses. It would also reduce working hours, but to my disappointment nothing of the kind has happened. My pay is still as low as it was in the first place. I work more than eight hours a day, but there is no overtime. When I told the Secretary about this he said that he would see my employer about it, but up to now he has done nothing about it. Leaders of this Union are more interested in collecting money than doing the things they promised to do for the members. I shall soon see the Secretary and get back all the money I paid for membership and monthly subscription.'

'I joined the General Workers when it started here in 1949. I saw that most of my friends were joining. I asked them what it was all about. They told me it would improve our wages and would fight against bad working conditions. But we uneducated people, we blind, just enter these organizations any old how. Once we are told by educated young men, we just agree with them even if they are wrong. We are like dogs which follow their master wherever he goes. Though he leads them to the snakes they would still follow. . . . I was told that the Union would fight for the improvement of our wages, just as I have said. But I see that my pay is just the same as it was. I am a full carpenter. I have worked for six years with this firm but I am only getting £5. What has the Union done for me?'

'I am a member of the General Workers' Union, but now I do not attend meetings because all the leaders who started the Union have resigned. The Union is not strong now because the President is a foolish man. He always agrees with the employers. Ngoni and Nyasalanders are always like that. They are all "yes men". If a Bemba were President of the Union it should have been very strong now. See, the Mine Workers are strong because its leaders are Bemba like Messrs. Katilungu and Puta. When we wanted to go on strike because the employers refused to give us an increment Shonga refused to support us. He agreed with the employers that they should give us tests so that the increment should be given only to those who passed. This is no policy of a Union that increments should be given to a few people, and not to others. This means that the Union fights only for a few people like Shonga himself and another "Ngoni" who passed a typing test. Because of all this I am losing interest in the Union. . . . The last meeting I attended was in June this year. I have not paid any dues since May [the interview took place in November]. I may join again if I see them go on strike or if another man becomes President in place of Shonga. But this man should be Bemba or some other tribe but not an Ngoni or Nyasalander. They are all useless people.'

'I may join the Union again if I see that it improves or becomes as strong as the Mine Workers' Trade Union. Since this Union [the General Workers] began it has never gone on strike, or increased the wages of its members. Instead, the leaders have made agreements with the employers that there shall be no increase until next year. I doubt if it will ever improve because all the leaders are uneducated, and know little of trade unions. Apart from this they are not to be trusted with money. Last year the branch secretary here stole all the money which belonged to the Union and went away with it. A few months ago the General Secretary stole about £19 and he is serving a sentence for this. My friends are also thinking of resigning for the same reason, that the leaders are stealing our money.'

The contrast between the African Mine Workers, where members tended to look to the Union for the solution of nearly all their problems, whatever their nature, and the General Workers, with its disillusioned and rapidly disappearing membership, is most striking. The Africans themselves are aware of this difference. The weakness of the General Workers is set off against the strength of the Mine Workers. Members of the former speak of the gains made by their fellows on the mine, and contrast it with their own lack of progress. As we see from the comments quoted above, many attribute the Union's lack of success to the poor quality of its leadership. And this in some measure is perfectly true. In comparison with the officials of the Mine Workers' Union, those of the General Workers are very much younger, are almost completely lacking in experience of negotiation, and have shown little organizing skill. But in fact the type of leadership possessed by the General Workers has itself to be seen as an effect rather than a cause, for the two Unions are faced with quite different problems of organization, arising out of the structure of the industries involved, and the kind of social structure with which those industries are associated.

On the African Mine Township everyone is an employee of a common employer. I have described its structure as 'unitary' in the sense that the mine organization is designed to cater for and to control almost every sphere of the workers' existence. The Mine Workers' Union has been able to work within and to utilize the framework provided by the organization of the mine itself. By contrast, the members of the General Workers' Union are employed by many different firms which are scattered about the

town and surrounding district. Most of the general workers live
in the Government Township, but many of them are dispersed
amongst the peri-urban settlements dotted around the area, where
contractors have their own private compounds.

The Municipal location is a residential unit, the structure of
which might be characterized as 'atomistic'. Not only do the
residents work for many different employers, but it is the employers themselves who are legally responsible for the payment
of rent. Each house is thus 'tied' to a particular employer for so
long as he requires it, and continues to pay rent. In order to get a
house in the location, a man must show that he is employed, and
he may only continue to occupy the house so long as he continues
in the employment.[1] The Housing Area or location is in charge
of a Location Superintendent. His responsibilities relate largely to
the problems of housing and hygiene: they do not involve the
further duties implicit in the relationship of employer and employee, which exists on the mine. For many years the Location
Superintendent has had the assistance of a body of Tribal Elders.
Their function has been confined mainly to the settling of petty
disputes. Unlike the Tribal Representatives on the mine, the
location Elders never conferred as a body with the Location
Superintendent on questions of wages or working conditions.
On the mine there was a long tradition of consultation by Management with committees of various kinds. Meetings of the African
Personnel Manager with Tribal Representatives, with Boss Boys,
and later with the Works Committee, brought the members of
these bodies into contact with the common authority, and enabled
them to acquire some experience in negotiation. Moreover, in the
earlier days, when the population of the Government Township
was still small, and opportunities for employment were few, it
seems likely that the ablest men were attracted to the mine. Thus
when the Mine Workers' Union finally emerged there were
already available older and more experienced men to take office.
But in the Municipal location the only representative body remained for a long time the Tribal Elders, and it is significant that
some of these are now leaders in the General Workers' and the
Shop Assistants' Unions. But the paid branch officials are generally

---

[1] The Location Superintendent may, in certain circumstances, permit a man
who has lost his job to continue to occupy the house for one month, provided
that he pays the rent for the month himself.

young men still in their twenties with little or no experience of negotiation, or of the trade or industry with which their Union is associated.

The fact that the General Workers are distributed among different firms, and different residential units, creates further problems for the Union organizers. One of my informants, a young man employed by a firm of building contractors as a capitao (foreman) in charge of a gang of labourers, once summed it up for me in this way:

'On the mines there are no departmental strikes. Usually a strike arises there because one of the employees has been ill-treated. When he complains to the Union then everybody would be informed at the public meeting, and they would all rise together like birds of a feather (*mucinshi wa nseba kwimina pamo*). They would not let one of their members suffer. They would all be willing to suffer for one person. . . . But in the General Workers we are employed by different firms. Here in Luanshya there is Richard Costain, Haywards, Bernards, Smiths and many others. When the trouble starts with Costain's employees, others do not feel affected even when the matter is explained to them by the Union leaders. They simply say, "We do not work for Costain." Then if a decision has been reached they say "Well, our employer gave us what we wanted, so why should we strike?" '

The wide distribution of the Union membership, in terms both of employment and residence, makes it virtually impossible to hold large public meetings of the kind held regularly on the mine. Such meetings as take place are of small working or residential units, and they tend, in this situation, to make for division rather than unity within the Union. Again, in the mining industry, wage rates and working conditions are generally standardized, so that on any specific issue the Union members are likely to have a certain amount of common ground between them. In less tightly organized industries there is more room for variation in these respects, and therefore less likelihood of all Union members, by whatever firm they are employed, taking a stand upon a common issue. Hence such strikes as take place tend to be confined to a single firm at a time, rather than to involve the local branch as a whole. Since the strikers are unable to win general support for their claims, these strikes have usually proved ineffective, and only serve to increase the individual members' feeling of disillusionment. Given the divisive and competitive character of the industry which the Union serves, the General Workers are themselves divided. Given, too, their residential scatter, and the fact that there exist no common activities to bind them together outside the work situation, they have thus far been unable to achieve the internal cohesion of the Mine Workers' Union. Consequently, too, their rôle in the political life of the town has been conspicuously less significant.

CHAPTER V

THE NATIONAL CONGRESS AND LOCAL POLITICS

I

IN an earlier chapter I attempted to show how through the development of Welfare Societies and Clerks' Associations, and their subsequent clash with the established administrative bodies, urban Africans were staking out their claim for recognition as full members of a new industrial society. Later, by their acceptance of trade unions, Africans showed that they were fully committed to an industrial system, and were engaged in a struggle to improve their position within that system. One aspect of that struggle has already been outlined in the discussion of African advancement in industry. The struggle also has a more specifically political aspect, and finds its expression in the development of the African National Congress.

A full account of the growth of Congress, and an analysis of its various policies, lie outside the scope of the present study.[1] Here I confine myself to an account of Congress activities in Luanshya, and an analysis of the relations between Congress, the trade unions, and the 'official' representative bodies in the town. I will attempt to bring out the nature of these relations by describing the 'social situation' created by the boycott of the European butcheries in Luanshya, which was organized by Congress. However, in order to understand fully certain of the events which took place in the town, it is necessary to sketch in a certain amount of the historical background.

I have referred earlier[2] to the visit of Mr. Charlie Harris to Northern Rhodesia in 1936. Mr. Harris was a European trade union leader on the Witwatersrand, and he came to the Copperbelt to try to organize the [European] Mine Workers' Union and amalgamate it with the South African Mine Workers' Union. Appalled to find that on the Copperbelt Africans were already

---

[1] This material will be presented in my paper 'The Rise of African Nationalism in Northern Rhodesia' now in preparation.

[2] See above, p. 102.

encroaching upon the preserves of skilled European labour, he emphasized the need for the Europeans to organize themselves. The South African Mine Workers' Union, he declared, was determined that Downing Street should not have its way. 'The White man's rights must be protected.' [1]

We have in these remarks a concise statement of two central themes in Northern Rhodesia's political history. When Mr. Harris spoke of the European's need to become organized, he meant 'organization' not so much for the protection of their interests against the employers, but against the encroachment of the Africans. He meant 'organization' so that they could bring pressure to bear on the employers to accept an industrial colour bar such as existed in South Africa, where certain categories of work were reserved solely for the European. It was a similar ideology which underlay the approach of the [European] Mine Workers' Union to the question of African advancement in industry, which I considered in the previous chapter.

But Mr. Harris's remarks carried a further implication. He implied that the White man's rights could only be protected if the European settlers were free to control their own political destiny. Economic privilege required to be buttressed by political power. Here the second theme is provided in the struggle which the Europeans have waged continuously to achieve independence from the Colonial Office, which took over the administration of the Territory from the British South Africa Company in 1924. This move for independence from 'Downing Street rule' has gone hand in hand with the move to amalgamate with Southern Rhodesia.

The various stages by which the European settlers have progressed towards a closer political association with Southern Rhodesia have been traced out by Professor Davidson.[2] After the war, the initiation by Mr. (later Sir) Roy Welensky and

---

[1] Quoted in J. Lewin, op. cit., p. 5.

[2] J. W. Davidson, *The Northern Rhodesia Legislative Council*, passim. Cf. 'The Bledisloe Report': *Rhodesia—Nyasaland Royal Commission Report*, Cmd. 5949 (1939). The Bledisloe Commission recommended the acceptance of amalgamation in principle, but considered that the time was inopportune. Among the reasons offered in support of this view were the differences of native policy between the Territories, and the general opposition to amalgamation expressed by Africans in Northern Rhodesia and Nyasaland.

other unofficial Members of the Legislative Council of proposals for Responsible Government marked the opening up of a new phase in the campaign for independence from the Colonial Office. The Africans immediately expressed their strong opposition to these proposals, which were described in a debate in the African Representative Council as a 'hoax' and wholly unacceptable in view of the Protectorate status of the Territory. The African Representative Council was an official Government body, and formed part of the machinery of Government. Its members were drawn from the Provincial Councils, and these in turn, in the case of the industrial areas, drew their members from the Urban Advisory Councils. But since membership of the Urban Advisory Councils at this time depended ultimately upon 'nomination' by the Provincial Commissioner, it followed that members of the African Representative Council drew their authority from the Government rather than from the people they were supposed to represent. Like the Tribal Representatives on the mine, the African Representative Council occupied an intercalary position within the wider political structure.

African leaders on the Copperbelt were quick to appreciate, and frequently pointed to, the difficulties implicit in this situation. They saw that the African Representative Council itself, by virtue of its intercalary rôle, was in no position to prosecute the African case as forcefully as they considered necessary, whatever the views of particular members of the Council might be. Now that the political battle had been joined over the issue of Responsible Government, they saw their problem as the need to mobilize African opinion and organize themselves on a territorial basis through some body which would be wholly independent of Government. As we saw earlier,[1] the various Welfare Societies had come together in 1946 to form a Federation of Welfare Societies. The Federation of Welfare Societies had held a number of conferences in Lusaka, and at one of these in 1948 it decided to disband and re-constitute itself under the name of the Northern Rhodesia Congress. After the publication in 1951 of the White Paper on the *Closer Association of the Central African Territories*,[2] Mr. Godwin Lewanika was replaced as President by Mr. Harry Nkumbula, and Congress emerged in its present

[1] See above, p. 71.   [2] Cmd. 8233.

form, adopting the name Northern Rhodesia African National Congress.

From his headquarters in Lusaka, Nkumbula at once set out to build up Congress organization. Leading figures in Congress toured the whole country, addressing Chiefs and mass gatherings of villagers, forming new branches, and collecting funds to send Congress delegations to England to express their opposition to a scheme which would 'betray Africans' national aspirations and rob them of their legitimate claims to ownership of the land'. Towards the end of 1951, an important Chiefs' and Delegates' Conference was called at Lusaka, at which the only two European members of Congress were also present.[1] At this Conference it was resolved to create a Supreme Action Council of nine members which was to include five places filled by the African Trade Union Congress. The task of this Council was to plan mass action, and it was to be empowered to call for such action at any moment, during the time of the Federation crisis, which it considered tactically wise. At the same time a Central Committee was set up on the Copperbelt to take active steps to oppose Federation, including a general strike should other action fail.

The publication in June, 1952, of the *Draft Federal Scheme*[2] called forth further expressions of African solidarity in opposition to Federation. A mass rally organized by Congress in Lusaka in August was attended by senior Chiefs, members of the African Representative Council, Trade Union leaders, and other figures prominent in African political life. The *Draft Federal Scheme* had made certain definite proposals concerning the nature of the Federal constitution, and had provided that time should be allowed for their full consideration by the peoples of the three Territories. Early in the new year (1953), a further conference was convened in London, and its findings were set out in the White Paper of January, 1953.[3] In March, Congress entered upon the final phase of its campaign against Federation, when Nkumbula called a further Chiefs' and Delegates' Conference in Lusaka. He analysed the proposals for Federation contained in the White

---

[1] These were Commander T. S. L. Fox-Pitt, O.B.E., R.N., a former member of the Provincial Administration, and Mr. Simon Zukas, a young engineer employed by the Ndola Municipality. Zukas was subsequently deported for his activities.

[2] Cmd. 8573.   [3] Cmd. 8753.

Paper, and restated the Africans' objection to them. After issuing a warning to the White settlers, he concluded his statement by formulating future Congress policy in the following terms. He referred to the burning of the White Paper, an act, he said, which would symbolize two things—that the Africans had rejected Federation both in principle and in detail, and that they had finally reached the end of the 'talking' stage. 'Both the Delegate Conference and the Supreme Action Council', he declared, 'have decided that should Federation be imposed against the opposition of the Africans, measures would be taken to paralyse the industries of this country. Among the industries that would be hard hit are farming, the railways, mining, and the general workers' industries. The Union leaders have at these meetings put it in express terms that their unions are behind the African National Congress. . . . Furthermore, I would like to announce that the Chiefs of this country have expressed their opinion that should Federation be imposed they would no longer co-operate with the Government. Their method of non-co-operation has already been decided upon by them—I now have the pleasure of announcing that both the Supreme Council, and the Delegates and Chiefs, have decided to have a "Two Day National Prayer".' With this final announcement, Nkumbula took a copy of the White Paper and publicly burned it.

The Lusaka Conference, with its announcement of full agreement in the decision to set aside two days for national prayer, was thus intended to demonstrate unequivocally and categorically not only the Africans' unanimous opposition to Federation, but also that that unity was embodied in the African National Congress. With its emphasis on the general consensus of the Chiefs, the trade union leaders, and the delegates, it was to be an expression of the unity of Congress itself. The 'two days of national prayer' was planned to take place at the beginning of April. Its complete failure brought into the open not only the organizational deficiencies of Congress, but also the divisions within the movement which the common opposition to the Europeans had hitherto managed to conceal. On the Copperbelt the African miners completely ignored the 'strike'. Nkumbula bitterly denounced Katilungu, the President of the African Mine Workers' Union, and the two African members of the Legislative Council, for failing to co-operate in a plan to which, he claimed, they had

M

previously agreed. Thereafter, although there were still strong Congress supporters within the Union leadership, there was open hostility between the two organizations.

Shortly afterwards the Federation of Rhodesia and Nyasaland was established: the campaign of opposition waged by the African National Congress had been lost. For many Africans the campaign against Federation was the sole *raison d'être* of the National Congress. There followed a period of uncertainty and disillusionment, which was reflected in the attacks and personal criticisms now being levelled at Nkumbula by his fellow Congress leaders. In August, 1953, there was a Congress conference in Lusaka at which Nkumbula called for a general election of office-bearers. With the exception of Nkumbula himself, all the leading members of the existing 'cabinet' were defeated, and replaced by men whose prestige in the movement was ascribed to their militancy. The Conference then went on to adopt a policy which was formulated as 'non-co-operation without violence towards any move considered detrimental to African interests'.

The policy of non-co-operation, as enunciated by Nkumbula, looked towards the complete withdrawal of African labour from the European farms. This aspect of policy was obviously addressed to the rural areas and, in particular, to the Southern Province, where European farming was most firmly ensconced. The withdrawal of African labour from contractors engaged in building houses for European immigrants was also urged; but the emphasis in the towns lay in carrying out organized campaigns to break down the colour bar in hotels, restaurants, public lavatories, churches, post offices, and shops.

The first steps in the campaign to 'break the colour bar' had actually been taken in June, when demonstrations were staged by Congress at Broken Hill, Kitwe, Lusaka, and Ndola, against the practice of racial discrimination in shops and other public places. For the most part the incidents were extremely mild. Congress officials, accompanied by a small band of followers, would take up their stand outside the selected shop. One of the leaders would make a speech to African passers-by, and then lead the way into the premises. In most cases the demonstrators were told that the management reserved the right of admission, and they left as peacefully as they had arrived. Now, however, it was hoped to wage a more intensive campaign against the colour bar, using the more effective weapons of the boycott and the picket line. Throughout January, 1954, the Lusaka branch of the Congress carried out a sustained picketing of all butcher shops in the town in protest against the practice of racial discrimination in the stores, and against the quality of the meat being sold to Africans. In February this boycott was extended to the towns of the Copperbelt. Thus the boycott in Luanshya, which I describe in detail in a later section, was the result of policies promulgated, and decisions taken, at a territorial level; it was not a purely local issue affecting only the Africans of Luanshya.

II

We have seen that the Federation of Native Welfare Associations was disbanded in 1948 and reconstituted as the Northern Rhodesia Congress. But for some time the new body continued to operate through the local Welfare Societies, which were affiliated to the Congress. However, by 1952 the Welfare Society at Luanshya had become moribund. A number of the leading members, including the chairman, Mr. Dauti Yamba, had left the town and taken up employment elsewhere. The mine members were now preoccupied with the affairs of the Union, of which they were office-bearers, and a new Co-operative Society on the mine, and had ceased to attend the Society's meetings. Much of the work thus devolved upon the secretary. He was a Southern Rhodesian African employed as an Agricultural Instructor by the Welfare Department of the Municipality. He had joined the Society originally because he was interested in social welfare, but he had come to feel that the Society was moving further away from its original purpose; by its frequent discussions of Federation, it showed that it was taking on too much the character of a political body. He was afraid that his participation in such a society might cost him his job with the Municipality, and he resigned shortly afterwards. Later in the year, when Congress made a Press appeal to all Africans to subscribe money to help Simon Zukas in conducting his legal defence, a number of individuals helped to organize a fund-raising campaign in the town. They spoke of themselves as Congress leaders because they were acting on behalf of the Congress, but none of the funds so collected appears to have been transmitted to Congress headquarters in Lusaka. Some of the money was said to have been handed over directly to members of Zukas' family who lived in the town, but it was widely believed amongst Africans that the money had been pocketed by one of the self-styled Congress leaders, and popular support for Congress declined sharply in the town.

Thus when I commenced my field-work in Luanshya in August, 1953, the position was that while there were individuals who were strong Congress supporters, no branch was actually in existence in the town. Then in November, 1953, Mr. Chitambala, the Branch Secretary of the Shop Assistants' Union, called together a small group of his fellow-leaders in the Municipal location to discuss the formation of a branch. Among these was Mr. Richard Banda, a senior clerk and labour supervisor employed by a large firm of building contractors. He had been at one time Branch Secretary of the General Workers' Union in Luanshya, but resigned when the Union appointed full-time paid officials. Banda had acted for some years as secretary of the Urban Advisory Council, on which he still sat as a location representative, and which he also represented on the African Affairs Committee of the Municipal Board. Banda expressed his opposition to the formation of a branch of Congress in the location. He claimed that a branch was already in existence on the mine which served the whole of Luanshya. He named as leaders of the branch some of those who had organized the campaign to raise funds to help Zukas, and said that to form a new branch would be to indicate a loss of confidence in these leaders. 'As I am an alien here'—(his home was in Nyasaland)—'I cannot take part in such an organization', he declared, and left the meeting. The remainder agreed that as there had never really been a Congress branch in the town, they ought to form one immediately. They agreed further that they should invite Mr. Puta, the Vice-General President of both the African Mine Workers' Union and the African National Congress, who was living temporarily in Luanshya at the time, and Mr. Chapoloko, the Secretary of the Roan branch of the Mine Workers' Union, to come and address them and advise on the formation and running of a Congress branch. A meeting, attended by about twenty people, was held a few days later. Chapoloko expressed his pleasure that 'Luanshya was at last becoming conscious', and the branch was formally inaugurated. A standing committee was appointed of which the chairman was Mr. Shitombwe, and the secretary Mr. Chitambala.

Shitombwe had been elected to the Urban Advisory Council in the election which had been held only a short time before, and he was also Chairman of the Hawkers' Association in Luanshya. At this time there were no trading-sites or stores in Luanshya available to Africans eager to trade, and such trade as there was in African hands was carried out by a small group who were known as 'hawkers'. On payment of an annual fee the hawkers were granted a Government licence which permitted trading within the Administrative District. They moved about the area selling second-hand clothes purchased from Indian dealers or sometimes smuggled across from the Belgian Congo, firewood, and grain bought in the adjacent tribal areas. The position of the hawkers is defined by law and they are, for example, forbidden to trade within a certain distance of established stores, or to occupy the same stand for more than a specified period of time. In order to protect and promote their interests they had come together in local branches of a Hawkers' Association, which claimed a membership in Luanshya of about a hundred and fifty.

About a fortnight after the inaugural meeting of the new Luanshya Congress branch, a second meeting was called. On this occasion there was a larger attendance, most of those present being members of the Hawkers' Association. There was no agenda, but it was quickly agreed that the new branch should do something to teach the public of the existence of Congress, of its aims, and of what it had already been able to achieve in other towns. After some discussion the meeting agreed that a most pressing issue was the need to see that Africans were allowed to open tea-rooms in the location, and it was decided to draft a letter on the subject to the Welfare Officer in the Municipal location. The Municipality itself ran a tea-room in the location, where it was possible for Africans to buy cups of tea, bread, biscuits, and the like. The letter pointed to the deficiencies in the service provided by the existing tea-room, and made general complaints about the kind and quality of stock carried, and about the hours of business. The Welfare Officer replied that he was not empowered to deal with the matter himself, but promised that he would raise the matter at the next meeting of the African Affairs Committee of the Municipal Board.

Early in the new year, Shitombwe, the branch chairman, led a small deputation to discuss the matter further with the Welfare Officer. The African Affairs Committee was a sub-committee of the Municipal Board, and met regularly under the chairmanship of the District Commissioner to discuss and advise the Board on local African matters falling within its jurisdiction. As described earlier,[1] the Africans had direct representation on the Committee. Mr. Richard Banda was a delegate of the Urban Advisory Council, and Mr. E. Mwamba was the nominee of the Urban Housing Board. Of these two, only Mwamba had a vote. The Congress deputation now complained that the African community was not properly represented on the Board, for if it were, then the question of the tea-room in the Mikomfwa would already have been discussed, and the necessary improvements introduced. The deputation asked that when the African Affairs Committee next met, Congress itself should be represented, and that leaders in other African organizations should also be invited to attend. The Welfare Officer's reply, that they already had their representatives on the Committee and that the matter should be referred to them, did not satisfy the members of the deputation. They were critical of their representatives who, they said, never consulted their constituents before attending meetings of the African Affairs Committee, and did not inform the constituents afterwards of the results of the Committee's deliberations. Following the meeting, therefore, the standing committee of the Congress branch met again and decided to call a further meeting of the members to discuss a proposal to boycott the Municipal tea-room in Mikomfwa. This proposal was quickly accepted and seventeen of those present, most of them hawkers, offered themselves as pickets. But on the appointed day only six of the pickets—all of them members of the standing committee—turned up, and the boycott was cancelled.

I obtained no explanation for the failure of the boycott, but clearly it represented a severe setback to the newly-formed branch. The proposed boycott had had two purposes. In the first place, it was directed towards extending Africans' opportunities for trading in the location by allowing them to open tea-rooms there, although the letter to the Welfare Officer was couched so

---

[1] See above, p. 19.

that it referred only to improvements being made to the existing service. Secondly, it was a calculated threat to the position of Mwamba and Banda, the two African representatives on the African Affairs Committee; and it is interesting to notice that both of these were absent at the next meeting of the Committee, although they had been regular attenders up to this point. Now that the first effort had failed, the Congress leaders decided to challenge their representatives on the African Affairs Committee through the Urban Housing Board.

Urban Housing Boards, it will be recalled,[1] were set up under the Urban African Housing Ordinance. The members of the Urban Housing Board were elected by the free vote of the African residents in the Housing Area.[2] The functions of the Board are to consider any matter specially affecting the interests of the Africans within the jurisdiction of the Municipal Authority, and to review any rules the local authority proposes to apply to the area. At Luanshya, the Urban Housing Board met once a month under the chairmanship of the Location Superintendent, and discussed such matters as complaints about the water supply, the repairing of the road leading to the cemetery, the building of stores in the Housing Area for African traders, conditions at the Beer Hall—in short, all matters affecting closely the day-to-day life of the inhabitants of the area. The Board also had political significance in that it had direct representation on the African Affairs Committee. By giving the Mikomfwa Housing Board some measure of financial responsibility, it was now hoped in Luanshya to develop the Board as an effective instrument of local government.

Having decided upon its next step, Congress despatched another deputation, this time to call upon the Location Superintendent. The deputation complained that residents in Mikomfwa did not know what was being discussed at meetings of the Urban Housing Board because they were never told, and that the members of the Housing Board did not address their constituents

---

[1] See above, p. 19.

[2] The arrangements for elections to the Urban Housing Boards may vary from place to place. At Luanshya, the Location Superintendent had the election announced throughout the location by the location 'police', and asked for nominations for the various sections or wards to be submitted to his office. The actual voting was by show of hands at a meeting conducted by the Location Superintendent.

either before or after meetings. The Location Superintendent agreed that, in future, Congress and trade union leaders in Mikomfwa would have copies of the minutes of these meetings circulated to them.

At the next meeting of the Urban Housing Board there was some discussion of a plan which the Municipal Board was considering for installing stoves in all houses in the location, provided that the residents were prepared to accept an extra rental. According to the minutes of the meeting, the members of the Urban Housing Board had said that their constituents were not prepared to pay this extra rental. They agreed that installation of the stoves should be on a purely voluntary basis, and anyone wanting a stove in his house could approach the Location Superintendent himself. This gave the Congress leaders the opening they required. They approached the Location Superintendent again, and said that there were many people in Mikomfwa who wanted stoves, but at no time had the people ever been asked by the members of the Housing Board whether they were willing to pay for these or not. The deputation declared that the members of the Board had only been speaking for themselves, and it asked the Location Superintendent to hold an election so that new representatives might be appointed to the Housing Board. A request was also made that the number of representatives on the Board should be increased. The Location Superintendent accepted the latter point, but explained that no election could be held until April, when the present Board's annual session expired. There the Congress leaders decided to allow the matter to rest for the time being, and they resolved that in April they would make every effort to ensure that each section or ward in Mikomfwa was represented by a member of Congress.

The actual membership of the branch at this time was still very small, and was made up mostly of hawkers. Denied the facilities for trading available to the European and the Indian shopkeepers, the hawkers shared a deep sense of grievance and frustration, all the more keen perhaps because they lacked the effective means to improve their economic and political position. They bitterly resented the barriers which stood in the way of their economic progress, and saw themselves as the victims of racial discrimination. It might be assumed, therefore, that the policies of Congress, with their emphasis on African rights and the breaking of the colour bar, would make an especial appeal to the hawkers. However, in the present instance, the factors which drew Luanshya hawkers towards Congress were more specific. For recently the Mine Management at the Roan had decided as a matter of policy, and for reasons which were never made clear, that it did not want hawkers on its premises. Now, as already explained, the mine lies on private property, and the Management is therefore entitled by law to debar from entry anyone whom it considers undesirable. Furthermore, under the Employment of Natives Ordinance, there is a provision to the effect that no person may enter a location which is occupied by natives engaged in mining operations without the permission of the Location Superintendent, unless authorized by law to do so. Since this permission had been refused the hawkers, their subsequent presence, selling goods in the mine compound, was an infringement of the regulations, and a number of prosecutions were laid in the Magistrate's court. There was no doubt that technical offences had been committed, and a number of the hawkers were convicted and given nominal sentences.

The hawkers felt that they had a genuine grievance. They argued that they had taken out licences to trade within the District, yet they were being excluded from the Mine Township, and had no means of redress. They knew no reason why they should be excluded, yet there was nothing in the law to compel the Mining Company to state its reasons for refusing them permission to enter and trade. Accordingly, the hawkers approached the Roan branch of the African Mine Workers' Union and, pointing out that they were satisfying a popular demand, urged the Union to take the matter up with the Mine Management. The Union expressed sympathy, but was unable to achieve anything because Management held that the matter lay outside the scope of its agreement with the Union. The case was then brought before the District Commissioner and the Urban Advisory Council, but here too, as we shall see later, the hawkers were able to make little headway. The only African body remaining which they considered could give them the support they required, was the African National Congress.

In the middle of January, 1954, shortly after the branch had been formed at Luanshya, an important Congress conference was called at Ndola, when it was hoped to establish Congress on the

Copperbelt on a firmer footing, and to infuse some fresh life into the flagging Copperbelt branches.

Shitombwe, the chairman of the Hawkers' Association, attended as one of the Luanshya delegates. He spoke of the arrests made at Luanshya, and the fines being imposed on hawkers for selling their goods in the mine compound. He appealed to the Conference for its assistance in redressing this wrong. One of the Kitwe delegates explained that similar arrests had also been made at Nkana; it was because there was a regulation which forbade them to enter the African Mine Township without proper permission. He said that there was little that Congress could do to change that regulation, and suggested that the best course was to take the case through the Urban Advisory Council right up to the Legislative Council, where the law could be amended. This suggestion was unanimously accepted by the Conference. But since the hawkers had already brought the matter before the Luanshya Urban Advisory Council, and made little headway there, Shitombwe was bitterly disappointed at this decision, which appeared to him to advance the hawkers' case no further than before. In the meantime there was a further circumstance which affected the attitude of the Luanshya hawkers towards the newly formed Congress branch there. The hawkers had hoped that Congress would be able to assist them in their dispute with the Mine Management; they also hoped that through Congress they would be able to exert sufficient pressure on the Municipal Board to gain permission to open tea-rooms in the location, using ordinary houses as their premises, as was the practice in other towns. The rule applied by the Luanshya Municipal Board at this time was that any African wishing to trade from premises in the location must show sufficient capital both to build and stock a suitable store before he could be granted a site. Since few Africans had the available capital, or the means to raise it, none had been able to take advantage of this opportunity. Thus the hawkers were extremely critical of the two African representatives on the African Affairs Committee for having accepted a policy which they, the hawkers, considered to be detrimental to African interests. But, in fact, the measure had been under the consideration of the Board for some time, and since it had become clear that no African was in a financial position to build his own shop in the location, the Board had now decided to build shops itself, and rent them to African tenants. It invited applications from Africans who wished to open shops and tea-rooms in Mikomfwa. The two representatives on the African Affairs Committee passed the information on to a number of the hawkers, and assisted them in filling in their application forms. The hawkers credited Mwamba and Banda with this success, and their prestige among the hawkers at least was thus restored.

It was the hawkers who had given the young Luanshya branch of Congress such strength as it had. Now, following the decision of the Ndola Conference and the new opportunities opened up by the changed policy of the Municipal Board, the hawkers saw little further advantage in their attachment to the branch, which they promptly abandoned *en masse*, save for their chairman Shitombwe, who was also chairman of the Congress branch. Had it not been for a fresh development which arose almost immediately, it appears likely that the defection of the hawkers would have resulted in the total collapse of the branch. This new event was the boycott of the butcheries which was organized by Congress. In the following section I describe its operation in Luanshya.

III

We have seen that following the establishment of the Federation, Congress had decided upon a policy of non-co-operation without violence in all matters considered detrimental to African interests. In line with this policy, Congress had been conducting throughout January, 1954, a protracted boycott of the European butchers in Lusaka, in protest against the treatment accorded to their African customers. It was believed that the boycott was being rendered less effective because the meat boycotted in Lusaka was being sold on the Copperbelt. Accordingly, towards the end of the month, Congress decided to extend the campaign. On January 29, two Congress members from Lusaka met the Luanshya branch committee. They pointed out that at Ndola it had been agreed to begin the boycott on February 1. The Luanshya committee replied that it could not begin so early in their town, because they were still poorly organized. However, they agreed to arrange a public meeting, in order to prepare to carry out a boycott of the Luanshya butcheries.

Only a short time before, the whole question of the butcheries had been discussed by the Luanshya Urban Advisory Council. It is quite probable, too, that the District Commissioner had foreseen the possibility of the boycott's extension to his own District. At any rate he had made arrangements for a meeting between the Urban Advisory Council, of which both the Chairman and Vice-Chairman of the local branch of Congress were already members, and representatives of the butcheries. This meeting was called at short notice for the same day as the public meeting arranged by Congress.

The public meeting took place first. A large crowd mustered at the market-place, and was addressed by the local Congress leaders. They set out a number of grievances they had against the butchers, and asked those present to express their views on the matter. One man said he spoke as a committee member of the Shop Assistants' Union. He agreed with what the previous speakers had said, and elaborated on their theme at some length. The Europeans still did not recognize the Africans as human beings. 'They treat us like animals,' he declared. 'But we have our freedom! We must complain when something hurts us.' Meat was being sold to Africans three weeks after it was slaughtered. When their wives went to the butchers they bought rotten meat, they were given nothing but bones. Finally he exclaimed: 'We have the same money as Europeans. The money with which we buy meat goes into their banks in the same way as the Europeans' money. There is no discrimination in money. If the Europeans do not agree to what we ask, we should boycott their stores on Monday.' Other speakers from the crowd followed, each in turn playing an individual variation on the central theme stated by the Union committee member, and all concluding with a statement that if the butchers did not comply with their demands, a boycott should be called on the following Monday. The meeting closed eventually with an announcement that there would be a further meeting on Saturday to learn the results of the discussion which was about to take place in the Urban Advisory Council.

The meeting of the Urban Advisory Council began shortly after the public meeting had come to a close. As at the public meeting, the members of the Council brought forward a number of complaints shared by the African customers about the treatment accorded to them in the butcheries, about the kind and quality of meat sold to Africans, and so on. A lengthy discussion followed in which each complaint was examined in detail, and in the end the butchers' representatives agreed to introduce many of the improvements which the Africans desired.

The Urban Advisory Council is a creation of the Administration, and has its place within the governmental structure of the Territory. In each urban district the Council is the body which officially represents the views of the African community to Government. The Luanshya Council's meeting with the butchers' representatives thus put the Congress leaders in a quandary, for they were themselves members of the Council, and therefore were a party to the agreement with the butchers. Furthermore, since the butchers had accepted many of the points brought up by the Urban Advisory Council, and had agreed to improve their service to African customers, there was no further justification for a Congress campaign, at any rate one which claimed to be founded upon a local issue. The matter was discussed at a meeting of the Executive Committee the following evening. Chimba, the chairman of the Ndola branch, who was also General Secretary of the Western Province division of the Congress, within whose jurisdiction Luanshya fell, was present at the meeting. He argued that even though the butcheries had agreed to abolish the practice of serving Africans through the hatch, and to make other improvements, nevertheless they should persist in carrying out the boycott until such time as the butchers agreed to meet Congress officials, and not the Urban Advisory Council. This view was also accepted by the local branch chairman, who doubted whether the butchers would abandon their discriminatory practices, since similar promises made to the Urban Advisory Council by other shop-keepers in the past had not been kept. Some members felt, however, that they should postpone the boycott until they had had the opportunity of seeing how far the butchers intended to keep to the terms of their agreement. They were overruled by Chimba, who stressed that it was the planned policy of the Congress that they should conduct a boycott. There could be no question of a postponement. Chimba returned to Ndola, saying he would come back again to review the progress of the boycott.

The next day (Friday) a meeting took place between members of the Executive Committee, and a number of leading personalities on the mine. Shitombwe, the Congress chairman, outlined the course of the discussions they had held in Mikomfwa, and reported that the people in the Municipal location were prepared to start a boycott on Monday. He repeated the reasons for holding the boycott, and he appealed to the people on the mine to join them on the same day. One of the mine spokesmen, a Union member and Secretary of the Roan branch of the Nyasaland National Congress, said that it would be difficult for people on the mine to carry on a boycott on Monday. A successful boycott required good organization, and a great deal of preparation. The first thing was to get the branch started and then to teach the people the aims of Congress. Only then would they be able to conduct a boycott or such other action as they considered necessary. Mr. Mwalwanda [1] then asked Mr. Musumbulwa, the Vice-Chairman of the Urban Advisory Council, to explain to them what the butchers had said at their joint meeting. After listening to Musumbulwa's account, he said that it was a childish idea to boycott the butcheries when the butchers had promised to do all that was being asked of them; he suggested that they should wait and see whether the butchers made any efforts to implement their promise. Mwalwanda was supported by the rest of the mine spokesmen. Chitambala, who was initially responsible for forming the Congress branch and was now its secretary, exclaimed that people on the mine were afraid to conduct the boycott because they were cowards. If they did not go through with it, he said, their fellows elsewhere would think of them as a lot of women. Another location delegate referred to those on the mine as 'Capricornists'.[2] The remark was deeply resented by the meeting. Musumbulwa sprang to his feet, and repeated that it was utterly childish to fight someone who had already agreed to do what you wanted of him. He added that if there were a boycott, this would

---

[1] See above, p. 147.

[2] The Capricorn Society was founded in 1949. Later, the Society identified itself closely with the campaign for Central African Federation which it regarded as the first step towards the long-term objective of a United States of Capricorn, in which men of all races would be able to share a common citizenship. 'Capricornist' became a term of abuse to stigmatize an African believed by his fellow-Africans to be a hired propagandist of the Europeans in favour of Federation. By extension, it then came to mean anyone who was opposed to Congress policy, or who appeared to be 'moderate' or pro-European in his views. It should perhaps be added that the Society has since admitted that it erred in having subordinated 'human values to the economic and administrative advantages of Federation'.

show that there was no co-operation between Congress and the Urban Advisory Council, for the Council had debated the subject, and the butchers had agreed that in future Africans would be served at the same counter as Europeans. It was a mistake to call other people cowards or 'Capricornists' simply because they were speaking the truth. 'It is a mistake', he said, 'to call for action when you are not yet organized.' He described those who wanted to carry out the boycott as inexperienced, and went on to recall how he had himself helped to organize the boycott of the Indian stores in 1947. That boycott had gone on for three months, but in the end it had failed because there were those wishing to buy things who visited the stores at night. He concluded by proposing that no action be taken, firstly because they were not yet properly organized, and secondly because they had the promise that there would soon be improvements in the butcheries. This view had the support of all the mine people present. One of them, a committee member of the Mine Workers' Union, said the people in the location could talk about a boycott, but they would not be able to organize it. 'They have never even organized a strike,' he remarked. He walked out of the meeting together with the other people from the mine.

On Saturday the public meeting organized by Congress was held as arranged, and some 400 Africans, men and women, gathered at the market-place. Shitombwe gave an account of what had taken place at the joint meeting between the Urban Advisory Council and the butchers. It had been explained that the Africans were prepared to carry out a boycott of the butchers should they continue to be refused service at the same counter as the Europeans. The butchers had accepted this proposal, provided that Africans entering the shops conducted themselves with propriety. Shitombwe added that African women with babies on their backs would not be admitted because the babies made such a lot of noise. This drew expressions of annoyance from the crowd. One man in the crowd began to make a speech. He said that only that morning he had found their vice-chairman buying sugar from one of the Jews' tea-rooms. They gave it to him in dirty wrapping paper. The Europeans, he said, were just like mice. First they would bite a man very slightly. Then when he began to feel the irritation the mouse blew air on it to still the pain. And so it went on until the wound was very big. That was what the Europeans were doing. For while they agreed to serve Africans together with Europeans they would not do it at all. The only thing was to stop buying from their butcheries until such time as the African women-folk were allowed in, and until they were supplied with better-quality meat. Others in the crowd wanted to know if the reduction of the price of meat had been discussed at the meeting. The vice-chairman replied that it had not, the price of meat was controlled by Government, and the butchers were not to blame in this respect. He leaned over to exchange a few words with one of his fellow committee members, but his act appeared to incense the people present, who cried out that it was a public meeting, and not a place for holding private discussions. One man called Phiri, a committee member in the Shop Assistants' Union, and an elder in the Free Church, demanded that the boycott should be called for Monday, and continue until the price of meat was reduced. His suggestion was greeted with cheering and clapping. But after their meeting on the mine, some of the Congress leaders had become irresolute, and eventually changed their minds when they saw that they would have no support from the Mine Workers' Union or other Africans on the mine. Now they attempted to persuade the meeting against the boycott. But the meeting was no longer prepared to listen. People began to fling curses at the leaders, saying they had not spoken as they had been told to do. They had been given no mandate to make an agreement with the butchers. One man screamed angrily: 'We have nothing to do with these leaders.' And though Shitombwe once more appealed to them to accept the agreement made with the butchers, none would listen and the crowd began to drift away, crying that on Monday they would boycott the butchers.

The Congress leaders remained undecided which policy they should adopt. During the weekend they met again in committee. One of them who had just returned from Kitwe reported that there, too, the Congress proposal to conduct a boycott had been rejected because the Kitwe butchers had also agreed to abolish discriminatory practices. So, after further lengthy discussion, it was finally agreed that no boycott should take place in Luanshya.

There had by now been two large public meetings organized by Congress, and the possibility of a boycott of the butcheries was of course known to the police. On the Monday morning, when it was expected that the boycott would begin, numbers of African policemen were on duty near the butchers' premises to ensure that citizens going about their lawful business were not molested by the Congress pickets. But since the Congress leaders had finally decided against the boycott, no pickets had in fact been posted. Banda, one of the location representatives on the Urban Advisory Council, and that Council's nominee to the African Affairs Committee, who, it will be remembered, had originally expressed his opposition to the formation of the Congress branch, was present at the butcheries: it was said that he told people there was no boycott, and persuaded them to enter and buy. At one shop he went in himself and bought meat, but the Africans refused to follow, claiming that they were frightened by the presence of the police. It appeared indeed as though an 'unofficial' boycott were being conducted—without pickets.

Later in the day a very large crowd gathered again at the market-place. Shitombwe acted as chairman, but as the meeting progressed his position became more and more difficult until he was finally ousted by Phiri and a Tribal Elder called Chitanda, who was also on the branch committee of the Shop Assistants' Union. Neither Phiri nor Chitanda had played any part in the formation of the Congress branch, but both had spoken in favour of the boycott at the previous public meetings. Now both of them urged that the boycott should continue until there was a reduction in the price of meat. Banda also addressed the meeting, and tried to persuade the people to call off the boycott. He pointed out that the question of the price of meat was one for the Government and not for the butchers. He was at once bitterly attacked by Phiri who said that Banda was afraid of the boycott because he feared that he would be repatriated to Nyasaland. He was a 'yesman' who had been bribed by the Europeans to 'blind' his fellow-Africans into agreeing with him in support of the Whites. At the same time he attacked Shitombwe for siding with Banda. Banda retorted that if they were going to boycott the butchers because the prices were high then they should also boycott all the other stores and go back to wearing bark-cloth. Chitanda replied that it was not a question of stopping all European things. The meat sold in the butcheries, he said, was of cattle bought from Africans in this country. 'We want a boycott because they buy it cheap from our people in the villages, and they sell it here at a very high price. We wouldn't mind that if it came from their country, from Europe.' Mwape, a schoolmaster and a member of the Urban Advisory Council, supported Banda, and was jeered by the crowd. Phiri exclaimed, 'All educated people are cowards': he announced that they would continue the boycott and declared the meeting closed.

Following this meeting Shitombwe and his Vice-Chairman Simukonda, who was Branch Secretary of the General Workers' Union, decided to present a memorandum to the District Commissioner telling him about the boycott, and to ask his assistance in explaining to the African public how the price of meat was fixed. They pointed out that the boycott was not in accordance with Congress policy, and had not been organized by Congress. They, the Congress leaders, had sought to persuade the people against it, but they had been unsuccessful.

Later that day there was a further public meeting, again attended by a very large crowd. Once again Banda was subjected to much criticism and abuse. It was alleged against him that he had written a note which was placed in a butchery window saying that he, Banda, was the only leader in the location, that there was no boycott, and that everyone was free to enter and buy meat. Phiri also attacked the Urban Advisory Council which was made up, he said, of useless people who never held meetings with the people to tell the people what they were discussing, or to hear the people's complaints. At length Chitambala, the Congress secretary, asked the public to appoint two men who would go and discuss the whole question with the butchers next day. Phiri and Chitanda were elected.

There were two main firms involved in the issue—I will call them A and B. The manager of firm A told the deputation that he had been instructed not to meet the Congress representatives, but to deal only with the delegates of the Urban Advisory Council. Firm B, on the other hand, agreed to meet the deputation and, pending the negotiations, the new leaders decided to lift the boycott on firm B, and to concentrate their activities on picketing firm A. This was agreed to by the people at another meeting. They said they would show the manager of firm A that Banda was not their leader. At this meeting, too, the Bemba Tribal Elder came in for much criticism and abuse for having associated himself with Banda in urging people to buy meat from the butchers. Incensed by these remarks, the Elder tried to speak but was ignored by the chairman. He began to declaim angrily, crying that the whole meeting was composed of a lot of nincompoops. He was slightly drunk at the time, and was hurling insults at various people, one of whom he caught by the jacket and wanted to fight. An Ngoni man standing beside the Elder berated him for wanting to fight in public. The meeting gradually dispersed and the Bemba Elder was left alone flinging his curses at all and sundry.

On the following day the boycott was confined to the premises of firm A. A number of the pickets, including the Congress branch secretary Chitambala, were arrested and subsequently fined for behaviour deemed likely to lead to a breach of the peace. The next day picketing had ceased. People had now begun to complain that although they could buy meat at firm B, that was really a mistake for it was firm B which sold poor quality meat. Further public meetings were called, but the attendances were falling rapidly. There were still a few who considered that the boycott should be continued until firm A agreed to meet the Congress leaders, but they could no longer muster a following, and within a short time African trade at the butcheries had returned to normal.

IV

The growth of the Congress branch at Luanshya, and the whole conduct of the boycott there, illustrate vividly the fluidity which marks the urban scene. The branch came into existence quite suddenly: had it not been for fortuitous circumstances, its demise would probably have been equally sudden. As we shall see, the conduct of the boycott itself was marked by much confusion, by personal rivalries between leaders, and by frequent changes in allegiance. Nevertheless these events were not completely haphazard: they took place within the political system of the town, and I will attempt to show how many of the features which characterized the conduct of the boycott, may themselves be explained in terms of that system.

To begin with, it may appear strange that, apart from the campaign to raise funds for Zukas in 1952, no serious attempt should have been made to organize a branch of the African

National Congress in Luanshya before the end of 1953. Nkumbula, the President-General of Congress, had visited the town only once, and then his stay was so brief that he was unable to address a public meeting. But this is not to say that Luanshya was hostile to Congress, or that the movement lacked sympathizers there. On the contrary, while the Federation campaign was still at its height all the leading African personalities in the town, whether trade union leaders or members of the Advisory Council, regarded themselves as Congress members, whether or not they actually held membership cards. (Indeed, I am not certain that Congress membership cards yet existed at that time.) They considered Congress as the proper mouthpiece of African opinion, and as representing their solid opposition to Federation. At this time, and on this score, they all spoke with one voice. After the Victoria Falls Conference of September, 1951, the Luanshya Advisory Council was most outspoken in its condemnation of the line taken by the African representatives at the Conference.[1] In November, delegates of the Council took part in a joint conference of Congress and the Urban Advisory Councils of the Copperbelt, when the policy of 'partnership' subscribed to by Government was denounced as a betrayal of the Protectorate status of Northern Rhodesia. Thus, in a sense, a distinct branch of Congress in Luanshya would almost have been superfluous. Indeed, the term 'branch' is perhaps inappropriate to describe Congress organization at this time, for it immediately suggests comparison with a trade union branch. One of the features of trade union organization is a relatively large membership paying regular subscriptions, and bound by trade union rules. Only a fully paid-up member is entitled to claim benefits. By contrast, Congress organization was built up through a large number of small nuclei or committees, each designed to organize the community as a whole on some specific issue or for some specific purpose. Its appeal is to a more generalized interest. In these respects Congress still approximated closely to the pattern of the older Welfare Societies which, with a membership of around

---

[1] At this Conference the African representatives had explained that they would be willing to consider the question of Federation on the basis of the *Report of the London Conference of Officials on Closer Association* after the policy of 'partnership' in Northern Rhodesia had been defined and put into progressive operation.

twenty or thirty, operated as committees to arrange sports and games for the children at Christmas, provide public entertainment for visiting chiefs, or arrange public meetings on some issue of the day. Indeed, during the early period of the development of Congress, the Congress branch and the Welfare Society were frequently one and the same thing.

The Luanshya Welfare Society had for some years been particularly strong and active. Its Chairman, Mr. Dauti Yamba, together with Mr. Godwin Lewanika of the Kitwe African Society, had been largely responsible for bringing the various Welfare Societies together to form a Federation, from which the Congress later emerged. But Yamba had now returned to the rural areas to take up a post in the Lunda Native Authority of Chief Kazembe, while the secretary, a post office employee, had been transferred to another town. The mine members of the Society had also withdrawn, for they were now actively engaged in the affairs of the Mine Workers' Union and the African Co-operative on the mine, the formation of which the Welfare Society had urged some years before. Then, too, the Urban Advisory Council was extremely active at the time, and there had been a number of special meetings with African representatives, and overseas visitors, to discuss the question of Federation. Amidst this welter of activity the Welfare Society gradually faded out of existence, and has not been revived. After the arrest of Zukas there appears to have been a decline of popular support for Congress on the Copperbelt. Consequently, although many individuals still spoke of themselves as Congress supporters, there was no impetus towards replacing the Welfare Society with a more firmly organized branch of Congress.

During September, 1953, the Urban Advisory Council, the composition of which had not changed in the past five years, was dissolved, and the District Commissioner announced that there would be an election by popular ballot for the new Council. I cannot enter upon a discussion of the election at this point. It is sufficient for the present discussion to record that, of the eighteen seats on the new Council, four were allocated to the Government Township. Each candidate wishing to stand for election had to fill in a nomination paper giving the names of his proposer, seconder, and supporters. Chitambala, the Secretary of the Shop Assistants' Union, was very anxious to stand. He claimed that he had filled in the nomination paper and given it to Banda, who had been secretary of the Advisory Council during the previous session, to deliver to the District Commissioner. Two others were also said to have given their nomination papers to Banda. None of these papers was in fact received by the District Commissioner, and four other candidates, including Banda, were returned unopposed. Chitambala and his supporters alleged that Banda, afraid that he might be defeated in an open contest, destroyed the papers so that there would be no election. A bitter enmity developed between the two men. Chitambala resolved to settle scores by putting himself in a position where he could successfully challenge Banda. As secretary of the Shop Assistants' Union, he was a leader in what was probably the strongest trade union in the location. Nevertheless, his influence was limited. So he decided upon the formation of a Congress branch since Congress was the one body which, since it cut across the divisions created by occupation and tribalism, could give him the strength and support he required.

Yet it would be a grave mistake to try to explain the rôle of Congress in Luanshya simply in terms of thwarted political ambitions and personal jealousies. Obviously these are factors of great significance, and we shall discuss shortly how they also operated within the context of the boycott itself: but the important point to notice is that Chitambala's political ambitions arose, and sought satisfaction, within a framework which was to some extent fixed. The constant shifting of forces, of alignment and realignment, that went on immediately prior to and in the course of the boycott, occurred in terms of the political structure of the town as well as in terms of personal rivalries. While Chitambala undoubtedly saw the possibilities of satisfying his ambition and settling scores with Banda by forming a local branch of Congress, he was only able to do this because the formation of a branch happened to coincide at that moment with the interests of the hawkers.

There were two issues of principal concern to the hawkers. Firstly, they wished to have the privilege of trading in the mine compound restored to them, for since the mine was the largest unit of population in the District this was their main market. If they were to be permanently excluded from the mine, their only hope of continuing in business lay in getting permission to open tea-rooms and stores in Mikomfwa. When it became clear to them that neither the Mine Workers' Union nor the Urban Advisory Council was in a position to help, the hawkers turned to Congress as the body most likely to help in pressing their claims. It is not quite clear what pressure they hoped to be able to bring to bear on the Mining Company. It is possible they were thinking in terms of the indirect pressures which could be created by an organized boycott of the stores on the mine itself, and in the Second Class Trading Area. On the second issue, however, their aim was perfectly patent. The power to grant trading sites in Mikomfwa was vested in the Municipal Board, and in these respects the Board was guided, though by no means bound, by the recommendations of the African Affairs Committee. Here the hawkers hoped that they would be able to exert pressure by replacing the African representatives on the Committee, of whom Banda was one. But when, on the first issue, Congress showed that it was no more willing or able to help than the Mine Workers' Union or the Advisory Council, and when on the second, the Municipal Board changed its policy in respect of trading sites, the hawkers did a complete *volte face*, and took no further part in Congress activities. Had the butcheries issue not arisen almost immediately, there seems little doubt that the branch would have collapsed, and Chitambala would have been left to nurse his resentment in isolation.

The boycott of the butcheries involved a much wider public interest than the issue of the tea-rooms in the location, and very large crowds gathered for many of the meetings organized by the Congress. Nevertheless, the whole conduct of the boycott revealed a great deal of confusion. The issue of the butcheries was not purely local to Luanshya, but had been seized upon by the African National Congress as the basis on which to wage a widespread campaign against the practice of the colour bar. Following their discussions with the Congress leaders from Lusaka and Ndola, the local branch leaders were committed to an attempt to carry out a boycott in Luanshya. But the branch leaders were hesitant, and delayed their final decision until it was too late to advise the public that they had decided to call off the boycott. People had left the public meeting on the Saturday, crying that they would hold the boycott until the butchers met their demands. On Monday, therefore, there was the strange spectacle of Africans being urged by Banda to enter the butcheries, and being 'restrained' by the presence of African police, acting, as it were, as involuntary and unwilling pickets. Then there was the discrediting of the 'official' leaders and their replacement at a public meeting by men who had played no part in forming the branch and who were not even enrolled as members of Congress. The new leaders at once urged the continuance of the boycott until the price of meat was reduced, thus introducing a fresh issue which had nothing to do with the claims on which the campaign had originally been based. Finally, there was the collapse of the boycott when, following the arrest of some of the pickets, people began to complain that they were wasting their time because the situation had by now become so confused that they found they were boycotting the wrong firm.

It is tempting to attribute the collapse of the boycott, and the general confusion, to the weak leadership provided by the Congress officials, the chairman and vice-chairman in particular. I feel this is inadequate. As in the case of the General Workers' Union considered in the previous chapter, weak leadership in the present situation has to be seen as an effect as well as a cause. Each of the major participants in the 'social situation' described played his part not simply as an individual, but also as the incumbent of a social position in the political and administrative structure. Both Shitombwe and Simukonda occupied dual rôles as leaders in Congress and as members of the Urban Advisory Council. And their vacillation, and the subsequent confusion which marked the general conduct of the boycott, stemmed in large measure from the fact that these different rôles were in contradiction and moved them to adopt different policies.

The nature of this divergence emerged plainly in the meeting of the branch committee attended by Chimba, and again at the joint meeting held at the mine. To begin with, once the Urban Advisory Council had received an assurance from the butchers that the service for African customers would be improved, there was no further justification for carrying on with the boycott. It had lost its *raison d'être*. But the campaign was not being waged over a purely local issue. The boycott of the butcheries called by the African National Congress had been deliberately extended to the Copperbelt in order to make more effective the boycott which had already been going on for some weeks in Lusaka. Once this policy had been communicated to the local leaders, they were bound to act upon it, irrespective of the concessions which the Urban Advisory Council had been able to gain in negotiation with the butchers. Here, therefore, the policies of Congress and the Advisory Council in respect of the boycott were diametrically opposed, and the conflict between the two bodies was expressed in the respective claims of each to be the acknowledged mouthpiece of African opinion in the town. Musumbulwa, the Vice-Chairman of the Urban Advisory Council, hinted at this conflict when he pointed out at the meeting on the mine that if there were a boycott it would show that there was no co-operation between Congress and the Council. Chimba, the Congress leader from Ndola, put a similar point before the Luanshya committee but stated it more bluntly. He told the committee that irrespective of the agreement reached with the butchers by the Urban Advisory Council, they should persist in their plans to conduct a boycott until the butchers agreed to meet the Congress officials and not the Advisory Council.

In the situation thus created by the boycott, Congress and the Urban Advisory Council stood opposed, and Shitombwe and Simukonda, as members of both bodies, were caught up in this opposition. After hearing Chimba, Shitombwe appeared to have accepted the need for carrying on with the boycott. But he began to waver after the meeting with the mine-leaders, when they made it perfectly plain that the boycott would receive no support from people on the mine; and it was undoubtedly Musumbulwa's speech which led him to speak against the boycott when he addressed the public meeting on the following day.

The lack of resolution of the Congress leaders was a function of their membership of two bodies, whose policies were in opposition to one another. But the behaviour of Banda, too, was affected by the struggle between Congress and the Urban Advisory Council. Throughout the course of the boycott Banda was subjected to much vilification and abuse because he had posted a notice in a butchery window urging Africans to come in and buy. Yet this action was not prompted simply by his personal feud with Chitambala; it was also guided by his rôle in the political system of the town. As the senior location representative in the Urban Advisory Council, and that Council's delegate to the African Affairs Committee, he was afraid that he would be suspected by the European authorities of having played a leading part in organizing the boycott. His action at the butcheries was taken in order to protect his position as a member of the Council. Furthermore, a few days before the boycott began he had received a letter from Musumbulwa telling him that the people on the mine were taking no action in the matter, and suggesting that Banda should advise his own constituents in the location against taking part in the boycott. Here again his behaviour in attempting to persuade a public meeting to call off the boycott—a task in which he was also assisted by his fellow-councillor Mwape—was guided by his position as a member of the 'official' Council.

As I have already stated, the waging of the boycott in the face of the agreement reached between the butchers and the Urban Advisory Council involved the claim that it was Congress and not the Council which 'truly' represented African opinion in the town. And it was as a member of the Advisory Council that Banda was publicly attacked. At the public meeting called on the day the boycott commenced, Chitanda said that he saw no reason why Banda should regard himself as the only leader in the location. 'It is because he is in the Urban Advisory Council,' he declared. 'But this does not mean that he is the only leader, there are three others.' Phiri was even more explicit in linking Banda and the Council in his criticisms. All members of the Council were useless, he said, because they did not hold meetings to inform the public of the Council's discussions, or to hear the complaints of the people. Banda and his like were just 'stooges' of the Government.

There was a good deal of personal animosity in Phiri's scurrilous diatribes against Banda. I was told that Phiri had a long-standing grudge against Banda because the latter had once accused him of neglecting his duties as a deacon in the church. Phiri resented the criticism, and attributed it to Banda's ambition to hold the post himself. Following the posting of the notice in the butchery window, it seemed to Phiri as if Banda were aiming at complete personal domination of every group or association open to him. Nevertheless, when Phiri publicly attacked Banda he did so not in personal terms, but in terms of Banda's failings as a representative on the Urban Advisory Council, and he denounced the Council itself for coming to an arrangement with the butcheries without prior consultation of, or any mandate from, the people. Since those views were accepted by the meeting, and since Phiri's criticisms also involved both Shitombwe and Simukonda as fellow-members with Banda in the Advisory Council, their leadership was entirely discredited. Chitambala, who was not a member of the Advisory Council, now had the support of his fellow-leaders in the Shop Assistants' Union in pressing for the continuance of the boycott, and the recognition of Congress as the representative body of African opinion in the town.

When the formation of a Congress branch in Luanshya was first mooted, it was opposed by Banda on the grounds that there was already a branch in existence on the mine which served the needs of all Africans living in the town. There was no branch on the mine, though even if there had been there was still no reason why another should not have been started in the location. But if Banda's argument is accepted for the moment then, conversely, in the absence of a branch on the mine, the Mikomfwa branch might also have been expected to cater for Africans living in the Mine Township. This did not happen. The new branch originated in Mikomfwa, and its membership was recruited entirely in the Municipal location. The issues with which the new branch immediately concerned itself were confined to the location, and when it did seek the co-operation of people at the mine on the issue of the butcheries, all the mine leaders came out in opposition to Congress policy, so that what picketing did take place subsequently did not extend to the butcheries in the Mine Township.

Why then did leaders on the mine refuse to co-operate with their fellows in Mikomfwa on an issue which, after all, did affect all Africans living in the town? Or putting the question in another way, why was it that Congress as a body made no real headway on the mine? One explanation which immediately suggests itself lies in the bitter hostility that had developed between Congress and the Mine Workers' Union over the failure of the 'Two Days of National Prayer' which Congress had organized in 1953 as a final statement of the Africans' opposition to Federation. This enmity persisted and little had been done since to heal the breach between the two bodies. For instance, at the Congress conference held at Ndola in mid-January, 1954, which Shitombwe had attended as a Luanshya delegate, there was some discussion about where Congress should establish its headquarters. There were those who favoured Kitwe because it was the centre of the Copperbelt, and had for many years been regarded as the 'Mecca' of African intellectual life. Others spoke in favour of Ndola, claiming that at Kitwe they would have to suffer interference from the Union, because the Location Superintendent would not allow them the use of the Welfare Hall without prior consultation with the Union: 'And could Congress kneel before trade union leaders just for the use of a meeting room?' Nevertheless, this hostility does not account in itself for the absence of Congress activity at the mine, and it does not appear to have entered directly into the issue of the boycott. Although the mine leaders were referred to as Capricornists, and thus, by implication, anti-Congress, none of them had made any attack on Congress. Nor, indeed, had they raised any objection in principle to the waging of a boycott. On the contrary, they objected that it would be foolish to conduct a boycott until they had been given the opportunity to see what measures the butchers had taken to implement the agreement; and that in any case the branch was not yet sufficiently well organized to conduct a boycott. One of the principal speakers at the meeting on the mine had been Mr. Musumbulwa, the Vice-Chairman of the Advisory Council. At one time he had been recognized as one of the leading figures in the Roan branch of the Mine Workers' Union, but he no longer took an active interest in Union matters, and there were some Africans at Roan who considered that if a Salaried Staff Association were founded there he would be its first chairman. It is all the more significant, therefore, that his views should have been endorsed by all the Union leaders present at the meeting, and later by Mr. Chapoloko, the Union Branch Secretary, whose advice had been sought in forming the Congress branch in Mikomfwa.

Thus it would appear that the rejection of Congress policy in the present instance cannot be explained solely in terms of the hostility between Congress and the Mine Workers' Union, but has to be viewed within the broader context of Congress's failure to organize a branch on the mine itself. I suggest that we must seek the explanation in the different forms of organization of the two bodies, and in the kind of administrative structure within which the African Mine Workers' Union developed.

We have already observed that one of the features of trade union organization is a relatively large membership, paying regular subscriptions. It is only through payment of dues that one becomes entitled to benefits. It is true, of course, that wage increases within the industry resulting from Union demands for strikes will extend to employees who are not paid-up members of the Union.[1] But, as we have seen previously, the work of the Union does not consist solely in spectacular strike action. Every day the branch officials are called upon to handle specific grievances and complaints brought by individual employees; and the first question put to a man who approaches the Union in this way is whether he is a paid-up member. The local branch of the Union is thus a 'permanent' organization which handles specific issues of day-to-day occurrence. This organization, in turn, has its place within a wider system possessing a regular machinery of negotiation. All this is in marked contrast to the loose-knit and volatile quality of present Congress organization. It has no regular subscribing membership, and for the most part has to depend on funds raised at public meetings.[2] Its local organization tends to centre on small committees which, from time to time, seek to rally the community on some broad issue which is a source of generalized feelings of resentment among the African public. Lacking official recognition, it lacks too a regular channel of access to Governmental and other authorities, such as that possessed by the Union. Unlike the Union, therefore, the activities of Congress are intermittent: indeed, it would seem fair to hold that the spasmodic eruption, such as the boycott in Luanshya, is not only the characteristic feature of the Congress, but for the present the very basis of its existence.

In addition to these differences in internal organization, we have to consider too the social framework within which the African Mine Workers' Union operates. As I attempted to show in the previous chapter, the Union developed within an organization already provided by the mining company. Jobs, housing and feeding, health—all these and more fall within the compass of mine administration: they also became the concern of the Union because, in the absence of any other local government body for the mine compound, the Union alone provided a means by which the grievances and wishes of the mine employees could be

---

[1] It is interesting to note in this connection that when a strike was called in January, 1955, the Union leaders threatened that their wage increase demands would apply only to members of the Union.

[2] A fuller account of these aspects of Congress organization will be given in my paper, 'The Rise of African Nationalism in Northern Rhodesia'.

effectively brought to the attention of Management. In this way, Africans have come to see the Union as their *'mfuti'*, their 'weapon' in the struggle for the betterment of their working and social conditions. When I was at Luanshya there were few issues arising on the mine which were not regarded as falling within the province of the Union. In all matters touching the Mine Township as a whole, the local branch leaders were regarded widely as the only appropriate spokesmen. This was well illustrated when it was announced early in 1954 that there would be a by-election to fill three seats in the Urban Advisory Council. Few people on the mine evinced much interest. Prior to the election, the District Commissioner called a public meeting in the Welfare Centre in order to explain the functions of the Council, and to introduce the candidates. Before this meeting began, the Union clerk was heard urging members paying their dues to hurry up so that they could all go along to the Welfare Centre. But the members were not impressed by his advice. One of them asked: 'Do you think the District Commissioner's meeting is more important than our Union? No, not at all. I'm not going there. Why should I waste my time?' Another immediately supported him by saying that on the mine they had the Union, they wanted no other organization. *Uwaikete fibili afwile ku menshi,* 'you can't serve two masters at the same time' (lit. he who grasped two things was drowned), he added, quoting a Bemba proverb.

These remarks were typical of the many comments recorded in the course of the election. The attitudes they revealed towards the Union were based upon its record of solid achievement. Its results were tangible; by contrast, the one major campaign which Congress had conducted against Central African Federation had been a failure.[1] Thus there were many who tended to see the

---

[1] The question why the 'Two Days of National Prayer' should have proved a fiasco falls outside the scope of the present study. The reasons are varied and complex. However, I am inclined to think that a major reason was that the Union leaders, from their wider experience gained through collective bargaining and negotiations, recognized earlier than the Congress leaders that the political campaign against Federation had been lost. If the prestige of the Union was not to suffer, it was important that the Union should be sharply dissociated, in the eyes of its members, from the failure of the Congress, so that at least the economic struggle for African advancement could be maintained. Later in the year, the establishment of the Federation resulted in the collapse of many

existence of any other body, however different or complementary its functions might be, as constituting a threat to the power and authority of the Union: as such it was suspect. Developing within a 'unitary' structure, the Union itself had developed unitary characteristics, and acquired functions far beyond the range of interests and activities usually associated with trade unions. Thus while Congress had a number of staunch adherents on the mines, after the loss of the campaign against Federation, there was little room for the development of a 'popular' movement independent of the Union. In the towns, it was only within the less closely-knit structure of the Municipal locations that Congress found the conditions in which it could emerge and flourish.

Thus mine and location have to be seen as distinct sections of a single community, each of which is built up around a different combination of principles of social organization. Far from being organized to serve the needs of a single industry, the location is essentially a housing unit for workers employed in a variety of occupations. The point is brought out strikingly in the different structural positions of the African Personnel Manager on the mine and the Location Superintendent in Mikomfwa. Whereas the latter stands in relation to the location residents as an administrator only, the rôle of the African Personnel Manager also involves the relationship of employer and employee. Consequently, the social organization of the location is much less closely integrated than that of the mine compound, and this has led me to describe its structure as 'atomistic'. Here the social system appears to be marked by a higher degree of flux, so that different and opposed principles of social organization may operate together much more easily than on the mine.

The implications of this statement are best illustrated in the position of the Tribal Elders. In Mikomfwa the Location Superintendent had no direct concern with the problems of labour, and the Elders had no responsibility at all in matters affecting the wages or working conditions of the Africans living there, for each man was responsible only to his own employer. Primarily, the Elders were concerned with the settlement of petty disputes and so were never too closely associated, in the eyes of the people,

---

Congress branches. See above, p. 181, and for further details my 'The Rise of African Nationalism in Northern Rhodesia', op. cit.

with the European authorities. Thus the Elders were never forced into the position, as were the Tribal Representatives on the mine, where they appeared to be acting in co-operation with the authorities against the interests of their own people. When the Mine Workers' Union finally emerged, it was soon able to establish its pre-eminence by having the Tribal Representatives abolished. But the Unions centred in Mikomfwa have been small and are, for reasons considered in a previous chapter, more poorly organized than the mine workers. Although the Union leaders in Mikomfwa speak from time to time of abolishing the Tribal Elders, in fact they have never been sufficiently strong to challenge their position.

Thus within the 'atomistic' structure of the location, there exists a multiplicity of groupings, each catering for different interests, each with its own small following: there is no general consensus on who the acknowledged leaders are, and no body which is generally accepted as representing the community as a whole. In these circumstances, the confusion which marked certain phases of the boycott becomes more understandable. The African National Congress is a territorial organization and its policies are promulgated at a territorial level. But in a local community, its organization reflects local cleavages, and its policies may be exploited to promote sectional or even individual interests. Chitambala, the Branch Secretary of the Shop Assistants' Union, was led initially to form a branch of Congress because he hoped that such a body, by cutting across the divisions created by membership of different tribes and different Unions, could then claim to represent the political unity of the location residents; and he hoped further, that as one of its leaders, he would be in a position to challenge successfully the claim of Banda, who sat on the Advisory Council. In this aim he had the support of the hawkers until they saw that their own interests would be better served in another direction. It was the vacillation of Shitombwe and Simukonda, stemming from their dual membership of both Congress and the Advisory Council, which produced the confusion and made it possible for a number of leaders to come forward and make their bid for popular authority. Urged on by a letter from Musumbulwa on the mine, Banda sought to explain the folly of the boycott, and was supported by Mwape, another member of the Advisory Council. The Bemba Elder intervened as the representative of the largest single tribal grouping in Mikomfwa, and also supported Banda. But it was Phiri and Chitanda, the two committee men of the Shop Assistants' Union—the strongest of all the Unions based on the location—who carried the day, and acted as the Congress delegates to the butcheries until the boycott collapsed.

V

In the preceding sections I have presented the boycott waged by Congress against the European butchers as a 'social situation', as that term has been used by Gluckman and others.[1] The situation consisted in a series of events, spread over the period of about a fortnight, which I recorded in the course of my field-work. Because the situation involved many members of the local community, it helps to throw light not only on the system of political relations within that community, but also on the process of change occuring within the developing social structure of the Copperbelt towns.

The whole issue of the butcheries had been raised by the African National Congress as part of its programme to test in action the theory of partnership which was the declared policy of the new Federation. In choosing to direct the first stages of this campaign against the butchers, Congress had seized upon an aspect of discrimination that had long been a source of resentment to many urban Africans—the treatment and service accorded to African customers in European shops and stores. At Luanshya, for example, the question had been raised by the Urban Advisory Council on a number of occasions in the past, and there had even been meetings with the local Chamber of Commerce, which resulted in the Council making some slight gains. The Council had also considered specific grievances against the butcheries before the boycott arose. Thus the issue was one which concerned the people as Africans; and it was in this sense that Congress could claim, through the organization of this and similar campaigns, to rise above the many differences which divided the African community and represent its political unity in opposition to Government and the European settlers.

---

[1] M. Gluckman, 'Analysis of a Social Situation in Modern Zululand', *Bantu Studies*, xiv (March, 1940), pp. 2, 10.

The policies of Congress are promulgated at a territorial level, but these policies can only be implemented by its branches inside their local communities. Here the emergence of a Congress branch, and the character of its membershp is affected by, and will in turn affect, the social structure of the community and the prevailing balance of forces within that community.

I have tried to show in earlier chapters how the growth of the urban community is associated with increasing social and economic differentiation. Such differentiation is given expression in the formation of associations and other bodies designed to cater for, and to promote the special interests of, its members. These in turn are led to seek a place for themselves within the existing political and administrative framework. We have already seen something of this process in the earlier history of the Urban Advisory Council, in the changing compositions of which we were able to trace the gradual elimination of the Tribal Elders and their replacement by younger and more educated men of the town. The case of the African hawkers provides another illustration of precisely the same kind of process. The hawkers were represented on the Advisory Council by their Chairman Shitombwe; and when the Advisory Council showed itself to be an ineffective instrument in protecting their interests, the hawkers sought through Congress to gain direct representation on the Urban Housing Board and the African Affairs Committee. As we saw,[1] the hawkers had been refused permission to trade in the African Mine Township. They then requested the Roan branch of the Union to intercede with the Management on their behalf. When this measure failed because Management declared that the matter lay outside the scope of its agreement with the Union, the matter was referred to the Urban Advisory Council. After some discussion in the Council, one member asked whether the District Commissioner would act as a mediator between the parties. The District Commissioner replied that he had already raised the issue with the mine on a number of occasions, but had always been met with objections which were based on certain health regulations. He added, however, that it would 'strengthen his hand' if he had a resolution from the Council. After some further consideration, the Council resolved that the Mine Man-

---

[1] See above, p. 169.

agement be asked to state its reasons for refusing permission to hawkers to trade on the mine. When the matter was raised at the next meeting of the Council about a month later, the chairman had to report that he had received no reply to his letter from the Mine Management. The hawkers' representative on the Council burst out angrily: 'It will be the same at the next meeting. You will say, "There is still no reply".' When the chairman explained that there was little further that could be done until a reply was received, the member commented sadly: 'Yes, so it seems this Council has no power.'

This case brings out what many Africans see as a major deficiency in the system of Advisory Councils. Since they are purely advisory bodies, their effective power is largely coincident with the influence that an urban District Commissioner is able to exert, and this, as I attempted to show in an earlier chapter, is considerably reduced in an industrial milieu. Nevertheless, the Urban Advisory Council still provides the sole official channel of communication between the Africans and Government in the person of the District Commissioner, and the other local centres of power. Furthermore, it constitutes the first rung of the political ladder which leads to Legislative Council. Consequently, African urban leaders have not been able to ignore the Advisory Councils, and have invariably been led to seek places within them. Thus when the new Council re-assembled at Luanshya in 1954 its membership included four members of the executive committee of the Roan branch of the African Mine Workers' Union, the Secretary of the local branch of the General Workers' Union, the Chairman of the Hawkers' Association, and others prominent in different organizations in the town.[1]

The Urban Advisory Council draws its members from all sections of the community. Since it is the only official link with Government, it purports to represent African opinion in the town. But the members themselves represent different groups whose interests in some situations may coincide, yet be opposed in others. At the same time, the Advisory Council itself occupies an intercalary position within the political structure of the town, so that the attitudes adopted by Africans towards the Council are sometimes diametrically opposed. Like the Tribal Representatives,

---

[1] See Table 14 below, pp. 242-3.

the Council is seen at times as a body in which the Africans have an interest, at times as a body too closely associated with the European authorities so that its members are regarded as 'stooges' of the Government. The nature of this contradiction was brought home to me most clearly in a conversation with a committee member of the Roan branch of the Mine Workers' Union at the time of the by-election to the Council. The committee member spoke of the Advisory Council as a body that was opposed and, indeed, dangerous to the Union. He pointed out that certain members of the Council were no longer members of the Union, while others who were now standing for election had never even joined. He went on to say that were the Council really striving to advance the interests of the African workers, Nkoma, the recently elected chairman of the branch, would also have stood for election to the Council. His attention was at once drawn to the fact that several leading figures in the branch had earlier sought nomination, and were already members of the Council. But the committee member remained unconvinced. Those people, he replied, attended meetings just to find out what was going on. They went as 'informers' to the Union. It was this contradiction, then, and the divisions within the Council itself which, in a situation like the boycott of the butcheries, enabled certain of the members to affirm their allegiance to the Council and others to range themselves in opposition to it without making the Council completely ineffective. In the case of the hawkers, Shitombwe had the full support of his fellows on the Council. But while all were agreed on the need for improvement in the general treatment of African customers in European-owned butcheries, the members decided to abide by the agreement made between the Council and the butchers rather than to ally themselves with the National Congress in the boycott.

The decision to reject Congress policy over the boycott was taken at the meeting on the mine, when all the mine spokesmen agreed that a boycott at that time was inadvisable. The mine leaders were influenced in their decision by the fact that the butchers had agreed to effect certain improvements, and should be given the opportunity to fulfil their promises. But I have also suggested that the roots of the decision lie deeper, and have to be seen in terms of the failure of Congress to organize a branch on the mine. This failure I attributed to the 'unitary'

structure of mine society. I have referred to the intercalary position of the Advisory Council. On the mine the Mine Workers'
Union, which at that time represented politically the unity of the
African mine community, was independent of the European
authorities; and where interests clashed, the Union was free to
express the opposition of the mine workers. By contrast, the
location lacked an 'indigenous' body performing the rôle of the
Mine Workers' Union, which would have served to integrate
its many separate components at a higher political level. Consequently, as new interest-groups emerged in the location, or
politically ambitious men arose whose interests could not be
served within the existing system, they could only promote
their case by becoming associated with a body such as Congress.
For by the very nature of its aims, Congress is a diffuse, loosely-
knit organization. Because it claims to be a National body, it
cannot become too closely associated with any particular tribe
or tribes or any one set of economic interests. Representing
Africans as a whole, it is anchored to no one local community.
In this way, paradoxically, Congress makes itself available as an
instrument for promoting sectional interests or even the interest
of dissident factions within existing bodies. For such interest-
groups, too small or weak to achieve their aims unaided, can only
make a bid for public support in terms of the values represented
by the National Congress.

CHAPTER VI

COURT AND COMMUNITY

I

ANTHROPOLOGISTS have found it convenient, for purposes of analysis, to distinguish between what can be called repetitive and changing social systems. The distinction is not an absolute one, and within a changing system some elements may display the characteristics of a repetitive system. A repetitive social system has been defined by Gluckman [1] as one in which conflicts can be wholly resolved and co-operation wholly achieved within the pattern of the system. The composition of the groups and the parties to the relationships which go to make up the system may change, but the pattern of the relations between the various elements of the system does not change. By contrast, a changing social system is one in which conflicts within the society can no longer be contained within the existing order, and can only be resolved, wholly or in part, by changes in the character of the elements which make up the system and in the pattern of the relations between those elements. Thus Gluckman describes modern Zululand as such a changing social system in which new types of groups and social personalities, in ever-changing relationships with one another, are emerging constantly.

In this sense an urban community on the Copperbelt also constitutes a changing, or perhaps developing, social system. In the preceding chapters I have tried to show how the process of growth is expressed in constant fission and the emergence of new bodies and associations. The new bodies do not represent 'like but competitive' interests, in the way that hiving off segments, in a repetitive system, do; they represent interests which are essentially different from those of the body from which they have split off. The major cleavages operating within an African Copperbelt community express conflicts of interest which can no longer be resolved in terms of a framework of norms and values commonly

---

[1] M. Gluckman, 'Some Processes of Social Change Illustrated from Zululand', *African Studies*, i (December, 1942), pp. 243-60, at p. 244.

accepted as binding on the community as a whole. Nevertheless, in its normative aspect, the urban social system also displays certain of the features characteristic of the tribal system. In the present chapter I want to consider this question in closer detail by examining the normative system of the urban community in so far as this is revealed in the work of the African Urban Court in Luanshya. Here I shall argue that in spite of the increased social diversification, there is still a broad general consensus amongst urban Africans on the applicability of tribal norms in regulating many of their social relationships in the town.

II

Urban Courts were established on the Copperbelt in 1938 and for more than a decade now have played a most important rôle in the urban administrative system. The four or five judges at each court are appointed by the Native Authorities in rural areas in order to provide as far as possible for the representation of all major linguistic and cultural groupings within the Territory. As we have seen,[1] this mode of appointment of the Court Members has been strongly criticized by urban Africans from time to time; but although the organization of the courts has been modified in certain respects, the basic principles and premisses on which the system of courts was founded have so far remained unchanged.

Most of the disputes among Africans in the towns which require legal settlement are dealt with by the Urban Courts. These have a wide jurisdiction in matters civil and criminal, and may impose fines not exceeding £5 or sentence of imprisonment not exceeding three months. The more serious cases, or disputes between Europeans and Africans, are dealt with in the court of the Resident Magistrate. With the exception of one or two minor statutory offences, the law administered in the Urban Courts is wholly unwritten. Claims are brought before the courts and are argued by the litigants themselves in terms of the customary law of the tribes. The cases are heard and settled within a framework of procedure that constituted a fundamental ingredient of tribal legal systems. Since a significant characteristic of that procedure is the tendency to argue in terms of general norms, rather than in

---

[1] See above, p. 77.

terms of specific claims, a consideration of a few cases which I recorded in the Luanshya court will provide a convenient point of departure for a discussion of the normative system of the urban community.

The first case, which I will refer to as the *Case of the Aggrieved Friend*, involved two women of the Lünda tribe from the Kawambwa District. The facts of the case are set out in the statement of the complainant, which I transcribe in some detail from my own record.

'I live with my husband on the mine. One day my friend [the defendant], who comes from the same part of the country as myself, came to see me. She said that things were not too good in the house. A short time ago her child had died, and since they had buried it she had not menstruated till yesterday. So she came to me to ask if I could find medicine to purify her. I said she had done well to come and discuss the matter otherwise later on she might have found "difficulties in the house". I found medicine for her. Some time later she came to see me again and said that things were now well in the house, and that she was pregnant.

'One day my husband gave me leave to go on a visit to our home in Kawambwa. When my friend heard this she gave me two pieces of cloth which she asked me to give to her mother at home. I took the material and put it with my own clothes. I started off, but when I got to Mufulira the clothes were stolen by thieves. So I came back to Luanshya and reported the matter to the District Commissioner. The District Commissioner said we could do nothing here in Luanshya, and that we should make a complaint at Mufulira where we might be able to recover the clothes. When I told my friend about it she did not believe me, and thought I was just saying the clothes were stolen. She said she would "bear it in mind".[1] When I heard this from *mukaya munandi*, my friend with whom I had grown up at home, my heart became sore, and I decided to bring the matter before the court.'

At the conclusion of this statement, the court questioned the defendant briefly as follows:

Court: 'In what way has your friend been lying in giving her statement?'—*Defendant:* 'No, so far as the matter of the medicine is concerned she has told it as it was.'

---

[1] In the vernacular the woman used a future continuous tense of the verb *kuisosha* which is difficult to render in English. Perhaps the sense is best conveyed by the vulgarism 'to go on about'. The term also carries undertones suggesting witchcraft.

Court: 'Then why were you 'complaining' about her? Did she come to you saying "let me take these things home for your mother"?'
—*Defendant:* 'No, I was just "grumbling" [*ukuisosha*].'
Court: 'Were only your clothes stolen?'—*Defendant:* 'No, from what she says both her own and mine were stolen.'
Court: 'You have been muttering about your friend. Now it is like this. If you have much money and then you take it to your friend that he may look after it, can there be a case if that money is stolen from him?'—*Defendant:* 'No, there is no case.'
Court: 'And so here too you cannot give your friend a case.'

The court then inquired if there had been any arrangement about the price of the medicine. The complainant replied, no, she had just sought for medicine because her friend was just as her 'sister'. 'Why then had she brought the case? What did she want?', the court asked. The complainant replied: 'No, there is nothing. What caused me to come to court is that my friend has done wrong.'

Court: 'As you sought medicine for her perhaps you feel that she should give you some small token that your heart should be at peace?'
—*Complainant:* 'No, it is not the matter of the medicine, for there was no arrangement in the past. She was my friend.'

The court addressed the defendant and proceeded to judgment. 'You hear that? Your friend has spoken very fine words indeed, words of truth and worth [*amashiwi ya chishinka*.] You have settled this case well between yourselves. Now, your friend has not asked for money. Are you asking for money? Is it for money that you have just come here? That is how you are getting all our customs mixed up. Your friend has "cut" this case. Do not do this sort of thing again, but now go and live peacefully together in the compound.'

The case is extremely simple and straightforward, and I cite it here because it brings out in a number of ways the significant differences between the African Urban Courts, and the Magistrates' and High Courts to the jurisdiction of which the African is also subject. In the latter courts English legal procedure is scrupulously followed: in the African Urban Courts the procedure followed is indigenous to African law. Here there are no statements of claims and rejoinders, no elaborate preliminaries to reduce the case to its simplest legal ingredients before the matter comes up for trial. This has important implications, the significance of which will emerge in the later analysis. The procedure itself is of the simplest: the case proceeds by way of statement and not by way of examination and cross-examination: and there is little attempt to exclude what might strike an English lawyer as irrelevant testimony. But perhaps the most interesting feature of the case is that, although the complainant brought the case before the court, she did not point to some specific breach of a legal rule and ask for compensation or some other specifically legal remedy in the generally accepted sense of that term. She had come to court with her *mukaya*, her friend from childhood, with whom she had grown up in the village, and she was asking whether the latter's behaviour was in conformity with the norms of friendship. Like Sinyinza in the case before the location Elders considered previously,[1] she came before the court that these norms might be publicly restated and her friend might be led to recognize her error. In this sense the Urban Court emerges as a repository of moral, as well as legal, norms.

The moral element in Urban Court procedure is well brought out in the hearing of the case itself. In introducing her case, the complainant went out of her way to explain how she had assisted her friend by seeking out medicines to make her ritually clean.[2] At first sight this would seem to have little to do with her later complaint about her friend's reaction to the loss of her pieces of cloth. In fact it is of the most immediate relevance. In the absence of any prior refining of the legal issues involved, before the hearing commences, the courts are able to entertain suits in terms of broad general principles, both legal and moral, rather than in terms of specific legal rules. *The Case of the Aggrieved Friend* is in essence an inquiry into the norms of friendship, and the defendant's breach of those norms is set off against the friendly behaviour of the complainant. The preliminary part of her statement, therefore, shows how throughout their relationship she had always behaved properly in terms of the norms of friendship. Later in the case she emphasized this point when, in reply to the court's question, she said she was not seeking compensation, an

---

[1] See above, p. 58.

[2] The medicine referred to here was to purify the woman after the death of the child. After her next menstruation, husband and wife perform an act of ritual intercourse. Early in the morning they rise and bathe themselves all over the body in the medicine prepared for them, *kuisangulula*.

attitude which won the immediate approval of the court members. She had spoken very fine words indeed, they said. In this way she had 'cut' the case: she had left little for the court to add save to bid the parties return home and live together in amity as they had done in the past.

III

Not all the cases which come before the courts are as straight-forward as this, but all reveal in their different ways the same underlying principles and concepts, the same concern with moral as well as legal norms. The *Case of the Disrespectful Son-in-law* provides an example where a legal claim, in its strict sense, was involved.

The case was brought by the Bemba Tribal Elder in Mikomfwa. 'Well, Mwamba,' the court inquired, 'what has brought you to court?' The Elder stated his case:

'What has brought me to court is this young man. He is full of contempt for me and wholly lacking in respect [*uwamusalula*]. He has been like this for some time; now I am tired of it, and I thought: "Let me take this case to the big people who will settle it. . . ."'

'I have a child, a daughter whom I sent to school at Mindolo [near Kitwe] where she was studying. When she returned to Luanshya a young man appeared who comes from our part of the country [i.e. Bembaland]. He became engaged to my daughter. During this time he looked after her, and did many things for me. After my daughter returned to school her younger brother became ill, and had to go to the hospital at Ndola where my "son-in-law" was then living. During the time he was in hospital my "son-in-law" was caring for him, and eventually paid his fare back to Luanshya. . . . Now when my daughter was back at school, another young man started to write to her saying that she should leave her fiancé, Simeo, and marry him. She agreed to this. I don't know what bad thing my "son-in-law" did. I know my daughter was stupid, she has no sense, for Simeo appeared to me to have a good heart. Now when this marriage was broken off I was very sorry. Simeo had "worked" very well, he did not ask that anything be returned to him, he just let matters be [*asulile fye*].'

'So I stayed and thought much about it. At last this young man here came and I thought well, it doesn't matter, he too is from our country. He brought £3 which I understood to be *matebeto* [i.e. one of the customary gifts exchanged between a man and his in-laws as a token of respect]. My daughter was now going to sweep out his hut, and to keep it nice. But then I found that sometimes she was coming back very late at night. I thought: "This young man just wants to destroy my child."[1] I stopped her going there. Some time later the young man sent £5 through *shibukombe*, the go-between in these matters. I thought to myself: "I am Mwamba. Can this young man decide himself what he shall give me as *ndalama sha cisungu*, as payment for *cisungu*?" I told the go-between to take the money back and ask the young man who sent him whether he was the one who begot the child. I said I could only decide the matter when I gathered together some of my people to discuss it.

'Now when the young man received this letter he did not hear the word which *shibukombe* brought. He wrote me a letter and asked why I had sent back the money. He said: "It was you who have stopped the girl from coming to sweep the hut; and it was you who sent back the money. It is because there is another fellow at Nkana whom you want her to marry." Seeing these words, I was very angry indeed. If he was not satisfied, why did he not send back the *shibukombe* with another message instead if writing to me as though I were a child? Now I too wrote a letter—for my heart was very sore—telling him to come right away so that we discuss the matter. I went and called some of the *bakalamba* [big people,] saying Chinkumba [Elder of the related Bisa tribe], Njovu [Elder of the Nsenga people], come and listen to the way young people are behaving here on the railway line. I also told Lukashi, Chikulye and Chipoya, for these are the people who would have to be present at the wedding, for they are my fellow *bakalamba*.

'In the evening, about seven o'clock, they all gathered at my house and this young man and another who came with him. I began to tell the "big people" how my son-in-law and I were troubling one another. They began to upbraid me saying that it was because I was angry that I wrote him a letter. They said that I should have sent the "go-between". I agreed that I was wrong there. Then they began to "instruct" the young man. They told him that in these matters the words were with the father-in-law. It was he who would decide what money he should pay for *mpango* and other matters. Then the young man agreed too. I told my daughter that the words were now finished, and that she could go and keep his house clean again.

'Now we were living well together. My wife prepared food which

---

[1] Here the father had in mind the fear that the young man would '*eat the cisungu*' by having pre-marital relations with the daughter. In Bemba custom the right to consummate the marriage is only conferred on the husband by a special payment, *ndalama sha cisungu*, made to the parents of the girl. For a more detailed account of the *cisungu* complex see A. I. Richards, *Bemba Marriage and Present Economic Conditions*, p. 52 et passim.

was taken to my son-in-law's house. We were now staying well. Then one day he gave my wife £1 with which to buy a sack of flour. So I was about to call the *bakalamba* together again so that we could discuss the amount he should bring for *cisungu*. Shortly afterwards another letter arrived from my son-in-law. He said: "I know you don't want me. So I am asking you to return to me £4." When I saw this I was angry again in my heart. I said this man has got no *mucinshi*, no feeling of respect. I had called the "big people" together, and the words were finished. Why then had he written again? So I wrote to him and asked: "This £4 you want me to return, of what sort is it?" He replied that he wanted £3 which he had brought me as part of the *ubuimashi* [marriage payment], and the remaining £1 was the one he had given my wife in order to buy flour. I was so angry that I did not answer this letter. I just rose and went to Chanda, the maternal uncle of the young man. When I arrived at Chanda's I found that my son-in-law was also present. I began to rate Chanda: "Is this how you teach your nephew?" I asked. "Is this what you do to your chief at home? Do you write letters to your father-in-law?" Chanda was very annoyed at this and asked: "Have you come here to curse and insult us? Very well, let us fight. This case must finish at the Urban Court." That is how I came to take out a summons.'

When the Elder had concluded this statement, the court turned to the young man and asked him in what way he considered his father-in-law had lied against him. The defendant gave his version of the case:

'In many things he has told lies, in others he is perfectly correct. I cannot say much in this matter, for I knew long ago that we would never marry. I took £3 to my "father" as *ubuimashi* [marriage payment], and then later £5 so that I might hear the word that I might now take my wife. And that £5 I took which my "father" returned, on that I said nothing. For I had not said it was for *cisungu* only. I wanted to hear the case so that he could decide what money would have to be added to it. But he just returned the money. He did not answer me properly. He sent back word: "Did this young man beget my child? Does he want to eat the *cisungu* of my daughter?" Then, after I had betrothed his daughter, he stopped her from sweeping out my house, saying that that young man would "eat the *cisungu*" and then would run away. He would "eat" nothing. Now all this angered me. Then, one day, a friend of mine came to see me and asked: "Why are you having troubles with your father-in-law?" I made no reply and he went on: "No, I know the reason. It is because he has in mind another fellow who lives in Kitwe, to whom he wants to marry his daughter."

So I saw that it was true, and I said that I must ask him to return all the money so that I should not waste any more time on the matter, and marry someone else.'

This concluded the statements of the parties, and the court now addressed the complainant.

Court: 'Now then, Mwamba, do you not hear how your son-in-law has spoken these good things? What do you think about it now? Would you not like us to "instruct" this young man and then he can marry your daughter?'—*Complainant:* 'No, the things you chiefs are saying I cannot listen to. This young man has disgraced me [*ansebanya*], and has no feelings of respect for me. I want simply that the marriage end, and I take my child and marry her elsewhere.'

The court asked the mother of the girl whether she also wished the marriage to be broken off. She replied: 'Yes, I too want it finished today. What has he ever done for me? He is just a dog. He has done nothing for me. Otherwise we could have lived well together. It is he who has broken my daughter's marriage.'

Court: 'We have heard the words of both of you, the parents of this girl. But this word "dog". It is not fitting to curse and use such words here in court. For that we can bring a case against you. Now you, young man, what do you say to these words of your parents-in-law?'— *Defendant:* 'I have heard what they say. The marriage ended a long time ago, and all I want is that the money I spent should be returned to me.'

Court: 'What money is that?'—*Defendant:* 'There is the £1 I gave for flour, £3 for *ubuimashi*, and then there is £2 which I spent to buy their daughter a pair of shoes.'

Court: 'Listen, Mwamba, you will have to return these sums the young man has counted.'—*Complainant:* 'The words you are saying, you chiefs, I cannot listen to. Also, you chiefs, you should think carefully of what you are saying in this case.'

Court President (angrily): 'What do you mean by saying that in this case we should think carefully about it? Why have you brought this case here instead of hearing it at your shelter in the location, you who are an Elder? The way you answer in court is not good. Do you think that here we are sitting at *chitenge*, the Elders' shelter? No, we are *kwisano*, at the Chief's quarters. If you talk in this way we can make you pay heavily for your contempt. You will take the money counted and hand it over right away in this court.'—*Complainant:* 'No, I cannot repay this money. In what way can it be returned? This sum of £3 was *matebeto*. We prepared food for him and sent it to his house, and then he brought this money. It was the money I laid out to perform *matebeto*. Nor can I return the £1. What about all the things I have spent on him? He has eaten all my flour, all my fish, all my cabbages. As for the £2, the one who can refund that is his "wife", for when we try to teach her she does not listen.'

The complainant had been stung by the President's remarks, and the Bemba Court Member now intervened to try to pacify him:

'These words which you have answered, Mwamba, are not good. It is not fitting for a *mukalamba* [a big man] to speak like that. You should just take the money and give it to him back for you have refused him.' He then addressed the defendant: 'Now, we have heard your case, and you are in the right. But you are a Bemba. That money you claim was for *matebeto*. Why have you said it was *ubuimashi*? No, you should deduct that £3.'

The young man agreed to this, and the Bemba Court Member addressed Mwamba once more:

'We are about to finish your case, Mwamba. Take £3 and give it to the young man, and he will go and marry elsewhere. Now you see, you big people, you must take care in arranging the marriages of your daughters. You are just coming to the court all the time over these matters. That is why many say that when a daughter is grown up she should go back to the village and contract a proper marriage [*cupo ca chishinka*]'.

Here, as in the *Case of the Aggrieved Friend*, the case proceeds by way of statement in which each of the parties is given the opportunity to set out at length and without interruption the nature of his grievances. In the absence of any form of technical pleading, the precise nature of the injury suffered and the redress sought is not always immediately clear and frequently emerges, as here, only towards the end of the case. The legal issue involved in the *Case of the Disrespectful Son-in-law* was whether certain payments made in consideration of a marriage could be recovered by the prospective son-in-law when the marriage was broken off at the instance of the girl's parents. The issue was joined when Mwamba refused the offer of the court to 'instruct' the young man on his duties as a son-in-law, and asked for a declaration by the court that the proposed marriage was 'dissolved'. The defendant did not dispute this point. So far as he was concerned, the proposed marriage had been stultified long ago, and all he asked was that he be allowed to recover the money he had laid out on account of the proposed marriage.

But while this simple legal issue lay at the core of the matter, there was no explicit legal argument on the point. The point of law involved was not put in dispute, nor did the court itself make any effort at explicit formulation of the legal rule applicable to the circumstances of the case. On the contrary, the universe of discourse of Court Members and litigants alike was the inquiry into the norms of behaviour which govern the relations between a man and his parents-in-law. In this way much of what would otherwise appear irrelevant in Mwamba's statement becomes meaningful. Like the complainant in the *Case of the Aggrieved Friend*, Mwamba began by a recital of certain incidents which might appear to have little direct bearing on the point of issue. He dwelt at some length on the virtues of his previous 'son-in-law', Simeo. Simeo had cared for his 'brother-in-law' when he was ill, and had shown solicitude for the parents of his fiancée in many ways. And when through his daughter's own stupidity the marriage was broken off, Simeo had behaved manfully and allowed the matter to drop, *ukusula*, instead of creating a fuss. In all this Mwamba was not concerned with Simeo as such, although I know personally that he was disappointed that Simeo had not married his daughter. Rather he was concerned to state how a good son-in-law ought to behave, and to show by implication how far the behaviour of the present defendant deviated from these norms. Here his argument was that the defendant had committed so glaring a breach of the norms of in-lawship that the young man was not only unfit to be considered as a son-in-law, but that by his conduct he had also estopped himself, so to speak, from recovering the sums of money he had expended.

The defendant's breach of the norms was shown in a number of ways. He had written a letter direct to his father-in-law, asking why his money had been returned to him. This was a gross discourtesy for, according to custom, all matters concerning the marriage arrangements have to be discussed through the channel of a nominated intermediary, known as *shibukombe*. Again, he had kept the girl at his house late at night, so that Mwamba was led to doubt his intentions. But while he listed these complaints against the young man, Mwamba was also careful to establish his own propriety, to show that he himself had acted in conformity with the norms attaching to the position of a father-in-law. He had also replied to his son-in-law by letter, but this, he argued, was a reaction reasonably to be expected, for his heart had suddenly become sore at the insult he had received. Thereafter he called together his fellow-*bakalamba* and his son-in-law so that they could hear and advise on the matter in the customary fashion. For, as Gluckman has shown,[1] in tribal societies where people are linked with one another in many ways through the same institutions, a law case or a dispute does not involve only the immediate participants to it. If the dispute is not quickly settled, it may ramify and spread friction throughout the whole group. Disputes thus tend to involve many people, and when a case arises there is a moral injunction to gather the local elders together so that they may settle it quickly and amicably. Here again, by acting as he did, and by admitting his own mistakes before the *bakalamba*, Mwamba was re-affirming the traditional norms of behaviour accepted amongst the tribes, and asserting at the same time the uprightness of his own conduct at the expense of the defendant.

Thus the argument is presented not in terms of specific rights and duties which are legally enforceable *per se*, but in terms of patterns of rightdoing and wrongdoing. To write a letter to one's father-in-law about the marriage arrangements is wrong, but it is not a legal wrong on which one can ground an action in an African court. Anyone who brought suit on such a flimsy pretext alone would be laughed out of court. The wrong only becomes significant in the context of legal action, as indicating a pattern of behaviour within the famework of a particular social relationship. I will return to this point shortly.

Mwamba's statement was thus directed towards showing that while he was an upright man whose conduct had conformed to customary norms of behaviour, his son-in-law's behaviour fell far short of these standards. And when the son-in-law replied, he too involved a similar line of argument. Mwamba had been angry because the young man took it upon himself to decide how much was to be paid for *cisungu*. But that was not the case, the young man said. The £5 he had sent was not for *cisungu* only.

---

[1] M. Gluckman, *The Judicial Process among the Barotse of Northern Rhodesia*, p. 16, et passim.

P

He was eager to have the matter discussed so that his father-in-law could decide how much should be added to it. Thus the young man did not attempt to deny the validity of the norms stated by Mwamba, or even to support his case by reference to other norms. On the contrary, he accepted the assumptions of Mwamba's argument, and tried to show how he had behaved as an upright son-in-law, whereas Mwamba had erred in refusing to allow his daughter to clean the house of her future husband.

In conformity with the views he was putting forward, the young man's attitude in court was extremely conciliatory. The breaking off of the marriage was none of his doing. It was Mwamba's fault, for he wished to marry his daughter elsewhere, and was trying to justify his action by accusing his son-in-law of wanting to 'destroy' the girl before her marriage. The action he had taken, therefore, had been forced upon him by his father-in-law. His attitude won him the approval of the Court Members who thought that with 'instruction' of the youth, the marriage might still be saved. By contrast, Mwamba and his wife showed themselves intransigent—conduct which earned them a sharp rebuke from the President of the court, and the court had no hesitation in finding in favour of the defendant.

IV

The *Case of the Aggrieved Friend* and the *Case of the Disrespectful Son-in-law* differ widely in their internal detail: but they have this in common, that they reveal the operation of a principle which is of fundamental importance for an understanding of the judicial process in African customary law.[1] Court Members and litigants alike operate not only with the same rules of law which regulate claims, but also with the same norms of behaviour, the same notions of how people ought to behave. Litigants describe their behaviour and evaluate it themselves in terms of commonly accepted norms, and they manipulate these norms to justify the propriety of their own conduct and at the same time to denigrate their opponents. In this way they provide the court with a kind of

---

[1] Gluckman has documented this principle in great detail for Barotse courts (*The Judicial Process among the Barotse*, op. cit.), and I have myself done so for African Urban Courts (*Juridical Techniques and the Judicial Process*, Rhodes-Livingstone Paper No. 23, 1954).

juridical tuning-fork which enables it to assess the behaviour or testimony of the litigants against the very norms they have them- selves invoked. The defendant in the *Case of the Disrespectful Son-in-law* attempted to show that he had acted at all times with customary deference for his father-in-law. If this was so then how could he, a Bemba claiming to act in conformity with Bemba custom, assert that the £3 he had given Mwamba was *ubuimashi*, which was part of the marriage payment, and not *matebeto*, which was part of a series of mutual gift exchanges. Viewed in this light, the judicial process becomes a kind of dialectic in which the litigants, working with the same premises as the Court Members, are led to admit, through the progress of the case, the error of their ways. The courts do not see their task simply as one of establishing the guilt of a party and punishing him for his wrong. They seek rather to proceed by bringing the parties themselves to recognize the nature of their wrong. Thus through breach the norms of society are reaffirmed.

In a separate paper [1] I have tried to work out some of the impli- cations of this principle for the judicial process in African cus- tomary law. But the principle also has implications which are important in a wider social context. Stemming from the mode of procedure it employs, the judgment of an African court is never simply a finding in terms of specific legal rights and duties; it is also a process in which judges and litigants alike work towards the reaffirmation of norms and values commonly recognized through- out the community. Thus the court is more than a court of law; it is a repository of the moral values of the community, and the Court Members are the upholders and arbiters of its moral stan- dards. If this is a correct assessment of the functions of an African court, how then do African courts continue to operate in the urban areas where, as we have seen, people are moved by widely divergent sets of interests and values? If the judicial process in African law is made to depend upon the acceptance by judges and litigants alike of a common body of norms, how does the system operate when the litigants are of different tribes and presumably follow different customs, or where traditional norms are in- appropriate to or do not cover the circumstances of some novel situation?

---

[1] Idem.

There are two problems to be considered. The first involves what lawyers call 'conflict of law', and arises through the dualism which exists in the legal structure of the Territory. Everyone, irrespective of race or creed, is subject to the laws in force in the Territory, and to the jurisdiction of its courts; but Africans are also bound by Native law and custom, recognition of which is provided for in the Charter of the British South Africa Company and later constitutional documents. They are also subject to the jurisdiction of the Native Courts which were set up or recognized under the Native Courts Ordinance of 1936. The recognition of Native law and custom has had the effect of bringing into being what is a system of personal laws. Instead of having a single system of law applicable to all Africans, each tribal group is deemed to retain its own body of laws and customs, and these continue to regulate the behaviour of its members when they leave their villages and come to the towns. So far as the Urban Courts are concerned, this means in effect that disputes before these courts will be settled in accordance with the law of the particular tribe or tribes involved.

In the two cases already cited here, the parties in each case were of the same tribe, and there was no conflict of law. But what of the case in which the parties support their claims by reference to different legal systems, where the rules of law or principles relied upon are opposed to one another? On *a priori* grounds it might be expected that where members of many different tribes are constantly interacting within the framework of a single community, the operation of a system of personal laws would pose very awkward problems for the Urban Courts. Yet this does not appear to be so. Although I have spent some considerable time listening to cases in these courts and in reading through case records and other documents, I have managed to collect very few records of cases involving a conflict of law.

Why is this? One explanation is that the comparative cultural homogeneity of the region as a whole enables the Urban Courts to administer a body of legal rules which is in fact common to most of the tribes of the Territory. In discussion Africans frequently refer to differences in custom which distinguish one tribe from another; but the customs invariably cited on these occasions, while often important in the context of a particular case, are rather badges of identity than statements of any legal rule. This point is brought out well in a note by Cunnison on the concept of custom amongst the Lunda of the Luapula Valley.[1] The Lunda state consists of a powerful Chief, known as Kazembe, and a number of territorial sub-chiefs. The whole area is thickly populated by the members of some twenty different tribes who have come from the surrounding plateau districts. Each tribe of the area is characterized by certain distinctive customs, although people of other tribes may in fact follow the same practices. Thus it is the custom of the Lungu to grow finger-millet as against the custom of the Lunda to grow cassava. It is the custom of the Lunda not to eat lion flesh on pain of death or madness, whereas it is the custom of the Luba to eat lion flesh as relish, and so on. As Cunnison points out, custom is indivisible in the sense that a certain body of customs is always associated with a particular tribe, while other bodies of custom are associated with other particular tribes. It is in this sense, too, that Africans on the Copperbelt speak of different tribal customs. Such customs may be invoked in the course of a case to assess the behaviour of a litigant, but rarely can they form in themselves the basis of legal action.

Thus while there are divergent tribal customs their existence does not markedly affect the broad uniformity of legal rule and doctrine as between the different tribes. But more important in explaining the general absence in the Urban Courts of cases involving a conflict of law, is a mode of hearing cases which appears to be common to all the tribal legal systems of the Territory, and which Gluckman relates to certain common features in the social structure of these tribes.[2]

As used by the jurist, the expression 'conflict of law' refers to that branch of the municipal law which comes into operation whenever a court is seized of a suit containing a foreign element. Its object is to determine for each type of case the particular system of law by reference to which the rights of the parties to the suit are to be ascertained. 'Conflict of law' in this sense is thus a body of principles which enables a court to decide what system of law is to govern a case when the claims of each party originate in different legal systems. But its operation and development as a

---

[1] Ian Cunnison, 'A Note on the Lunda concept of custom', *Rhodes-Livingstone Journal*, xiv (1954), pp. 20-9. Cf. M. Gluckman, *The Judicial Process among the Barotse of Northern Rhodesia*, ch. 4.

[2] Ibid., passim.

branch of the law is only made possible by a mode of procedure in which pleading has become a technical and refined art. The conflict of law is set out immediately in the pleas of the respective parties, and legal argument follows on what law ought to govern the dispute. This is markedly different from the procedure which obtains in an African Urban Court. Here there are no technical pleadings or other devices whereby extraneous issues are pruned away prior to the trial, so that when the hearing commences, the legal issues involved may be presented to the court in a straightforward fashion, on which the court then hears legal argument. Litigants in an Urban Court rarely speak about the law; they address themselves to the 'facts', leaving it to the court to decide whether the 'facts' disclose a cause of action and what the appropriate remedy should be. Although therefore legal argument is rarely explicit, the drift of the argument itself is always clear from the way in which the 'facts' are presented. For each statement of fact is at the same time 'loaded with ethical implication' (Gluckman). When, for example, the plaintiff in the *Case of the Aggrieved Friend* described how she had sought 'medicine' to purify the defendant following the death of her child, she was not just making a bald statement of fact; she was asserting that this was the kind of behaviour one could reasonably expect of a friend. She was building up her case to show that while her own behaviour conformed to the norms of friendship, that of her friend did not.

Gluckman has shown for the Barotse that their courts are primarily concerned to re-establish harmony in those cases which arise out of kinship and similar relationships. As we see from the two cases I have cited here, Urban Courts show a similar concern. In the *Case of the Disrespectful Son-in-law*, the court was eager to reconcile the two parties, and offered to 'instruct' the young man so that in future he would show proper deference for his father-in-law. It desisted from this attempt when it became convinced by the intransigence of Mwamba and his wife that no harmonious relationship could exist between them and the young man. This concern with social relationships rather than with right-and-duty-bearing units, which form the core of English legal procedure, compel the Urban Courts to take a much broader view of a particular case than would a European Magistrate. An Urban Court deals with patterns of rightdoing and wrongdoing within the context of a given social relationship, rather than with the enforcement of specific legal rights and duties.

It is this factor which explains most satisfactorily the general absence of cases in the conflict of law. Tribal custom may be widely divergent in many cases, but on the norms of behaviour which underlie a given social relationship there is general consensus. Lozi and Bemba may differ, for example, in their modes of contracting a marriage and in the legal incidents which attach to such a union, but they are in complete agreement that mutual respect, aid and co-operation are among the supreme values of the new relationship created. And because an Urban Court is primarily concerned with these supreme values, it becomes possible for the majority of disputes to be settled by methods which are traditional, yet involve no reference to any particular system of tribal law.

V

We have seen now how Urban Courts are able to work and to handle disputes in which parties of different tribes are involved, because judges and litigants are operating for the most part with the same norms and values. In the main these norms and values derive from the tribal system: they are part of tribal culture. At the same time the courts function in a social system which is in the process of rapid development. In this situation the traditional norms may no longer be appropriate, or may be unacceptable to a section of the urban population. New forms of social relationship come into being for which the old norms offer no adequate guide to behaviour, and so forth. Here the problem is how the Urban Courts, which are bound by their constitution to administer a system of law rooted in the past, can develop that law to meet the novel sets of circumstance which may arise in a Copperbelt community.

In its wider aspect, of course, the problem is not peculiar to the Copperbelt nor to the Urban Courts. For fundamental to every legal system is the problem of achieving some balance between the needs of stability and the needs of social change. It is one of the paradoxes of law, as Dean Pound has observed, that it must be stable yet it cannot stand still. Part of the solution to the general problem is generally to be found in the division of function of

judiciary and legislature, where it is the task of the judiciary to
'apply' the law, and the task of the legislative body to amend old
law or introduce new laws. But on the Copperbelt, in the absence
of an Urban Native Authority or other body equipped with legislative powers, both these tasks are thrust upon the courts alone.

I have shown in separate papers on the Urban Courts that this
dual task imposes heavy strains on the judges. Caught between the
injunction to administer customary law on the one hand and the
necessity to create new law to meet the needs of an urban situation on the other, the Court Members become involved in a
series of contradictions which sometimes have the effect of stifling
the judicial process.[1] Nevertheless the developmental process is
never completely stifled, for the judicial process carries within
itself the possibilities of change and legal development. It is this
problem which I wish to examine in the present section.

We have seen how in the cases considered here litigants seek to
justify their behaviour by appealing to traditional norms. They
seek to show that their conduct conformed to customary standards of behaviour. But in doing this they do not attempt to
pose as saints or paragons of virtue. The standard invoked is
always that of the reasonable man, and the argument presented
is always in terms of reasonable expectation, of how a man might
reasonably be expected to act in a particular situation. For example,
when Mwamba received a letter from his son-in-law saying that
Mwamba wished to marry his daughter to another man, he
himself replied to the young man by letter instead of sending
shibukombe, the go-between. Here Mwamba was in the wrong, as
he later admitted to his fellow-*bakalamba;* but he had acted out of
anger for his 'heart was made sore' by the behaviour of the son-
in-law. Here he was arguing, in effect, that although he was himself guilty of a breach of custom, his sudden display of anger was
perfectly reasonable because the behaviour of his son-in-law
reflected on his dignity as a father-in-law and as an Elder.

Thus litigants seek to vindicate themselves by establishing themselves as reasonable men, and they do this by appeal to the norms
and customs of the group. Mwamba explained how after the
engagement of his daughter he had sent her to sweep out the hut

---

[1] For fuller discussion of this point see my *Juridical Techniques and the Judicial
Process*, pp. 31–4.

of her fiancé, and how his own wife prepared food which was sent down to the house of their son-in-law. This was old Bemba custom, and by enumerating these things Mwamba was showing that he was behaving as a Bemba father-in-law is expected to do. In this way customs, beliefs, and presumptions, none of which would be legally enforceable in themselves, are constantly being channelled into the judicial process, when they are seized upon by the Court Members in order to assess the behaviour and the claims of the litigants. Working with precisely the same tools as the litigants, the Court Members themselves are able to import into their judgments their experience of the whole way-of-life of the people—their habits and customs, their ethical code and system of knowledge. Untrammelled by the fiction of judicial ignorance, the Court Members bring to their task their whole experience of society, which now includes the Copperbelt as well as the tribal areas from which they came. Thus new customs can be recognized, or changes introduced in the law, where they are capable of restatement in terms of indigenous law and ethics.

In order to illustrate this process I cite briefly the following cases. In the *Case of the Butcher's Assistant* all the parties lived in the African Township of Fisenge, a few miles outside Luanshya, where the defendant owned a butchery. One day the plaintiff sought out his kinsman, who was the butcher's assistant, and asked him if he would sell a cow through the butchery. The assistant agreed, and some time later brought the sum of £8 15s. to the owner of the cow. The owner of the cow was angry at the small sum realized from the sale of the meat, for he had bought the beast for £8 10s. And how could the sale of a slaughtered cow show a profit of only five shillings? Feeling that he had been cheated, he brought the case to the Urban Court. The owner of the butchery claimed that he knew nothing of the matter, while his assistant argued that the cow was young and still undeveloped. Moreover, he added, when the beast had been killed the plaintiff had removed all the innards for himself. The Court Members were unconvinced by this argument, and asked why he had agreed to sell it in the first place when he saw it was so small and would bring in a low return. The Court Members discussed the case between themselves at some length. The President of the court, who had then served as a Court Member at Luanshya for fourteen years, led the discussion. He argued that if one sold a slaughtered cow, one could not fail to make a profit. Were it a big beast, he said, here on the Copperbelt the sale of the meat would have brought in nearly £50. His own view of the case was that the owner of the butchery was practising *bucenjeshi*, cunning or deceit. He and his assistant had come to an agreement between themselves to deprive the owner of the cow of the profit to which he was entitled. Two of the other Court Members shared this view, but the fourth was more hesitant. It was sometimes very difficult where Africans are concerned, he said. Sometimes a man would take meat for himself, and then he found the money he received was less than he expected. The President disagreed. He said that he was well acquainted with the place where they killed the cattle, and knew the market prices. From the sale of a cow a man would make much money. After further discussion they all agreed that the owner of the cow was entitled to a further £3 as his profit on the beast. Passing judgment, the court told the assistant that he was being 'given a case' on account of his deceitfulness. The sale of the meat had brought in much more money, but he had 'eaten' that money himself and would pay the plaintiff £3. The butcher's assistant accepted the judgment but added that although the owner of the beast was his maternal uncle when the cow was brought to him, now there was no relationship between them.

The second case involved the sale of a tea-cart and was heard in the Urban Court of Appeal which was set up on the Copperbelt in 1953. The appellant Nshindano said that he agreed to purchase a tea-cart from the respondent Greenwell for £30. He had paid £11 as a deposit and was to pay the balance within two months. At the end of the first month the balance outstanding was still unpaid and Greenwell took the cart, sold it to another, and claimed interest on the profit Nshindano had made in the period the cart was in his possession. The Urban Court of first instance found for Greenwell. Nshindano appealed on the grounds that if Greenwell was entitled to claim interest then he, Greenwell, was also liable to pay interest on the £11 paid over as a deposit. The appellant argued further that since he had not failed to carry out his part of the bargain the respondent had no grounds on which to support a case. The appeal was upheld. The judgment of the Appeal Court is set out in the case-record as follows:

. . . the respondent and the appellant made an agreement that the latter was to pay the rest of the money at the end of two months. The respondent did not stick to his part of the agreement but arranged with somebody else to buy the tea-cart. After this the appellant had to claim back his deposit of £11 since he had not failed to carry out his side of the bargain. He had not been given the chance to pay the money outstanding and he had been evicted. After this it is surely unreasonable for the respondent to claim interest on the profit made during the tenure of the cart by the appellant. It would be in order if the appellant had failed to fulfil his promise. But if the appellant had failed to pay the amount as agreed, the respondent should have come to the court where the terms of the agreement would have been enforced.

The economy of the tribal societies, within which customary law had its origins, was dominantly a subsistence economy. There were some tribes, of course, that had achieved a relatively complex economy which was marked by a developed internal trade. For example, the Lozi of the Central Barotse Plain formed a powerful and politically centralized state made up of many tribes, between whom an elaborate system of trading existed. Yet even amongst the Lozi, whose legal system was among the richest and most intricate in the Territory, contract formed the least developed branch of the customary law. Yet today on the Copper-belt, in the towns that lie along the railway strip, and in the rural areas too, there are many Africans who earn their livelihood in trade and commerce. The two cases just cited reflect the way in which Africans are coming increasingly to participate in commercial enterprises. This state of affairs creates fresh sources of dispute: new legal interests arise for the protection of which the assistance of the Urban Courts is sought.[1] Cases of this nature therefore have to be settled in accordance with customary law, since no other body of law is available. How do the courts cope with this problem?

The answer, I believe, lies in those characteristics of the judicial processes which we have already considered. Faced with a set of facts, however novel or unprecedented, an Urban Court has to make some attempt to order them and to pass judgment upon them. Some decision is necessary, and the fact that the vast majority of decisions do appear to satisfy the litigants springs

---

[1] It is of course possible for an African to bring a civil suit in a Magistrate's Court, but the number of civil suits involving Africans only which are heard in these courts appears to be negligible.

from the fact that an Urban Court is not simply a court of law: it is also a court of morals and of equity. This emerged clearly in the *Cases of the Aggrieved Friend* and the *Disrespectful Son-in-law*; it also lies at the core of the *Case of the Butcher's Assistant* and the *Case of the Tea-cart*.

In the *Case of the Butcher's Assistant* the Court Members argued that nobody goes to the expense of starting a business without the intention that the business shall pay. Every businessman aims at making a profit. Was it reasonably to be expected therefore, the Court Members inquired of the owner of the butchery, that a man could sell the meat of a cow in the normal way without showing a substantial profit? Since in their experience this seemed most unlikely, they were led to conclude that the behaviour of the butcher or his assistant, or of both together, had been motivated by *bucenjeshi*, cunning or deceit. Deceit is not a term of purely legal import; it also carries strong overtones of moral opprobrium. And it is the moral element which the Urban Courts invoke in applying the concept of *bucenjeshi* to a wide variety of situations in order to develop the law. Thus in the present case the court was able to give recognition to the claim for a reasonable profit, because it would not countenance a man being allowed to profit by his own wrongdoing.

Equitable doctrine was similarly invoked in the *Case of the Tea-cart*. As I have said, the law of contract is the least developed branch of tribal jurisprudence, and it is interesting to notice that in the present case the court made no effort to inquire into the nature of the title passed by the agreement between the parties. It did not hold, as conceivably it might have done, that the respondent was guilty of a breach of contract for which the appellant might claim damages or even specific performance. The court confined itself to the issue raised by the plaintiff in the court of first instance, and held that it would be unreasonable, that is inequitable, to allow him to claim interest on the profits made by the appellant while the cart was in the appellant's possession, when the respondent was himself guilty of a prior wrong. It does not seem inappropriate to see in the case an application of the maxim that 'he who comes to equity must come with clean hands'.

VI

Cases of the kind I have just been considering involve legal claims of a kind uncommon, if not wholly unknown, in African customary law. In each case the court reached its decision by reformulating the claims in terms of indigenous ethics. Cases selected from the field of domestic law would show a similar process at work, where the courts are able to give recognition to certain changes in the patterns of relations between husband and wife by considering these patterns in the light of the general moral value which tribal society placed upon this relationship. But the judicial process carries within itself a further potential source of legal growth and development. For the constant channelling into the judicial process of customs, beliefs, and practices, which are not legally enforceable in themselves, enables the Urban Courts to give increasing recognition to 'Copperbelt practice'.[1] Thus claims in respect of marriage payments or actions for seduction which in some cases would not have been recognized in the tribal law of the parties involved, and in others would be far in excess of anything that a tribal court would sanction, are upheld by Urban Courts on the grounds that the upbringing of a girl in the towns often represents a considerable financial investment on the part of the parents which ought to be recognized. Similarly, orders for compensation or sentences of fine and imprisonment are made in terms of urban practice, not in terms of the practice prevailing in remote tribal areas. In this way there is gradually emerging a recognized body of urban 'customary' law in terms of which urban African litigants present their claims.

Yet one must be careful not to press the argument too far. While it is true that the Urban Courts have been able to develop the law to cope with many novel sets of circumstances, and with novel sets of relationships and patterns of behaviour, the very nature of urban societal growth and the present organization of the courts themselves set limits upon the developmental process. We have already had occasion to observe[2] how the Urban Courts have more than once been subjected to intense criticism by African representatives, and we have related their attacks to the struggle

---

[1] See, for example, the discussion of the *Case of the Burnt Hut* in my *Juridical Techniques and the Judicial Process*, p. 30.

[2] See above, p. 79.

going on for political leadership within the urban communities. But the criticisms levelled against the courts are also a reflection of increasing social differentiation, and an indication that the population of a Copperbelt community no longer operates with a common set of norms of behaviour. From time to time cases are heard in the courts which make it apparent that the litigants are appealing to norms irreconcilably opposed to those of the traditional tribal system. In matrimonial disputes, in particular, it is common to hear young men protesting in the most vehement terms—though unavailingly—against the power of the wife's kin to break up marriage and home. It is interesting to recall in this connection, that in 1950 Copperbelt delegates to the Western Province Provincial Council introduced a motion calling for the abolition of the principle of matriliny, around which the social organization of many of the tribes of Northern Rhodesia is built. The motion was lost; but it is evident that given this process of increasing social diversification within the urban communities, a judicial process which is based on the principle that Court Members and litigants alike are operating with the same norms and standards must ultimately break down, or at least undergo radical transformation.

There is no evidence at present that such a breakdown is immediately imminent. One possible index of the impending collapse of the system would be a relatively high proportion of cases where there was an appeal against the decision of the Urban Court of first instance. Before 1953 all appeals from the decisions of the Urban Court lay to the District Officer or District Commissioner, and ultimately to the High Court. Today appeals are brought before an Urban African Court of Appeal which is composed of the Presidents of the Urban Courts, and which travels on circuit round each of the Copperbelt centres once every three months. It is still too early to say whether this innovation will lead to an increase in the number of cases taken to appeal: certainly, what has been most striking thus far in the history of the Urban Courts is that, considering the amount of litigation they deal with annually, the number of cases in which there is an appeal is very small indeed.[1] The reasons for this are fairly complex,

---

[1] See Table 3 in Epstein, *The Administration of Justice and the Urban African*, p. 40. This showed that in the total of over 7,000 cases handled by the five

but undoubtedly a factor of major importance is the fact that Court Members and litigants, as I have attempted to show, are working with the same body of norms, beliefs, and attitudes. Given the kind of legal procedure I have outlined above, a litigant may express dissatisfaction with the decision of the Court, but in most cases he has little room for further complaint, for the whole aim of the court's inquiry is to lead him to see for himself the error of his ways, or at least the weakness of his arguments. In explaining his case he has put his own moral evaluation on the facts, and it is in terms of this evaluation that his behaviour is measured.

Summing up, therefore, we can say that in the vast majority of cases the Urban Courts arrive at decisions which still appear to give general satisfaction to the litigants, and they are able to do this because there is an underlying consensus about the norms of behaviour associated with particular forms of social relationship. In the main, though not entirely, these norms form part of an ancient tribal heritage, and appear to be common to most of the indigenous peoples of the region. This close link between the Urban Courts and tribal culture is further emphasized in the current mode of appointing Court Members from the tribal areas. The present Court Members are all nominees of important chiefs whose names they carry in the urban areas. In this connection it is worth recalling the words of the Court President in the *Case of the Disrespectful Son-in-law*. Reprimanding Mwamba, he said: 'The way you answer is not good. Do you think that here we are sitting at *chitenge*, the Elders' shelter? No, we are *kwisano*, at the Chief's quarters.' The Court Members provide in some cases an important link between the urban dwellers and the tribal chiefs, and they themselves see it as one of the most important aspects of their task to uphold and reaffirm the norms and values of tribal society. The evidence from the Urban Courts suggests that over a wide area of the social field these norms and values continue to operate in regulating the behaviour of urban Africans, and that within that area the authority of traditional spokesmen is still widely recognized.

Urban Courts of the Copperbelt during 1950 the number of appeals lodged was 69, or less than 1 per cent.

CHAPTER VII

TRIBALISM AND THE URBAN SOCIAL SYSTEM

THE growth of large, modern towns in Africa represents one major aspect of the revolutionary changes now overtaking all African society. But while 'social change' has been an important theme in much recent work in the field of African sociology, there have as yet been relatively few intensive investigations into the problems of African urban society.[1] As a field of study, African urbanism is still largely virgin territory, in which much of the preliminary spade-work has yet to be done. So the present study, which is confined to an analysis of African political institutions on the Northern Rhodesia Copperbelt, is essentially exploratory in character. In this chapter, therefore, I have tried to set out some of the ideas which seem to me to emerge from my analysis, and which may be relevant to the understanding of urban communities emerging elsewhere in Africa.

There are always certain dangers inherent, I think, in the approach of the anthropologist. Caught up in the minutiae of events which make up the social life of the community he is studying, he sometimes finds it difficult to avoid over-emphasizing the unique features of 'his' community at the expense of features held in common with similar communities in less 'exotic' regions. Urban communities in Africa do have their unique features and specific problems, but in other respects they often reveal startling similarities to urban communities which have grown up outside Africa. It may be instructive, therefore, by way of introduction, to glance briefly at the way in which an American anthropologist approached his study of a slum district in one of the Eastern cities of the United States.[2]

Whyte carried out his study in a slum district, known as

---

[1] See the valuable survey by Merran McCulloch of recent and current studies in this field, *Industrialization in Africa*, a report prepared by the International African Institute for the Social Sciences Division of UNESCO, and presented to the Conference on the Social Impact of Industrialization in Africa held at Abidjan in October, 1954.

[2] W. F. Whyte, *Street Corner Society*, University of Chicago Press, Chicago (1943).

Cornerville, which was inhabited almost exclusively by Italian immigrants.

To the rest of the city [Whyte remarks] it is a mysterious, dangerous, and depressing area. Cornerville is only a few minutes' walk from fashionable High Street, but the High Street inhabitant who takes that walk passes from the familiar to the unknown.

Respectable people have access to a limited body of information upon Cornerville. They may learn that it is one of the most congested areas in the United States. It is one of the chief points of interest in any tour organized to show upper-class people the bad housing conditions in which lower-class people live. Through sight-seeing or statistics one may discover that bathtubs are rare, that children overrun the narrow and neglected streets, that the juvenile delinquency rate is high, that crime is prevalent among adults. . . . Those who are concerned with Cornerville seek through a general survey to answer questions that require the most intimate knowledge of local life. The only way to gain such knowledge is to live in Cornerville and participate in the activities of its people. One who does that finds that the district reveals itself to him in an entirely different light. The buildings, streets, and alleys that formerly represented dilapidation and physical congestion recede to form a familiar background for the actors upon the Cornerville scene.

With certain minor emendations, Whyte's description could readily fit many of the urban communities of modern Africa. Like Cornerville, the population of an urban African community is an immigrant one, though these immigrants have a widely different background from, and more diversified origins than, those in Cornerville. Again, throughout southern Africa, urban Africans live in segregated residential areas, generally known as locations, which are as unfamiliar to the European population of the town as Cornerville was to the middle-class residents of Eastern City. Finally, we may note how closely Whyte's description of social conditions in Cornerville parallels many of the available accounts of African urban life: poverty,[1] inadequate housing,[2] and general conditions of squalor are the almost

---

[1] 'The most outstanding single characteristic of non-European urban communities, and particularly of urban Natives, is their poverty.' See Ellen Hellmann, 'Urban Areas' in *Handbook of Race Relations in South Africa*, Oxford University Press, London (1949), pp. 268 et seq.

[2] Ibid., pp. 253–7. For West Africa see, for example, K. A. Busia, *Report on a Social Survey of Sekondi-Takoradi*, Crown Agents for the Colonies, London (1950), pp. 5–10.

Q

universal features of African life in the towns. But in our concern to document these social conditions, I think we sometimes tend to overlook the fact that a new system of social relations is also growing up in the towns. The urban African community is not 'a formidable mass of confusion, a social chaos'. On the contrary, as Whyte found in Cornerville, it has its own form of social organization, and this organization provides a general framework for the understanding of a good deal of the behaviour of its inhabitants. The analysis of this organization is the major task now confronting sociologists working in urban African communities.

In speaking of 'organization' I refer here to the pattern of observable regularities of behaviour by reference to which people are seen to order their social relationships amongst themselves. But the analysis of this pattern presents considerable problems because the form of social organization with which we are dealing is an emergent rather than an established one. Fluidity and richness of contrast are the characteristics which perhaps most clearly stamp the developing town. Thus a major characteristic of the African population of the Copperbelt is its high degree of mobility. People move freely between town and country, and between town and town. If we had data on the movement of people within any particular town we should probably find that the instability is even greater, and that on the average a family stays in any one particular area for only a very short time.[1] Such mobility obviously affects the growth of stable urban social groupings and institutions. A further problem, and for the present discussion a more important one, is that social relationships develop within a setting which is itself continually changing, and they are also affected by increasing diversification of custom and standards. Consequently, as Hellmann observes of the South African situation, there is no one 'pattern' of African urban life, there is no one 'type' of urban African.[2] Fallers' remark that much of what we observe appears to be a patchwork of diverse and conflicting elements is as apposite to the Copperbelt as it appears to be to the Kingdom of Busoga.[3] In this kind of situation, Fallers

---

[1] J. C. Mitchell, 'Africans in Industrial Towns in Northern Rhodesia' (unpublished MS.).

[2] Op. cit., p. 271.

[3] Lloyd Fallers, 'The Predicament of the Modern African Chief', *American Anthropologist*, vol. 57, no. 2 (1955), p. 292.

remarks, 'institutions are constantly getting in each other's way, and individuals are constantly being institutionally required to do conflicting things'. But what is important to note is that, in the main, these conflicting elements do not hinder the effective working of the urban system as a whole. They do not lead to a breakdown of the system because they operate within it. Thus I would suggest that the deeper understanding of the urban social process in Africa requires a formulation in which inconsistency and disharmony are recognized not only as an integral part of the nascent social system, but also an important source of its dynamic.

The notion that inconsistency or contradiction may form an integral part of a system is not novel in anthropological literature. Evans-Pritchard's analysis of Zande beliefs about witchcraft, oracles, and magic provides a classic exposition of this theme.[1] The vast body of Zande beliefs about these matters forms a coherent ideological system, perfectly intelligible once its basic premises and inner logic have been grasped. As Evans-Pritchard points out, it is only when the beliefs are presented as 'a conceptual system that their insufficiencies and contradictions become apparent'.[2] Because in real life the beliefs function in 'bits' rather than as a whole, Evans-Pritchard is able to show how contradictions are 'contained' by the system through the principle of situational selection. In any given situation a single event may evoke a number of different and contradictory beliefs among different persons: each selects what is most relevant from his particular standpoint. In this way the possibility of situational selection serves to reinforce the system of belief as a whole. The system is, indeed, 'self-sealing', so that logical objections or personal experience which might seem to deny the validity of certain beliefs are themselves explained in terms of the system, and in fact strengthen it.

The kind of system which Evans-Pritchard was analysing among the Azande may perhaps be characterized as 'closed' in the sense that within the context of Zande society the whole complex of beliefs about witchcraft and magic was both self-contained and self-perpetuating. For example, there were sceptics among the

---

[1] E. E. Evans-Pritchard, *Witchcraft, Oracles, and Magic among the Azande*, Clarendon Press, Oxford (1937).

[2] Ibid., p. 540.

Azande who would point to the deceits practised by magicians; but their doubts extended only to individuals whose obvious human failings left unimpaired the belief in the 'genuine' magician and in magic forces. Here scepticism, far from presenting a challenge to the system of belief, actually operates to support it. The system is a 'closed' one because it provides no avenue for internal development and change. In antithesis to this, an 'open' system is one in which fresh sources of conflict are continually generated in the developmental process itself: here conflict and its resolution provide part of the momentum to further social adjustment and change. In this sense the nascent social system of the new town provides an example of an 'open' system. In the remainder of this chapter I have attempted to illustrate and develop this formulation by considering briefly the place of tribalism within the urban social system.

The views expressed on the place of 'tribalism' in the modern situation often appear to be diametrically opposed. On the one hand, for example, Parker writes of the urban situation in Kenya that there are definite signs of the passing of tribal cohesion, and observes that new forms of social discipline are to a measure replacing tribal sanctions.[1] On the other hand, Busia notes that loyalty to the tribe and home village remains strong even among those who have lived in the towns for many years. He adds that one result of this is that very few of the large population manifest civic loyalty or responsibility for the new towns in which they make their living.[2] In a recent discussion of the question, Professor Harlow refers to a widely held view that tribalism in Africa is on the way out, and asks whether this assumption is valid. 'We may be misled,' he remarks, 'if we mistake revolutionary changes in tribal custom for decay.' The potency of 'resurgent tribalism' should not be underestimated, he argues. On the contrary, 'its dynamic power should be harnessed to the task of nation building'.[3]

There is of course an explanation of these divergences of viewpoint which will at once spring to the mind. Over a continent

---

[1] M. Parker, *Political and Social Aspects of Municipal Government in Kenya*, unpublished MS. quoted in McCulloch, op. cit., p. 52.

[2] Quoted by McCulloch, ibid., p. 23.

[3] Vincent Harlow, 'Tribalism in Africa', *Journal of African Administration*, vii, 1 (1955), pp. 17–20.

marked by wide regional differences, where there is no uniform pattern of imperial dominium or of industrial and commercial development, and where the degree of European settlement is an important variable, it is clearly to be expected that there will be a wide range of variation in the process of urbanization itself. On this view, divergences of opinion between different writers may simply reflect the different conditions, or patterns of development, prevailing in different parts of Africa. But a further possible explanation is that the divergent views held on the scope of tribalism in the modern situation are correct in themselves, but represent only a partial view of that situation: they are an expression partly of ambiguities in the concept of tribalism itself, partly of ambiguities in the emerging social system of the town.

The nature of these ambiguities is to be seen clearly in Hellmann's account of African urban life in the Union of South Africa. Dr. Hellmann notes a suggestion frequently made that the African in the towns is becoming aware of wider political loyalties than the tribe: 'Through his many contacts with Natives of other tribes and through perceiving more keenly the inequalities and restrictions he suffers in common with them, he is tending to become a Bantu citizen, and not remain merely a tribesman with special loyalties.' Dr. Hellmann observes that urban life yields many instances of harmonious co-operation between members of different tribes in the most diverse activities. Nevertheless, she adds, a constant undercurrent of strong tribal feeling still exists: 'The customs of other tribes are referred to with contempt, and each man avers that sorcery is more prevalent in tribes other than his own.'[1] In other words, the urban African remains a tribesman, and yet is not a tribesman.

In our study of Luanshya, we come upon an apparent contradiction of precisely the same kind. Briefly, it is this: in our account of the growth of Luanshya we saw the political development of the community in terms of the emergence of new groups and associations and new social personalities, and the forms of authority associated with them. More precisely, we noted a tendency for new groups to emerge in opposition to existing

---

[1] Ellen Hellmann, 'The Native in the Towns' in *The Bantu-Speaking Tribes of South Africa*, ed. by I. Schapera, Routledge, London (1937), pp. 405–34, at p. 432.

bodies, or at least to come into conflict with them. Thus in considering the growth of the Urban Advisory Council at Luanshya we saw, for example, how over the period of a decade the Tribal Elders and the Tribal Representatives who had formerly dominated the Council were gradually ousted from membership by an emerging urban leadership. By 1953, when elections to the Council were conducted for the first time by popular ballot, only one of the original Tribal Representatives remained. He had been a member of the Council for close on fifteen years, but, significantly, after the new Council re-assembled he ceased to attend its meetings almost at once. The new Council was made up almost exclusively of trade union officials, Congress officials, and other leading urban personalities. The clear breach with the earlier Councils is well brought out in the fact that for the first time in its history the Council was able to dispense with the services of an interpreter at its meetings. The composition of the Council is set out in Table 14 which should be compared with Tables 4 and 5. Thus the evidence from the Urban Advisory Council points to the sharp decline of tribal authority in the field of political representation within the town. The evidence from the Urban Housing Board confirms this view. For instance, in 1949 a conference of Location Superintendents discussed ways and means of electing members to the new Housing Boards to be set up under the terms of the Urban Housing Ordinance. One Location Superintendent considered that the time was not ripe for elected Boards, and felt that the average African still clung to his respect for the Tribal Elders. The introduction of fully elected Boards was only likely to benefit a small section of the African community, he said. Another speaker, who expressed an open mind in the matter, confidently anticipated that the men who were at present acting as Elders would most likely re-appear on the Housing Boards after elections. The Urban Housing Board at Luanshya was established in 1953, and there have now been two popular elections. Individual Elders have stood for election, but in no case has a Tribal Elder been returned. Thus the composition of representative bodies in the town would tend to suggest that 'tribalism' is no longer a political force in this urban society. But when we look at other aspects of the social and political system of the town we see that in fact 'tribalism' is still a most important factor. This is brought out most clearly in our analysis of the position occupied in the community by the Urban Court. The evidence from the Urban Court shows that not only do the majority of urban Africans regulate much of their social behaviour in terms of tribal norms and values, but that in this sphere they also respect the authority of Court Members who are the nominees of important Tribal Chiefs. To resolve this contradiction it is first necessary to examine a little more closely the different ways in which the term 'tribalism' is used.

For most Africans in Northern Rhodesia to be a member of a tribe means to be involved in a complex set of social relations which centre on the social personalities of chief, hereditary councillors, village headmen and elders, and so forth. In addition, it means, at least in theory, that a man's behaviour will tend to conform to certain type-patterns which are prescribed by the customs of the tribe. The total body of custom provides the basis of those mutual expectations which are necessary to social intercourse. It is in this sense that Harlow speaks of a tribe as a social, economic, and political unit. Thus the concept of 'tribalism' has two distinct points of reference. On the one hand, its application is intra-tribal and refers to the persistence of, or continued attachment to, tribal custom. On the other, it refers to the persistence of loyalties and values, which stem from a particular form of social organization, and which operate today within a social system much wider than that of the tribe. These two aspects must be carefully distinguished, since it is clear that there may be 'revolutionary changes in custom' while the tribe itself remains an important category of interaction within a wider social system. It is in the second sense that I speak of 'tribalism' on the Copperbelt.

On the towns of the Copperbelt Africans can no longer live and work together on the basis of kinship and affinity as they do in their rural villages, and many of the customs and features of the tribal system fall into desuetude. Nevertheless, 'tribalism' continues to exert a powerful influence on African urban life. The African population of a Copperbelt town is both extremely heterogeneous and polyglot, so that personal association often tends to take place on the basis of cultural and linguistic affinity. The mutual unintelligibility of many of the Bantu languages of the region creates obvious barriers to intercourse across tribal lines, and many prejudices and stereotypes develop around the various tribes which serve to reinforce tribal solidarity in the towns. Again, although there is a considerable degree of inter-tribal marriage, Copperbelt Africans still tend in the majority of cases to marry within the tribe.[1] Finally, one of the most popular sources of entertainment on Sundays is the tribal dancing in which teams of young men accompany their dances with ribald songs directed against the customs and characteristics of other tribes. Taking one of these teams as a starting point for the analysis of urban social relationships, Mitchell has been able to show how certain tribes are linked together through historical connections or linguistic and cultural affinities, or through special joking relationships. Further, he has been able to demonstrate that from the point of view of any one tribe the others can be arranged in an order which reflects the social distance between them.[2] In this way the network of tribal relationships operating within the town provides a framework by means of which any African is able to fix his relationship with any other. Here therefore 'tribalism' is a category of interaction in day-to-day social intercourse.

But at the same time the African in the town is involved in a variety of sets of social relationships, many of which perforce cut across tribal lines. A second source of the confusion which sur-rounds the discussion of 'tribalism' arises from the failure to distinguish those sets of relations in which tribal factors remain important, and in those in which other factors are dominant. In its common connotation 'tribalism' tends to become a unitary concept, and carries the implicit assumption that, because the evidence points to the persistence in the towns of strong tribal loyalties, those loyalties will operate with the same strength over the total field of social relations in which the urban African is involved. This difficulty is avoided if we approach the town as a field of social relations which is made up of sets of social relations of different kinds, each of which covers a distinct sphere of social interaction, and forms a sub-system. Although it is the inter-relations of these various sets which make up the total system, each set may have a certain measure of autonomy so that the tempo and character of change are not evenly distributed over the whole field. Indeed, one of the points which emerges most strik-ingly from the present study is the way in which the tempo and

[1] Information supplied by Dr. Mitchell, based on a survey which he carried out at Luanshya in 1952.

[2] J. C. Mitchell, *The Kalela Dance*, Rhodes-Livingstone Paper No. 27 (1957).

character of change may differ significantly within the different sub-systems.

The thesis being advanced here is well illustrated in the changing pattern of African leadership in the towns. Over the years representatives whose appointment was on a tribal basis have gradually been supplanted by men whose prestige and authority among the new urban dwellers owed little to high status enjoyed within a tribal polity, but derived from their education and conscious approximation to European standards. When African trade unions came to be formed in Northern Rhodesia it was men of this stamp who emerged as leaders, and the authority they enjoyed was reflected in the abolition of tribal representation on the mines. We have seen that the explanation of the eclipse of the Tribal Representatives lay partly in the intercalary position they occupied within the authority structure of the mine, partly in the fact that trade union growth and activity relates to that part of the field of social relations which is primarily concerned on the Copperbelt with the relations of White employer and Black employee. At the same time, while the relationship of employer and employee is fundamental in the social system of the Copperbelt, and ultimately must come to affect all other social relationships, there are parts of the field which are to some extent 'sealed off': here the tempo of change is much slower and its character less obvious. The set of relations which makes up the domestic system provides a good instance of this. There is abundant evidence to show that here too there have been profound changes, and that under urban conditions the traditional system of domestic relations is undergoing a continuous process of modification and readjustment. But the break with traditional practice is less radical than in the sphere, for example, of political relations. Of course many of the customs and characteristic features of the indigenous system have been abandoned, or have become impracticable under urban conditions.[1] But many of the customs, if sometimes difficult to comply with, are not fundamentally incompatible with the conditions of urban life. They continue to be adhered to by sophisticated and unsophisticated alike.[2] Thus the

---

[1] See, for example, Godfrey Wilson's account of Bemba marriage in Broken Hill, op. cit., ch. xi.

[2] See also, Z. K. Matthews, 'The Tribal Spirit among Educated South Africans', *Man*, xxxv (1935), no. 26. Professor Matthews, who is himself an

African trade union leader who marries may pay bride-wealth to his parents-in-law, may be most meticulous in his observance of the in-law and other domestic taboos, and may apply customary precepts in his relations with his children, all without doing violence to his rôle of Union official: these various activities relate to quite distinct sets of relations and no necessary conflict of rôles is involved. It would be potentially much more difficult were he to attempt to combine his rôle of Union leader with that of tribal elder, for essentially these rôles are in contradiction and would inevitably clash. No such clash of rôles is involved in the position of Urban Court Members. Their influence is confined for the most part to the sphere of domestic relations, and since they handle disputes in terms of norms to which the majority of urban Africans continue to subscribe, their authority, though it has been challenged in the past, continues to be recognized. But in other parts of the social field the authority of Tribal Representatives has been overthrown because the additional political functions they came to acquire related to the total field of Black-White relations. Here 'tribalism' was irrelevant: its continued operation in the form of tribal representation could only raise impediments to the effective unity of the mine employees vis-à-vis the employers.

The Copperbelt, then, has to be seen as a single field of social relations which is composed of different sets of relations, each of which forms a distinct sub-system. Fundamental to this social system is the dominant cleavage between Europeans and Africans, and this cleavage influences behaviour and institutional growth within each part of the social field. At the same time, each sub-system enjoys a certain measure of autonomy: they do not react in the same way and at the same time towards the external stimuli making for social change. The various sub-systems are interdependent, but they are not synchronized. Hence the contradiction whereby African urban dwellers give allegiance to tribal leaders in some situations and in others have moved away completely from representation on a tribal basis, is explained by the fact that these situations refer to different sets of social relations, and belong to different departments of social life.

African, writes: 'Even the individual who feels that for him the old political organization of the tribe does not adequately meet his needs . . . still thinks that as far as his private married life is concerned the old code need not be entirely abandoned.'

However, this is but part of the problem. The principle of situational selection would provide a barrier to understanding if it simply meant, for example, that 'tribalism' operates in the domestic set of relations but ceases to operate as soon as we move into the political set of relations. In the emergent social system of the Copperbelt, we also have to face the problem that the tribal factor does intrude into situations where, on our analysis, it would seem to have no place. For example, I have argued that a system of representation which is based upon the tribe is incompatible with the needs of a heterogeneous working population, the members of which are linked primarily within the framework of a wage economy. 'Tribalism' is no longer a relevant category here because questions relating to jobs, wages, and promotion are decided without reference to the employees' tribe. Tribal leaders may still be able to handle effectively matters relating to tribal custom; but in a situation in which workers stand together in opposition to their common employer their interests can only be effectively represented by a body which cuts across tribal ties. The African Mine Workers' Trade Union provides an example of such a body. Yet when the first election for offices in the newly-established Union took place at Kitwe in 1949 the principal candidates based their campaign on an appeal to tribal loyalties.[1] At a later date, the cleavages developing within the Union appeared to follow tribal lines. Thus when an African Mines Salaried Staff Association was formed at Nkana in 1953 and subsequently spread to other Copperbelt centres, these events were widely interpreted by Africans as yet a further manifestation of the hostility between Nyasalanders, Lozi, and Bemba. We have already noticed the derogatory reference to Mr. Katilungu as the Paramount Chief of the Bemba Trade Union. Similarly, when the Union called a strike towards the end of 1954, it was announced in the Press that the members of the Nyakyusa tribe intended to break away from the Mine Workers' Union and form their own association through which they could make representations to the mining companies. Thus we have the strange paradox of 'tribalism' re-appearing in situations in which a man's tribal affiliations would appear to be completely irrelevant.

How are these events to be interpreted, and how do they affect

---

[1] See above, p. 92.

the operation of the principle of situational selection? If we assume for the moment that they are instances of the persistence of tribal loyalties in an urban and industrial milieu, it is important to examine the situations and circumstances in which these forms of persistence are expressed. The Nyasaland Africans are drawn mainly from a number of small tribes, none of which ever achieved any high degree of effective political cohesion. In the towns of Northern Rhodesia they describe themselves and are referred to by local Africans by the national rather than the tribal designation. Because of the earlier establishment of Christian Missions in Nyasaland, Nyasaland Africans have had a long start in the field of education over their fellows in Northern Rhodesia, and from the earliest days of the Copperbelt have held, together with the Lozi, the best-paid jobs on the mines. As a group they formed a very obvious élite. The Lozi, too, have always tended to be an important group in this sense and, in the earlier days at least, mine clerks tended to be exclusively Lozi and Nyasas. The very fact that the latter are referred to as Nyasalanders and are not differentiated as Henga, Tonga, Tumbuka, etc., makes it evident that we are not dealing with some situation of 'resurgent tribalism' or persistence of loyalties and values stemming from a traditional social order. Moreover, between these various groups—Lozi, Nyasas, and Bemba—there was no traditional hostility. Their present hostility springs from the efforts of other tribes, led by the numerically preponderant Bemba, to advance themselves to posts in which the Lozi [1] and Nyasas had become strongly entrenched. In other words, these inter-tribal relations are a function of the developing social system of the towns, in which as a result of historical accident the lines of an emerging class structure are tending to coincide with tribal divisions. [2]

If this is a valid assessment of the situation we may well ask why it is that the Africans themselves express these cleavages in tribal terms. And how do we account for the threat by the Nyakyusa to break away and form their own tribal union? I believe that the answers to these questions are to be sought in two

---

[1] It should also be noted here that the special constitutional position of Barotseland, and the policies followed by the Lozi Paramount Chief during the discussions on Central African Federation, have been a further source of tension between Lozi and Africans of other tribes.

[2] J. C. Mitchell, *The Kalela Dance*, op. cit.

directions. The first is to be found in the social system of the Copperbelt itself, the second in the much wider field of social relations of which the Copperbelt forms one sector.

We have spoken of the Copperbelt as a single field composed of different sets of social relations. We have noted, too, that each set enjoys a certain degree of autonomy, so that the total field appears to be characterized by contradiction and discontinuity. Describing a similar situation in the Sierra Leone Protectorate, Little has argued that the different ideas held by Africans there of what constitutes social value and prestige makes it impossible to conceptualize their behaviour in terms of a single system. It has to be analysed, he says, in terms of social situations.[1] The importance of situational analysis has been underlined at a number of points throughout the present study, and particularly in the present discussion of 'tribalism'; but Little's further argument can only be sustained if the various spheres of interaction within the social field are completely autonomous. In fact they are in a relation of interdependence, so that events in one set of relations continuously 'feed back' and influence events in another. The development of new rôles within the urban social system becomes in itself a further source of incompatibility, so that established patterns of behaviour in one set of relations may hinder the effective fulfilment of a new rôle in another set of relations: the incompatibility is resolved by a modification of the established pattern of behaviour. For example, we have observed that an African trade union leader may order his domestic life in accordance with traditional and customary values without any obvious ambiguity. But it is conceivable that if, in the course of his Union duties, it became necessary for him to entertain important delegates and other visitors at his home, a considerable re-ordering of his domestic life might be involved. In these circumstances, a wife whom he had married many years ago in his rural home might prove an inadequate hostess, and he would be led to take a younger and more sophisticated woman in her place. These various events relate to very different sets of social relations, but they all have to be interpreted in terms of the one system.

A similar process of 'feed back' would seem to explain the

---

[1] Kenneth Little, 'Structural Change in the Sierra Leone Protectorate', *Africa*, xxv, no. 3 (1955), p. 232.

behaviour of the Nyakyusa in the strike called at the beginning of 1955. We have already observed how personal association amongst Africans tends to take place on the basis of linguistic and cultural affinity. Primary interaction between urban Africans thus tends to be in terms of tribe, and the primary obligation to help a tribesman is still universally honoured. In a strike many mine workers could count on support from urban and rural kin. The Nyakyusa, coming all the way from Tanganyika, could count on no such local support. Furthermore, the majority of the Nyakyusa are unmarried and live in the mine single quarters, so that they would have no women to make gardens for them. Hence, as one of their leaders pointed out, during a strike they were always the first to suffer. Here again, therefore, the position of the Nyakyusa in one set of relations 'fed back' and influenced their behaviour in another. Nevertheless, it is interesting to notice that in spite of this, following the criticism of Mr. Lewanika,[1] the President of the African Mines Salaried Staff Association, the idea of forming a separate tribal organization appears to have been dropped, and the Nyakyusa later took part in the strike alongside members of all the other tribes represented on the Copperbelt. Here the tribal factor had obtruded into the political sphere, but in the actual situation of the strike it was outweighed by other considerations.

Thus far our focus of study has been the field of social relations which make up the urban social system. In fact of course the social field is always a continuum: its boundaries are only arbitrarily set to meet the needs of a particular study. The Copperbelt is itself only a sector of a wider field which embraces both the rural and the urban areas of Northern Rhodesia. Developments in the towns reach back and have a profound influence on the life of the villages: but the rural influence on the towns is also continuous and very strong. Under existing conditions, there is little place in the town for the African once he ceases to be employable. Thus the distinction between the townsman and the countryman often tends to be blurred since, however long the African may have lived in town, he is compelled by circumstance to retain a

---

[1] Lewanika is reported as saying that it was a 'pity' that the Nyakyusa as workers were planning to dissociate themselves on a tribal basis from well-organized industrial organizations. Tribal isolation among workers could not go unchallenged, unless it was confined to purely tribal affairs (*Northern News*, December 23, 1954).

foot in the rural camp. This state of affairs not only militates against the growth of a stabilized urban population; it also serves to maintain the Africans' interest in the land, and consequently in the tribe from which their claims to land derive.[1]

To sum up, therefore: the rural background of the African, with its concomitant cultural diversity, provides the basis for the classification of the urban population into different tribal categories. But the inter-tribal relatioṇs on the Copperbelt which we have just described, and the cleavages within political organizations along tribal lines, cannot be explained simply as vestiges from a tribal past which have survived into the present. On the contrary, they reflect processes at work within the urban social system. Tribalism on the Copperbelt refers to a significant category of interaction in everyday social relationships amongst Africans. The African who comes to the town is already involved in a complex network of social relations which originate in the tribal system: he brings with him certain patterns of behaviour, values and attitudes, and all of these he continues to utilize in the town. The present evidence suggests, indeed, that personal association most frequently takes place upon the basis of kinship and the possession of a common language. Through the linking together of certain tribes on the basis of historical connections or cultural and linguistic affinities, or by special joking relationships, 'tribalism' provides a framework for organizing interpersonal relations amongst urban Africans.

Nevertheless, while the urban African remains in many situations primarily a 'tribesman', his presence in the town also involves him perforce in other sets of relations which cut across tribal lines. The wage economy of the towns, the urban forms of local grouping and administration, and the increasing assimilation of European patterns of behaviour, give rise to new sets of relations and interests. Here 'tribalism' ceases to be a relevant category, and new forms of association, and new types of leadership, come into being to express the new sets of interests involved. The authority of leaders appointed on a tribal basis may continue to be recognized in situations involving purely domestic and

---

[1] Land has a further significance at the present time, for it is their present possession of the tribal lands which provides the symbol of African national freedom. It was the fear of dispossession of the land which provided one of the main driving forces in the struggle against Federation.

inter-personal relations; in the political sphere, where interests of a different kind are involved, they become caught up in a conflict of rôles and are replaced by leaders of a different stamp.

Thus the principle of situational selection operates within a developing system that is marked by the continuing conflict of different principles of social organization. Although 'tribalism' is an irrelevant category in many of these new sets of relations, it does not thereby cease to operate within them. Because primarily interaction between Africans still tends to be in terms of tribe, and because the various sets of relations which make up the urban social system are interdependent, 'tribalism' tends to be carried over into, and to operate within, all the sets of relations in which the urban African is involved. But as we move from the sphere of inter-personal relations into the sphere of political relations other factors come into play. Here, as in the case of the Nyakyusa in the strike of 1955, the tribal factor may be out-weighed by the strength of the other interests involved. The evidence of the present study shows that in situations involving the total field of Black-White relations the tribal factor tends to be overborne. In situations involving relations within the African field, tribalism remains a potent factor. But, as we have just noted, tribalism is not the only category of interaction operating within the African field. Mitchell's study of the *Kalela* dance brings out clearly the increasing significance of prestige or 'class' as a further category of social interaction in African urban life. Here the 'civilized way of life' provides a scale along which the prestige of Africans in the towns may be measured: one's position in the prestige continuum, or 'class' affiliations, increasingly deter-mines one's behaviour and attitudes in a wide variety of situations. Similarly, the formation of the African Mines Salaried Staff Association, although interpreted by some Africans as an expression of tribal antagonism, points to the growing divisions within the urban communities along the lines of 'economic class'. We may perhaps speak of 'tribalism' and 'class' as pervasive concepts in the sense that they pervade and operate within all the various sets of relations which make up the urban system. Their complex interplay in different situations pose important problems for further research in the field of African urbanism.

TABLE 14

COMPOSITION OF THE LUANSHYA URBAN ADVISORY COUNCIL
MAY, 1954

Name	Tribe	Representing	Age in 1953	Present Occupation	Membership in other organizations, or other social position, with additional Biographical Notes
G. Musumbulwa	Lungu-Bemba	Mine Township	38	Mine Clerk in African Personnel Department	Former Secretary Luanshya Welfare Society; Founder Member Roan Clerks' Association; Former Committee Member A.M.W.T.U. (Roan).* Chairman Roan Parent-Teachers' Association; Chairman Roan Branch Co-operative Society; Member of African Representative Council and Member of Luanshya Urban Advisory Council since 1948. Formerly Headmaster Roan African School.
J. Chapoloko	Bemba	,,	32	Branch Secretary A.M.W.T.U. (Roan)	Former Leader Bemba *Mbeni* Tribal Dance Association (Kitwe); Former Committee Member Kitwe African Society; Former Elder in Seventh Day Adventists; Founder Member African National Congress and Former Chairman Nkana Branch; Founder Member and Vice-General Secretary A.M.W.T.U.; Member of Western Province Provincial Council. Formerly a Clerk in the Provincial Administration, and later a Senior Clerk in the African Personnel Department, Nkana Mine.
D. Nsabashi	Bemba	,,	29	Vice-Branch Secretary A.M.W.T.U. (Roan)	Former Treasurer A.M.W.T.U. (Roan) and Member of Supreme Council of the Union; Former Secretary to Fisenge African Township, and later employed as a Mine Clerk.
C. M'hone	Tumbuka	,,	38	Mine Clerk in African Personnel Department	Former Member Roan Clerks' Association; Former Representative on the Works Committee; Treasurer and Elder in Free Church; Vice-Treasurer Nyasaland African National Congress in Northern Rhodesia and Chairman Roan Branch.
A. Chambeshi	Lala	,,	38	Mine Clerk in African Personnel Department	Former Member of the Clerks' Association; Former Member of the Works Committee; Former Member Luanshya Welfare Society; Founder Member African National Congress; Former Chairman and now Vice-Chairman in Roan Branch A.M.W.T.U. Formerly a Schoolmaster.
			26	Mine Clerk	Treasurer Roan Branch A.M.W.T.U.; Secretary Ballroom Dancing Society.

Name	Tribe	Location	Age	Occupation	Remarks
				in African Welfare Department	
J. Sichone	Namwanga Tabwa	"	34	Mine Clerk in African Personnel Department	No information
D. Lisulo	Lozi	"	24	Welfare Assistant	Secretary of Cinema Club (Recent arrival at Roan from School).
R. Chisulo	Aushi	"	32	Mine Clerk in African Personnel Department	Former Committee Member Nkana Branch African National Congress (Recent arrival at Roan from Nkana).
R. Mwansa	Bisa	"	25	Temporarily unemployed	Former Member Northern Province African Provincial Council; Formerly employed as Clerk in Northern Rhodesia Police and later in African Personnel Department at Roan.
J. Simukonda	Namwanga	Municipal	22	Trade Union Secretary	Branch Secretary General Workers' Trade Union; Vice-Chairman Luanshya Branch of African National Congress.
R. Banda	Tonga	"	33	Head Clerk to Contractor; Tea-Room Proprietor	Former General Secretary General Workers' Trade Union; Chairman Luanshya Parent-Teachers' Association; Elder in Free Church; Member of African Affairs Committee of Municipal Council; Member Western Province African Provincial Council; Trained as Medical Assistant.
D. Shitombwe	Kaonde	Municipal Location	38	Private Trader	Chairman of Hawkers' Association; Chairman Luanshya Branch of African National Congress; Formerly a Clerk in the Provincial Administration and later Manager Roan African Co-operative Society.
D. Mwape	Aushi	"	28	Schoolmaster	Secretary Luanshya Parent-Teachers' Association (Recently arrived in the Town).
L. Muma	Bemba	Fisenge Township	30	Private Trader	Member of Fisenge Township Board; Founder Member of Fisenge Branch African National Congress; Formerly a Carpenter.

* A.M.W.T.U. = African Mine Workers' Trade Union.

APPENDIX I

Basic Rates of Wages of African Mine Workers before and after the Guillebaud Award

Source: Report of the Arbitration Tribunal, 1953

	Surface			Surface	
	Pay per ticket before the Award	Pay per ticket after the Award		Pay per ticket before the Award	Pay per ticket after the Award
Group 1:			**Group 4 contd.:**		
	45/–	80/–		87/6	127/6
	47/6	82/6		90/–	130/–
	50/–	85/–			
	52/6	87/6	**Group 5:**		
	55/–	90/–		172/6	217/6
	57/6	92/6		175/–	220/–
	60/–	95/–		177/6	222/6
	62/6	97/6		180/–	225/–
	65/–	100/–		182/6	227/6
	76/6	102/6		187/6	232/6
Group 2:				192/6	237/6
	52/6	87/6	**Group 6:**		
	55/–	90/–		190/–	235/–
	57/6	92/6		195/–	240/–
	60/–	95/–		200/–	245/–
	62/6	97/6		205/–	250/–
	65/–	100/–		210/–	255/–
	67/6	102/6		215/–	260/–
	70/–	105/–		217/6	262/6
Group 3:			**Group 7:**		
	62/6	97/6		222/6	272/6
	65/–	100/–		227/6	277/6
	67/6	102/6		232/6	282/6
	70/–	105/–		237/6	287/6
	72/6	107/6		247/6	297/6
	75/–	110/–		257/6	307/6
	77/6	112/6		267/6	317/6
Group 4:				270/–	320/–
	75/–	115/–	**Special Group:**		
	77/6	117/–		290/–	340/–
	80/–	120/–		300/–	350/–
	82/6	122/6		310/–	360/–
	85/–	125/–		320/–	370/–

Underground		Underground	
Pay per ticket before the Award	Pay per ticket after the Award	Pay per ticket before the Award	Pay per ticket after the Award

Group 1:

55/–	90/–		
57/6	92/6		
60/–	95/–		
62/6	97/6		
65/–	100/–		
67/6	102/6		
70/–	105/–		
72/6	107/6		
75/–	110/–		
77/6	112/6		

Group 5:

Pay per ticket before the Award	Pay per ticket after the Award
187/6	232/6
190/–	235/–
192/6	237/6
195/–	240/–
197/6	242/6
200/–	245/–

Group 2:

Pay per ticket before the Award	Pay per ticket after the Award
65/–	100/–
67/6	102/6
70/–	105/–
72/6	107/6
75/–	110/–
77/6	112/6
80/–	115/–
82/6	117/6

Group 6:

Pay per ticket before the Award	Pay per ticket after the Award
197/6	242/6
202/6	247/6
207/6	252/6
212/6	257/6
217/6	262/6
222/6	267/6
225/–	270/–

Group 3:

Pay per ticket before the Award	Pay per ticket after the Award
77/6	112/6
80/–	115/–
82/6	117/6
85/–	120/–
87/6	122/6
90/–	125/–
92/6	127/6

Group 7:

Pay per ticket before the Award	Pay per ticket after the Award
232/6	282/6
237/6	287/6
242/6	292/6
247/6	297/6
252/6	302/6
257/6	307/6
260/–	310/–

Group 8:

Pay per ticket before the Award	Pay per ticket after the Award
257/6	307/6
262/6	312/6
267/6	317/6
272/6	322/6
282/6	332/6
292/6	342/6
302/6	352/6
305/–	355/–

Group 4:

Pay per ticket before the Award	Pay per ticket after the Award
90/–	130/–
92/6	132/6
95/–	135/–
97/6	137/6
100/–	140/–
102/6	142/6
105/–	145/–

Special Group:

Pay per ticket before the Award	Pay per ticket after the Award
325/–	375/–
335/–	385/–
345/–	395/–
355/–	405/–

APPENDIX II

CHRONOLOGY OF MAIN EVENTS CITED

Year	Event
1926–8	Development work begins on the mines of the Copperbelt.
1930–1	Production of copper begins at the Roan Antelope.
	Tribal Elders are introduced at Roan.
	Sharp drop of prices begins in the copper market. In February, 1931, Bwana Mkubwa mine closes suddenly. Later, all Northern Rhodesia copper mines suspend operations with the exception of Roan Antelope and Nkana.
1935	The Alison Russell Commission reports upon the serious disturbances which occurred on the Copperbelt, particularly at Luanshya. The Native Industrial Labour Advisory Board is established, and discussions also take place on administrative policy in the urban areas.
1936	Administrative re-organization begins. Luanshya is established as a separate administrative district under a District Commissioner. The Government Township of Luanshya is gazetted as a Municipal Board.
	Mr. Charlie Harris, European trade unionist from the Rand, visits Northern Rhodesia.
1937	Formation of the Northern Rhodesia [European] Mine Workers' Union.
1938	Urban African Courts begin to operate on the Copperbelt. The Urban Advisory Committee comes into existence at Luanshya.
1939	The Royal Commission under the chairmanship of Viscount Bledisloe reports on the amalgamation of the two Rhodesias and Nyasaland.
1940	Strike of European miners on the Copperbelt. This is followed by an African strike and disturbances in which seventeen Africans are killed, and many more injured. The Forster Commission raises the question of African advancement in industry.
1941	Tribal Representatives replace Tribal Elders, and come into existence on mines where formerly there were no Tribal Elders. Urban Advisory Councils established on the Copperbelt.
1942	Sir Stewart Gore-Browne, leader of the 'Unofficials' and nominated Representative of African Interests, raises in the Legislative Council the question of African political representation.
	The mining companies recognize Boss Boys' Committees to represent the interests of boss boys or charge hands. The African Welfare Society is introduced at Luanshya.
1946	Major strike of European artisans on the mines. First meeting takes place of the newly established African Representative Council.
1947	Africans in Luanshya organize a boycott of Indian stores.

Year	Event
1948	Mr. (now Sir) Roy Welensky, leader of the Unofficials in the Legislative Council, raises the question of Responsible Government. The Dalgleish Commission reports upon African advancement in industry. Two African representatives take their seats in the Legislative Council. Africans take their first steps in organizing trade unions and co-operative societies. The Urban Advisory Councils are dissolved and re-constituted.
1949	Union branches on the Copperbelt amalgamate to form the African Mine Workers' Trade Union. The African National Congress is formed.
1951	*March.* Report is published of a Conference held in London on the closer association of the British Central African Territories. *September.* The Victoria Falls Conference accepts proposals for closer association.
1952	Further conferences and discussions on Central African Federation. The African National Congress organizes a campaign of opposition. *April.* Deportation proceedings brought against Simon Zukas. *October.* First organized mass strike of African miners.
1953	*March.* African miners vote on abolition of tribal representation. *April.* The failure of the Congress-organized 'Two Day National Prayer'. *August.* The Federation of Rhodesia and Nyasaland is established. Preparations begin for elections to the Federal Parliament and Territorial Legislatures. *September.* Urban Advisory Councils dissolved, and elections take place for the first time by popular ballot. At its Annual Conference, the African Mine Workers' Trade Union discusses the implementation of the *Dalgleish Report*. *November.* African Mine Workers' Union begins collection of its own subscriptions itself. A local branch of Congress is formed in Luanshya.
1954	*January.* The African Mine Workers' Union is invited to participate with other interested parties in the discussions on African advancement. *February.* Congress organizes the boycott of the butcheries in Luanshya. Roan branch of the African Mine Workers' Union holds its election for the post of branch chairman. *March.* Sir Will Lawther, President of the National Union of Mine Workers of Great Britain, flies to Northern Rhodesia at the invitation of the European and African unions.

BIBLIOGRAPHY

BARNES, J. A. 'The Village Headman in British Central Africa' (with Mitchell, J. C. and Gluckman, M.), *Africa*, xix (1949).
—— 'Some Aspects of Political Development among the Fort Jameson Ngoni', *African Studies*, vii (1948).
BRADLEY, K. G. *Copper Venture*, published privately for the Rhodesian Selection Trust (1953).
BRONOWSKI, J. *William Blake: A Man without a Mask*. London: Pelican Books (1954).
BUSIA, K. A. *Report on a Social Survey of Sekondi-Takoradi*, London: Crown Agents (1950).
CLAY, G. C. R. 'African Urban Advisory Councils on the Northern Rhodesia Copperbelt', *Journal of African Administration*, i (1949).
COLE, G. D. H. *A Short History of the British Working Class Movement*, London: Allen & Unwin (revised edition, 1948).
COLSON, E. 'Modern Political Organization of the Plateau Tonga', *African Studies*, vii (1948).
CONYNGHAM, L. D. 'African Towns in Northern Rhodesia', *Journal of African Administration*, iii (1951).
CUNNISON, I. 'The Lunda Concept of Custom', *Rhodes-Livingstone Journal*, xiv (1954).
DAVIDSON, J. W. *The Northern Rhodesia Legislative Council*, London: Faber & Faber (1948).
EPSTEIN, A. L. *The Administration of Justice and the Urban African*, London: H.M.S.O. (1953).
—— *Juridical Techniques and the Judicial Process*, Rhodes-Livingstone Paper, No. 23, Manchester University Press (1954).
EVANS-PRITCHARD, E. E. *Witchcraft, Oracles, and Magic among the Azande*, Clarendon Press, Oxford (1937).
FALLERS, Lloyd. 'The Predicament of the Modern African Chief', *American Anthropologist*, lvii (N.S.)(1955).
FORTES, M. *The Dynamics of Clanship among the Tallensi*, Oxford University Press, London (1945).
GLUCKMAN, M. 'The Zulu of South-East Africa' in *African Political Systems*, ed. by M. Fortes and E. E. Evans-Pritchard, Oxford University Press, London (1940).
—— 'Analysis of a Social Situation in Modern Zululand', *Bantu Studies*, xiv (1940).
—— 'Some Processes of Social Change illustrated from Zululand', *African Studies*, i (1942).
—— 'Malinowski's "Functional" Analysis of Social Change', *Africa*, xvii (1947), republished in *Malinowski's Sociological Theories*, Rhodes-Livingstone Paper No. 16, Oxford University Press, Cape Town (1949).
—— *The Judicial Process among the Barotse of Northern Rhodesia (Zambia)*, Manchester University Press (1955, 1967) and for the Institute for African Studies (1973).

GLUCKMAN, M. 'The Village Headman in British Central Africa' (with Barnes, J. A. and Mitchell, J. C.) *Africa*, xix (1949).

GOLDSCHMIDT, W., 'Social Class in America—a Critical Review', *American Anthropologist*, vol. 52, no. 4 (1950).

HAMMOND, J. L. and Barbara. *The Rise of Modern Industry*, Methuen, London (1937).

HARLOW, V. 'Tribalism in Africa', *Journal of African Administration*, vii (1955).

HEATH, F. M. N. 'No Smoke from the Smelter', *Corona*, April (1953).

—— 'The Growth of African Councils on the Copperbelt of Northern Rhodesia', *Journal of African Administration*, v (1953).

HELLMANN, Ellen. 'The Native in the Towns' in *The Bantu-Speaking Tribes o, South Africa*, ed. by I. Schapera, Routledge, London (1937).

—— 'Urban Areas', in *Handbook on Race Relations in South Africa*, Oxford University Press, London (1949).

KUCZYNSKI, R. R. *A Demographic Survey of the British Colonial Empire*, vol. 2, Oxford University Press, London (1949).

LEWIN, Julius. *The Colour Bar in the Copperbelt*, South African Institute of Race Relations, Johannesburg (1941).

LITTLE, Kenneth. 'The Study of Social Change in British West Africa', *Africa*, xxiii (1953).

—— 'Structural Change in the Sierra Leone Protectorate', *Africa*, xxv (1955).

McCULLOCH, Merran. *Industrialization in Africa:* Survey of Recent and Current Field Studies on the Social Effects of Economic Development in inter-tropical Africa prepared by the International African Institute for the Social Science Division of UNESCO, London (1950).

MATTHEWS, Z. K. 'The Tribal Spirit among Educated South Africans', *Man*, xxxv (1935), art. 26.

MERLE DAVIS, J. *Modern Industry and the African*, Macmillan, London (1933).

MITCHELL, J. C. 'The Political Organization of the Yao of Southern Nyasaland', *African Studies*, vii (1948).

—— 'The Village Headman in British Central Africa' (with Barnes, J. A. and Gluckman, M.), *Africa*, xix (1949).

—— 'A Note on the Urbanization of Africans on the Copperbelt', *Rhodes-Livingstone Journal*, xii (1951).

—— 'The Distribution of African Labour by Area of Origin in the Copper Mines of Northern Rhodesia', *Rhodes-Livingstone Journal*, xiv (1954).

—— *African Urbanization in Ndola and Luanshya*. Rhodes-Livingstone Communication, No. 6 (1954).

—— *The Kalela Dance*, Rhodes-Livingstone Paper, No. 27 (1957).

—— 'Urbanization, Detribalization, and Stabilization in Southern Africa: A Problem of Definition and Measurement', Working Paper prepared for the Abidjan Conference on the Social Impact of Industrialization and Urban Conditions in Africa, 1954.

—— 'Africans in Industrial Towns in Northern Rhodesia', (unpublished MS.).

MOORE, R. J. B. *These African Copper Miners*. Revised edition by A. Sandilands, Livingstone Press, London (1948).

ORDE-BROWNE, Major G. St. J. *Labour Conditions in Northern Rhodesia*, Colonial No. 150, London, H.M.S.O. (1938).

PRAIN, R. L. 'African Advancement on the Copperbelt', *African Affairs*, liii (1954).

RICHARDS, A. I. *Bemba Marriage and Present Economic Conditions*, Rhodes-Livingstone Paper, No. 4, Livingstone (1940).

SPEARPOINT, F. 'The African Native and the Rhodesia Copper Mines', *Journal of the Royal African Society*, vol. xxxvi, July (1937), (supplement).

WHYTE, W. F. *Street Corner Society*, University of Chicago Press, Chicago (1943).

WILSON, Godfrey. *The Economic of Detribalization*, Rhodes-Livingstone Papers, Nos. 5 and 6, Livingstone (1940).

OFFICIAL PUBLICATIONS CITED

United Kingdom Government:

Bledisloe Report: Rhodesia-Nyasaland Royal Commission Report, Cmd. 5949, 1939.

Central African Territories: Report of Conference on Closer Association, Cmd. 8233, March, 1951.

Draft Federal Scheme for Central African Federation, Cmd. 8573, June, 1952.

Report by the Conference on Federation, Cmd. 8753, January, 1953.

Northern Rhodesia Government (Government Printer, Lusaka):

Report of the Commission appointed to inquire into the Disturbances in the Copperbelt, Northern Rhodesia, 1935 [Recommendations and Minutes of Evidence].

Report of the Commission appointed to inquire into the Disturbances in the Copperbelt, Northern Rhodesia, 1940.

Report of the Commission appointed to inquire into the Advancement of Africans in Industry, 1948.

Report of the Commission appointed to inquire into the Finances and Administration of Urban Locations, 1944.

Report of a Committee appointed to consider the Constitution of Management Boards, 1949.

Annual Report on African Education, 1947.

African Affairs, Annual Report, 1951.

Northern Rhodesia Legislative Council Debates.

Proceedings of the African Representative Council.

Proceedings of the African Provincial Council of the Western Province, 1951.

INDEX

Administration (Provincial), 20; approach to urban problems, 29–31, 83; assumptions underlying urban administrative policy, 32–6, 43–4; perception of the urban situation, 34; policy on urban stabilization, 35; re-organization in urban areas, 30. See also Conference of District Commissioners, Conference of Provincial Commissioners

African advancement in industry, 101–110; African views on, 145–7. See Unions

African Affairs Committee, 19, 24, 166. See also Municipal Board

African Mine Workers' Trade Union (A.M.W.T.U.), see Unions

African Miner, quoted, 93, 108, 149 fn.

African National Congress, see Congress

African Personnel Department, functions of, 14–17; internal organization, 16–17

African Personnel Manager, 4, 14, 16; central importance in mine administration, 23; structural position of, 124, 127, 191. See also Compound Manager

African Provincial Council (Western Province), 25, 76, 78, 222

African Representative Council, 72, 159

African Trade Union Congress, see Unions

Arbitration tribunal, 97, 101. See also Guillebaud

Banda, R., 75, 164, 166, 177, 182

Beer Halls, 9, 50, 66, 124–5; use of profits, 18; expenditure of funds, 40

Bemba tribe, 5, 6, 31, 236; Katilungu's influence among, 92; part played in the disturbances of 1935, 44; 'right' to urban leadership, 5, 152

Boss Boys' Committee, 63, 64, 82, 89, 132; meetings of, 63

Boycott of European butcheries, account of in Luanshya, 171–9

Broken Hill, 13, 47, 93, 94

Bwana M'kubwa, 1

Capricorn Africa Society, 174 fn.

Case of the Aggrieved Friend, 200–1, 202, 207, 208, 210, 214

Case of the Butcher's Assistant, 217–18, 220

Case of the Disrespectful Son-in-law, 203–7, 210, 214, 223

Case of the Tea-cart, 218–20

Chambeshi, A., 126, 135–43

Chapoloko, J., 92, 164, 188

Chingola (Nchanga), 1; strike at, 93

Chitambala, P., 164, 174, 179, 181. See Boycott

Chitimukulu, Paramount Chief, 5, 44, 92 fn.

Clerks, 16, 82; criticism of, 142–3; membership of Advisory Council, 76; as trade union organizers, 73, 134; special social importance of, 82, 132. See also Leadership

Clerks' Association, 82, 86, 132

'Closed shop', 103, 112

Colour bar, in industry, 89, 107; Congress campaigns to break, 162

Commission of Inquiry into the Disturbances on the Copperbelt (1935), 2 fn., 21, 26, 29–32, 44, 87

Committee of Seventeen, 65, 82

Community, as a field of social relations, xii–xiv, 232–4

'Community study method', xiii

Compound Manager, relations with Tribal Elders, 27–8, 36; relations with Boss Boys' Committee, 63. See also African Personnel Manager

Comrie, W., 90, 150

Conferences, see District Commissioner, Provincial Commissioner

Congress, 67, 86, 157–97; 'branch' organization, 180–1; campaign against Central African Federation, 160–2; decline in popular support for, 181; failure to organize branch on the mine, 187–91; formation of, 160; formation of Luanshya